CAMBRIDGE IBERIAN AND LATIN AMERICAN STUDIES

GENERAL EDITOR
P. E. RUSSELL F.B.A.
Emeritus Professor of Spanish Studies
University of Oxford

ASSOCIATE EDITORS
E. PUPO-WALKER
Director, Center for Latin American and Iberian Studies
Vanderbilt University
A. R. D. PAGDEN
Lecturer in History, University of Cambridge

Seneca and *Celestina*

This book examines the reason and intent behind the many Senecan and pseudo-Senecan quotations in Fernando de Rojas' masterpiece *Celestina* (1499), which enjoyed enormous popularity in sixteenth-century Europe.

The author considers the importance attached to Senecan thought in the oral, scholarly and literary traditions of fifteenth-century Spain, and demonstrates how readers' tastes and sensibilities were shaped by it. The main themes of *Celestina*, such as self-seeking friendship and love, pleasure and sorrow, gifts and riches, greed, suicide and death, are shown to be rooted in this intellectual background. The Senecan tradition, albeit treated in a satirical vein, is also seen as underlying the later additions and interpolations to the text, with a shift towards Seneca's tragedies in response to changes in fashion; Professor Fothergill-Payne reveals that even the Petrarchan quotations in *Celestina* have Senecan sources.

Seneca and 'Celestina' thus offers an entirely new perspective on the literary and intellectual sources that shaped this famous book.

T0371059

Seneca, the *amicus principis*. Woodcut frontispiece of the first edition of *Las epístolas de Séneca* (Zaragoza, 1496). (*Reproduced by permission of the Biblioteca Nacional, Madrid.*)

Seneca and *Celestina*

LOUISE FOTHERGILL-PAYNE

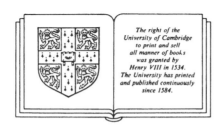

The right of the
University of Cambridge
to print and sell
all manner of books
was granted by
Henry VIII in 1534.
The University has printed
and published continuously
since 1584.

CAMBRIDGE UNIVERSITY PRESS

CAMBRIDGE

NEW YORK   NEW ROCHELLE   MELBOURNE   SYDNEY

CAMBRIDGE UNIVERSITY PRESS
Cambridge, New York, Melbourne, Madrid, Cape Town, Singapore,
São Paulo, Delhi, Dubai, Tokyo

Cambridge University Press
The Edinburgh Building, Cambridge CB2 8RU, UK

Published in the United States of America by Cambridge University Press, New York

www.cambridge.org
Information on this title: www.cambridge.org/9780521121187

First published 1988
This digitally printed version 2009

A catalogue record for this publication is available from the British Library

Library of Congress Cataloguing in Publication data
Fothergill-Payne, Louise.
Seneca and Celestina / Louise Fothergill-Payne.
p.   cm. — (Cambridge Iberian and Latin American studies)
Bibliography.
Includes index.
ISBN 0-521-32212-X
1. Rojas, Fernando de, d. 1541. Celestina—Sources. 2. Seneca,
Lucius Annaeus, ca. 4 B.C.-65 A.D.—Influence.   I. Title.
II. Series.
PQ6428.F6   1988
862'.2—dc19   87-27216 CIP

ISBN 978-0-521-32212-6 Hardback
ISBN 978-0-521-12118-7 Paperback

To Peter,
my best friend and husband,
'nullius boni sine socio iucunda possessio est'
Seneca, Epistula 6, 4

Contents

Illustrations

Preface

The very suggestion that Seneca might have been the main source for the composition of *Celestina* generally meets with disbelief if not outright rejection. The reasons usually put forward against this argument are that Seneca is such a stern moralist, cold and unsympathetic to human plight, while *Celestina* is cherished as a book full of life, humour and deeply human insights.

This study, therefore, faces the double task of convincing the disbeliever that in the fifteenth century Seneca was considered to be the opposite of all the negative things he represents to many today, and that *Celestina* is squarely rooted in a fifteenth-century Senecan tradition. In both the medieval and the modern context, then, we are faced with a problem of transmission.

Transmission, then as now, was as much a question of oral communication expressed by a *vox populi* or *vox auctoritatis*, as of written testimony in the form of texts, their dissemination, translation and the literary criticism that concerns itself with them. The main reason for the ups and downs in Seneca's reception is that his words have always been more cited than read and that his message is so applicable to contemporary needs and expectations in all ages. In *Celestina* all these various aspects of Seneca's reception and transmission come together. Chapter 1 therefore traces how the medieval Senecan tradition was a curious mixture of myth, hearsay and second-hand sources, all nurtured in Spain by heavily glossed translations. These vernacular versions are anything but a true reflection of the 'real' Seneca; in fact they mainly excerpt semi- and pseudo-Senecan works.

In chapter 2 I study how early attempts at literary criticism in the form of introductions, prologues and notes to the translations reflect and define a fifteenth-century intellectual frame of reference into which the *Comedia de Calisto y Melibea* fits so neatly.

It is generally accepted that *Celestina* is not the work of a single author; therefore we should not consider the development of its intent as if it were. With this in mind, I have divided this study into three different parts: the first act, the 16-act *Comedia* and the 21-act *Tragicomedia*.

The Senecan influences in Act 1 have already been well documented. As early as the mid-sixteenth century, an anonymous commentator was alive to various textual borrowings from the *Epistulae* and *De Beneficiis*, which were picked up by Castro Guisasola, by Heller and Grismer, and by Blüher. However, one should not content oneself solely with pinpointing sources but should inquire into the reason and the intent of such quotations. This is what I attempt to do in chapter 3, through the examination of the first author's skill in fitting the 'sentencias dos mil' into the general framework of his 'dulce ficción'.

Fernando de Rojas, whom I have accepted as being the author of the 16-act *Comedia*, then develops the subtext of the first author's *sententiae* into a full-scale plot, continuing the first author's gentle mockery of the new reader's superficial knowledge of Seneca's *De Vita Beata* and *De Beneficiis*. His immediate source is that used by the first author, Seneca's *Epistulae Morales*, to which Rojas adds Seneca's *De Ira* as an important factor in the development of the story. Chapter 4 thus follows the continued Senecan presence in *Celestina*, a presence reinforced by a host of quotations from the pseudo-Senecan *Proverbios* and other popular words of wisdom.

And then there is Petrarch, that other important source of *Celestina*, so expertly studied by Alan Deyermond. The Petrarchan quotations reflect the same Senecan tradition as informs the moral context of *Celestina*, simply because many stem from *De Remediis Utriusque Fortunae*, a book modelled on the pseudo-Senecan *De Remediis Fortuitorum*. The other great storehouse of quotations is Petrarch's Index, which, as I show in chapter 5, served Rojas as a rich source for pedantic name-dropping, metaphors and other contrived poetics.

Finally, in chapter 6, taking the *sententiae* as a point of departure, I analyse the interpolations and added Acts which transformed the 16-act *Comedia* into a 21-act *Tragicomedia*. And again we detect the same Senecan tradition as underlies the previous acts, but with one major shift. While the *Comedia* was inspired by Seneca's prose work, the *Tragicomedia* now shows a much greater debt to Seneca's tragedies – apparently in answer to readers' changing tastes and sensibilities.

In choosing the title *Seneca and Celestina*, I wanted to give equal prominence to the Roman philosopher and to the book that fictionalizes his message. By abbreviating the title of this book to *Celestina* I pay tribute to Keith Whinnom who first suggested we drop the article. In a study which basically deals with translations, quotations could not be translated into English without doing the text an injustice. I also trust that readers with an interest in *Celestina* are sufficiently conversant with Spanish to appreciate the original language. Finally, it is my sincere hope that modern students may discover Seneca's sound advice and committed concern for humankind in much the same way as the fifteenth-century 'new readers' did.

The longest book Seneca wrote on any single topic is *De Beneficiis*. In it he analyses how free and disinterested gifts form the basis of our society. This is particularly true in a community of scholars who benefit most from each others' precious gifts of wisdom. I want here to express my deep gratitude to all those who have given so freely of their time and knowledge in advising, helping and encouraging me to study the Senecan connection further. Some colleagues may not even remember a casual reference in conversation or a subtle pointer to untapped information, but each of them has contributed immensely to the completion of this book. My greatest debt, however, is to Nick Round, Alan Deyermond and Dorothy Severin, who each have taken the time and trouble to read parts of this book in draft and, by doing so, have opened up new perspectives and prevented major disasters. Any error of judgement, therefore, is entirely mine. A special word of thanks is also due to Charles Faulhaber, who trusted me with his entire card-index, and Joseph Snow, who, as friend and editor of *Celestinesca*, created a bond between us all. I am also grateful to Lisa Storozynsky, whose assistance extended beyond the call of duty because of that same disinterested commitment to research.

The year I spent working in Oxford was made both more profitable and congenial by the welcome extended to me by the Sub-Faculty of Spanish and Portuguese and the Principal and Fellows of Linacre College. My special thanks are due to Ian Michael, Tom Earle and Leighton Reynolds. As always in the past, I was immeasurably assisted by the ever-patient and resourceful staff of the Taylor Institution Library.

A particular word of gratitude must be addressed to the Social Sciences and Humanities Research Council of Canada, who through the award of a generous Release Time Stipend and other research support allowed me the leisure to work in the great libraries of Europe unshackled from the cares of office.

And then there is my family, who through the years have Stoically accepted the Senecan presence in their life, and especially my husband, who continuously processed my words and thoughts in more than the technical sense of the word. Without his unfailing belief and his daily encouragements this book simply would never have become a reality.

Abbreviations

Anth.	*Las epístolas de Séneca* (see p. 152, (a) II)
BN	Biblioteca Nacional, Madrid
CL	*Los cinco libros de Séneca* (see p. 152, (a) II)
D.	Deyermond, *The Petrarchan Sources of 'La Celestina'*
De Ben.	*De Beneficiis*
De Brev.	*De Brevitate Vitae*
De Prov.	*De Providentia Dei*
De Tranq.	*De Tranquillitate Animi*
DVB	*De Vita Beata*
Ep.	*Epistulae Morales*
Helv.	*De Consolatione ad Helviam*
Marc.	*De Consolatione ad Marciam*
M.	Marciales (ed.), *Celestina. Tragicomedia de Calisto y Melibea*
NQ	*De Naturalibus Quaestionibus*
Poly.	*De Consolatione ad Polybium*
R.	Riss (ed.), *Los proverbios de Séneca* (see p. 152, (a) II)
S.	Severin (ed.), *La Celestina*

I

Towards a Senecan tradition

The fifteenth century in Spain was a truly Senecan age. From the early 1430s on, translations of Seneca's genuine and putative writings circulated in various manuscripts, and they figure among the first incunabula to come down to us. But his name evoked a very different image from that of today. In contrast to the prevailing modern view of Seneca as the cold and impassive observer of humankind, the fifteenth century read his moral philosophy as a compassionate guide to the good life. This late medieval reception of Seneca was the result of a long process of transmission characterized by the arbitrary adaptation, distortion or even pure invention of his words.

In order to understand Seneca's unique position in late medieval Spain, it would seem useful in this chapter to examine the steady rise of his fame accompanying the dissemination of relevant texts and to determine how the creation of a legend surrounding the Roman philosopher in early Christian times promoted a pseudo-literature; then to follow the steps whereby the fifteenth-century translators' selection of what should be made available to an emerging lay readership subsequently reduced and transformed Seneca's canon into a set of rules for good conduct and prudent behaviour. Finally, mention will be made of the first booksellers' choice of what should be printed – a choice which was responsible for a yet more restrictive perception of this pagan philosopher.

In this way, Seneca's medieval transmission can be seen as a continuing process of expansion, transformation and exclusion which was moreover greatly influenced by a powerful *vox populi*.

Seneca's changing image

From the start, an ambiguous reputation accompanied the reception of Seneca's works. For some, Seneca was the *amicus principis*, given his office as adviser to Nero; for others, he was a provincial upstart from Cordoba and, last but not least, the fabulously rich man who advocated poverty.

However, prejudice against this influential statesman was not unanimous during his lifetime. In the tragedy *Octavia* an unknown dramatist portrays Seneca as the brave and virtuous adviser to the tyrant Nero; Juvenal praises him on the same grounds, adding his appreciation of Seneca's generosity as a patron – a gratitude repeated thirty years later in the words of the poet Martial.

Shortly after his death, Seneca's fame as statesman and author enters the realm of historiography and literary criticism. Tacitus, evoking an *imago vitae suae* in his *Annales*, questions Seneca's morals, while Quintilian, in his evaluation of Seneca's style in the *Institutio Oratoria*, condemns his dialectics as too facile. Nevertheless, neither the criticism of Quintilian and Tacitus nor the more damaging statements of later historians such as Suetonius and Dio Cassius could stem the rising tide of Seneca's popularity. As Imperial Rome gave way to Christian Europe, Seneca's image began to change. New meanings were being discovered in his teaching, and his words were interpreted in Christian terms. In due course, his message was appropriated by Christianity to such an extent that the pagan philosopher became *Seneca noster*.[1]

In response to this urge to accept him as a Christian writer, legends about Seneca's conversion to Christianity and his friendship with St Paul soon began to circulate. This, in turn, produced a fictitious exchange of letters known as *Epistulae Senecae ad Paulum et Pauli ad Senecam*. All in all, there are a mere eight letters from Seneca and six from Paul, a scant correspondence which leaves much to be desired in both style and content. It is all the more surprising, then, that this fictitious exchange of letters was taken so seriously. From the eleventh century on, the letters were either joined to Seneca's genuine *Epistulae Morales* or circulated independently in manuscript collections together with other genuine and apocryphal works.

The main transmitter of the legend was Jerome (*c.* 348–420), who used the letters as a justification for including Seneca in his famous *De Viris Illustribus 12*, in which he states: 'Lucius Annaeus Seneca of

Cordoba, pupil of Sotion the Stoic and uncle of Lucan the poet, lived very temperately.' This preamble is then followed by the much-quoted line 'but I would not have included him in the catalogue of Saints were it not for these letters between him and Paul which are read by many'. Although Jerome meant by 'catalogus sanctorum' only a list of writers on Christian topics, his words gave Seneca's name an aura of near-saintliness, especially as they were uttered in the context of his correspondence with the apostle.[2]

Another interesting feature of the sentence is Jerome's mention of the widespread reading public of these letters: 'quae leguntur a plurimis'. Jerome then goes on to say that, according to these letters, Seneca 'wished he had the same position among his people as Paul had among the Christians', and that 'he was killed by Nero two years before Peter and Paul were crowned with martyrdom'.

With one stroke of the pen, an authority such as Jerome redresses the precarious balance between praise and slander. Seneca, who not long before had been portrayed as teacher of Nero's vices, now surprisingly becomes associated with the Christian martyrs, like them meeting a violent death. Jerome does not say that Seneca was killed by Nero because of his friendship with Paul, but subsequent readers could deduce this from his words and did.

The authority of Jerome's testimony was such that his words were repeated in all Catalan, French and Italian translations of the Letters. As such they were quoted in the Prohemio to the Spanish translation of the *Epistulae Morales* and printed in 1496, thus giving wide diffusion to Seneca's image as a saintly sage. In the style of a dust-jacket blurb, the Prohemio lists all the virtues of the book, finishing with 'Deste sabio Séneca hizo San Jerónimo muy especial mención en el libro que él compuso de los varones claros por tales palabras . . .'. The words in question, of course, refer to his abstemious life, the equally misleading mention of the 'catálogo de los santos' and the letters between Paul and Seneca, 'que de muchos son leídas'.

In Spain, Seneca's status as a native son of Cordoba was as important as his legendary friendship with the apostle. Following in the footsteps of the chroniclers, Alonso de Cartagena (1384–1456), another 'image-maker', proclaims the Roman philosopher as King John II's favourite subject, 'Porque Séneca fue vuestro natural y nacido en vuestros reinos y tenido sería, si viviese, de vos hacer homenaje' (*CL* 4). Cartagena's words, recorded in the Prologue to his translation of

Seneca's *De Providentia Dei*, subsequently appeared in print in 1491, thus authorizing the myth of 'Séneca español'.

Meanwhile, thanks to an equally bizarre process of transmission, Seneca's literary fame increased by leaps and bounds. More than any other Latin author, he enjoyed the questionable honour of having his work pillaged and reattributed to him, his canon rearranged beyond recognition, his words quoted out of context and, what is more, his name attached to work by other hands.

Apart from the apocryphal correspondence between Seneca and Paul which began to circulate in the fourth century, there was another dubious early transmission, the *Formula Vitae Honestae*. This was a sixth-century treatise on the four Stoic virtues, based on a presumed lost work by Seneca entitled *De Officiis*. Although its true author, Martin of Braga, does not mention his source, this hugely popular treatise reappeared in the twelfth century under Seneca's name with the title *De Quattuor Virtutibus*. The popularity of the treatise was due mainly to its analysis of *prudentia*, a virtue which, if used properly, promised to pay great dividends.[3]

Another pseudo-Senecan work which began to circulate at this time was *De Remediis Fortuitorum*, a treatise which is still considered by some to be by Seneca. Like the *Formula*, it was probably extracted from a genuine Senecan treatise. However, like the apocryphal correspondence with Paul, its contents are of dubious stylistic and philosophic merit.[4] It is a short treatise of only a dozen or so folios, taking the form of a dialogue between a querulous Sensus and a comforting Ratio. The complaints advanced concern all types of misfortune, including sickness, old age, poverty, shipwreck, enemies and the loss of family or friends. Meanwhile, Ratio's consolatory words are rather cynical, admonishing Sensus to wipe away his tears and get on with life. The interest of the treatise resides in its relation to the second book of Petrarch's *De Remediis Utriusque Fortunae*; however, his point of reference is not the pseudo-*Remediis* but Seneca's genuine work, and the *Epistulae Morales* in particular.

It was not until the twelfth century that Seneca was to conquer the hearts and minds of all medieval readers. At first, *De Clementia* and *De Beneficiis* were the most cherished treatises, and they could be found, together with the first 88 of the 124 *Epistulae Morales*, in the main religious libraries of Europe (Reynolds 1965: 12). The first two books were particularly valued by rulers and princes, *De Clementia* because it dealt with political ethics in its advocacy of tolerance in the name of expediency, and *De Beneficiis* because it taught how, when and by how much to reward one's dependants. Of these three genuine Senecan texts, however, the *Epistulae Morales* would prove to be a perennial favourite.

By contrast with the seven books on gifts and the long volume on mercy, Seneca's letters to Lucilius attracted those readers in search of short answers to a wide range of practical problems. In fact, Seneca's moral precepts proved so applicable to contemporary life that he soon became the stock-in-trade of those in search of quotable maxims. The medieval need to quote Senecan *sententiae* and *exempla* was best met by diverse sentence collections, of which the apocryphal *De Moribus* and *Proverbia Senecae* are the most conspicuous examples.

By its very title the first collection shows how Seneca's ethics were taken to be a set of rules of good conduct, while the second brings out the proverbial quality of his words of wisdom. Even so, the *Proverbia*, a list of some 365 *sententiae* arranged in alphabetical order, are mostly by other hands. Two-thirds of them (A–M) come from the maxims of the Roman mime Publilius Syrus, the remainder (N–Z) from *De Moribus*, itself a collection of aphorisms culled from Seneca's *Epistulae*, Vincent of Beauvais' *Speculum*, the Church Fathers and other sources.[5]

This type of miscellaneous compilation, on which the label 'by Seneca' was stuck to lend it greater authority, fits perfectly into the new learning of the emerging schools and universities. In response to an academic interest in source and commentary, twelfth-century scholasticism evolved an ingenious system affording quick reference to *auctoritates*; by *auctoritas* they meant the famous sayings of an author rather than the author himself. To facilitate location of texts, the material was organized into books and chapters, each with its running titles, rubrics and marginal glosses.

Compiling *auctoritates* required the co-operation of many scholars such as the humble scribe (*scriptor*), the compiler (*compilator*), the commentator (*commentator*) and finally the author (*auctor*), who added his own glosses to those of the compiler and commentator, and so put his final mark on the work. The *auctor* most responsible for elevating the *compilatio* to an art form was Vincent of Beauvais, whose *Speculum* would in turn serve as a source and inspiration for later compilations.[6]

Of interest to those researching the Senecan tradition in Spain is the *Tabulatio et Expositio Senecae* by the Italian Bishop Luca Mannelli, who dedicated his immense compilation to Pope Clement VI in the mid-fourteenth century. A selection from this compilation was translated by Alonso de Cartagena in the early fifteenth century and proved so popular that it was printed in 1491 as the last book of *Cinco libros de Séneca*.[7]

The collection reads like a genuine anthology of Seneca's work, divided into short treatises, each dealing with a particular topic. The subject under discussion is then illustrated with an extract from a particular passage in Seneca's work, while the glosses give the source of similar sayings, explaining obscure passages and refuting a heretical thought wherever necessary. Thus the medieval reader was able to take note of the whole of Seneca's canon, including the tragedies, and could compare his moral philosophy with that of other classical and Christian thinkers.

Other *compendia* of Seneca's words of wisdom comprise the anonymous *De Institutis Legalibus*, a list of maxims collected from various sources, the *Copia Verborum*, a condensation of the *Formula Vitae Honestae*, the *De Paupertate* and *De Sapientia*, both containing extracts from the *Epistulae Morales*.

Finally, mention should be made of the legalistic *Controversiae* by Seneca the Elder, which were commonly attributed to the son until the end of the sixteenth century. This is a collection of declamatory samples, replete with the sayings of famous orators and organized in an argumentative dialogue. Another work on which the label 'by Seneca' was often stuck was Flavius Vegetius' *Epitome Rei Militaris* on knightly virtues. Thus, to put it in the words of Leighton Reynolds, it is clear that 'Seneca's fame grew fat on works which he had never written' (Reynolds 1965: 112).

Although certain medieval scholars had expressed legitimate doubts as to the authenticity of some of the transmitted texts, genuine and apocryphal works as a rule happily co-existed in medieval manuscript collections and were copied, anthologized, translated and printed as if they were all authentic.

Seneca's medieval transmission and reception end with Erasmus' critical editions of 1515 and 1529 (Blüher 1983: 123–42). The humanist's philological inquiry into the validity of each text once and for all separated the genuine from the apocryphal works, with the exception of the anonymous *De Remediis Fortuitorum* and Seneca the Elder's rhetorical writings. True to his own predilection for clarity and simple language, Erasmus came down rather heavily on Seneca's style, which he condemned even more than Quintilian had done for being bombastic and disorganized. With these reservations, however, Erasmus still recommended the moral philosopher, and so 'Seneca castigatus' survived the humanist's surgical knife, thus starting a new era of Senecan reception.

Interestingly, the reduction of Seneca's canon was no impediment to a new wave of interest, dissemination and imitation. On the contrary, the growing neo-Stoic movement chose Seneca as the exponent of fortitude under hardship, a repository of all practical wisdom and a fountain of consolation in the face of increasing disillusion. Montaigne, Caspar Schoppe, Thomas Lodge, Justus Lipsius, Quevedo and countless other men of letters unanimously hailed the Roman philosopher as their favourite teacher of Stoicism. Moreover, a late sixteenth-century anti-Ciceronianism wholly rehabilitated Seneca's style, as witness Justus Lipsius' commentaries in his celebrated new edition of Seneca's complete works printed in 1605.[8]

Although by now Tacitus' *Imago Vitae Suae* was widely read thanks to Lipsius' edition of the *Annales*, this potentially damaging account of Seneca's life did not stop the humanists from considering him an *auctoritas* on ethics. Thus his eminently portable and quotable sentences continued to be a rich source of epigrams, mottoes and other notable sayings.

Concurrently, the sixteenth century renewed its acquaintance with Seneca's tragedies, not because of their moral content, but because of their passionate portrayal of love, death and revenge on the stage. The Elizabethan playwrights in England, their counterparts in France and the *trágicos españoles*, as well as the writers of *comedias*, all owe much to Seneca's dramatic analysis of behaviour dominated by passion rather than reason.[9]

In striking contrast to Seneca's medieval reception as a master in the *ars vivendi*, the neo-Stoics admired him on account of a perceived *ars moriendi*, due in part to the survival of the spurious and death-dominated *De Remediis Fortuitorum*. This modern view of Stoic impassivity in the face of suffering and death on the one hand and of violence and bloodshed on the other persisted through subsequent generations of readers and, in certain respects, is still with us today.

Translation as a means of transmission

A good way to measure the extent to which an author is adopted by a foreign readership is to note the quantity of his work in translation. In the case of Seneca, we come to the startling realization that the number of his translated books is more than quadruple that for any other classical author in fifteenth-century Castile. If we add to the genuine works the even more popular semi- and pseudo-Senecan translations, the list becomes truly extraordinary (see below, pp. 153–5).

In fact, the success of other authorities fades considerably when compared to that of Seneca's books which circulated in translation throughout the fifteenth century. Of Aristotle's work, only the *Ethics* were translated and printed, while a compendium to these was used in the schools. Plato's *Phaedo* was translated by the same Pero Díaz de Toledo who glossed and translated the *Proverbia Senecae*, but, unlike these, it never reached the European presses. Cicero has long been considered a formidable influence, but in actual fact only three of his shorter treatises were translated by Alonso de Cartagena, who was later to translate six of Seneca's genuine books and six semi- and pseudo-Senecan texts.[10] Despite this, it should be pointed out here that Plato, Aristotle and Cicero remained the cherished authors of the educated classes, who, by definition, did not need the crutch of a translation.

This wide interest in Seneca's moral philosophy seems to be uniquely a Spanish phenomenon. In Italy, the discovery of Cicero's rhetorical works in 1421 sparked a new interest in language and style.[11] The orator's writing was studied, diffused and imitated, and Ciceronianism spread to the rest of Europe. Spain, however, remained faithful to her favourite son, openly preferring Seneca to Cicero.

Castile's preference for Seneca over Cicero cannot be explained in terms of national pride alone. Throughout the fifteenth century Castilian literati consciously valued moral philosophy more than the study of rhetoric, tending to dismiss the latter as a fruitless exercise – as witness Pérez de Guzmán's statement in *Los sabios de España*: 'Asaz emplea sus días/en oficio infructuoso/quien sólo en fablar fermoso/ meta sus filosofías' (Blüher 1983: 169).

Perhaps the most eloquent example of this resistance is the long polemic between Alonso de Cartagena and Leonardo Bruni concerning the latter's translation of Aristotle's *Ethics*.[12] One of Cartagena's objections to the humanists' new translation was to his use of neologisms and a Ciceronian concision of expression, which, he argued, detracted from its clarity and meaning. Too much attention to form, Cartagena maintained, obscures the message and invites misinterpretation. Hence his own adoption of plain language in translating

Seneca: 'siguiendo el seso más que las palabras' (Prologue to *De la providencia de Dios* (*CL* 4)).[13]

In comparison to Bruni's elegant style, Cartagena's technique must have seemed pedestrian, old-fashioned and over-scholastic. In reality, however, Castile's initial opposition to Italian humanism should be seen as a genuine concern for truth and understanding coupled with a fear that too much attention to form would lead to artificiality and hollow rhetoric.

Nor does he speak without experience in this matter. While ambassador to Portugal, and prior to embarking on his translations of Seneca, he had been commissioned by the Portuguese crown prince to translate Cicero's *De Senectute*, *De Amicitia* and *De Inventione* (see Salazar 1976). It seems, however, that he shared his own sovereign's preference for Seneca, judging by his words in the Prologue to his translation of *De Providentia*.

Addressing himself to his patron, King John II of Castile (1406–54), he explains: 'E aunque a Cicerón todos los latinos reconozcan el principado de la elocuencia . . . siguió [i.e. Cicero] su larga manera de escribir y solemne como aquel que con razón en el hablar llevó el principado' (*CL* 4). The same Prologue gives us other clues as to the why and how of Seneca's popularity. First, Cartagena found it necessary to point out that the king was well acquainted with other classical authors but that he often preferred Seneca: 'Y aunque muchos lees pláceos escoger a las veces a Séneca y no sin razón.' Apart from Seneca's being a Spaniard, the main reason was his talent for giving such poignant advice that it went straight to the heart: 'tan cordiales amonestamientos ni palabras que tanto hieran al corazón'. Then, contrasting Seneca's colloquial style to Cicero's solemn rhetoric, Cartagena becomes quite florid in describing the former's impact on the reader: 'mas Séneca tan menudas y tan justas puso las reglas de la virtud con estilo elocuente como si bordara una ropa de argentería bien obrada de ciencia en el muy lindo paño de la elocuencia. Porende no lo debemos llamar del todo orador ca mucho es mezclado con la moral filosofía'.

Clearly, moral philosophy in fifteenth-century Castile was still the preferred subject of inquiry, and Seneca was seen as a mirror in which man could recognize 'sus costumbres cuáles son buenas o malas' (Cartagena's gloss to 'espejo', *De la clemencia*, BN 6962, fol. 59v).

In addition to offering pointers to good conduct, Seneca's philosophy was considered to be of great psychological value on account of the *animi remedia*, which were so applicable to contemporary problems. Seneca himself has many a thought on the transmission of these 'remedies'. For instance, in Epistula 64, he talks about the continuous process of passing on previous knowledge, summed up as 'Animi remedia inventa sunt ab antiquis; quomodo autem admoveantur aut quando, nostri operis est quaerere' (*Ep*. 64, 9). In the Spanish anthology this reads: 'Los remedios del corazón son hallados por los antiguos, mas a nos pertenece conocer y escoger la sazón y la manera de la usanza' (Anth. 55, fol. 56v).

A very early example of putting Seneca's 'remedios del corazón' to good use is the translation of his *De Ira*, the first vernacular version of a Senecan treatise in Spain and possibly in Europe. It was translated at the end of the thirteenth century in the court of Sancho IV 'el bravo', a man reputedly prone to fits of anger. It is significant that Seneca's first translated book deals with what he calls an *affectus*, that is to say an affliction or a mental disturbance. This is the word Seneca uses to refer to the Greek *pathos*, by which the Stoics meant a disease of the mind. Of all the *affectus*, Seneca says in *De Ira*, anger is the most destructive, as it causes irreparable harm to oneself and to others. Stressing political ethics but leaving out the philosophical polemic concerning this *affectus*, the Spanish *Libro de Séneca contra la ira y saña* became a suitable 'Mirror for Princes', as the Prologue brings out: '. . . e hízolo [Seneca] a provecho de todos universal, y más señaladamente para los príncipes y grandes señores; porque en los semejantes la ira y saña es muy más peligrosa' (Rubio 1961: 120). Its impact was such that in 1445 Nuño de Guzmán, unhappy with the first translation, commissioned a reworking of the text.[14] This fifteenth-century revision of *La ira y saña* itself forms part of a proliferation of Seneca translations initiated in the court of John II in the early thirties.

Aware of the eminent applicability of Seneca's moral philosophy, the king wished to make the information available to others as well: 'Y no vos contentastes de lo vos entender si por vos no lo entendiesen otros', as Cartagena puts it (*CL* 4). The very phenomenon of translation, a relative novelty in those days, reveals a love of antiquity outstripping their knowledge of Latin. Cartagena's mention of the king's wish to have Seneca translated so that others might benefit from his words points to a lack of Latin among the nobility. A more explicit statement in this respect comes from Pero Díaz de Toledo, who, in the Prologue to his translation of the *Proverbia Senecae*, says that King John had commissioned the translation for 'los de vuestro palacio y si se pudiera hacer todos los de vuestra corte y reino que no saben latín o si lo saben no lo entienden expedidamente' (R. 4).

King John was very wise to choose Cartagena as the man to transmit Seneca's philosophy to the layman. Then Dean of Santiago, Cartagena was soon to become Bishop of Burgos and famous for his writing on theology as well as for his role at the negotiating table at the Council of Basle.[15]

His fame as a sage and scholar was to endure after his death. In the *Coplas* commemorating Cartagena's death, Pérez de Guzmán, himself an admirer of Seneca, tells us: 'aquel Séneca espiró a quien yo era Lucilio' (Blüher 1983: 145). Juan de Lucena makes Cartagena the protagonist of his book *Diálogo de vita beata* and introduces him with the words: 'Tú de cavallería, de república, de fe cristiana escribiste vulgar, y las obras famosas del moral Séneca nuestro vulgarizaste.'[16]

It is very possible then, that in the first instance it was Cartagena who inspired the Court of John II with his example, erudition and personality. His influence was such that the nobility themselves soon started collecting and exchanging manuscripts, with the result that they assimilated much of Seneca's thought into their own literary compositions.[17]

The Senecan translations

Cartagena translated six genuine Senecan treatises, *De Providentia Dei*, *De Constantia Sapientis*, *De Clementia*, *De Vita Beata*, *De Otio* and *De Septem Artibus Liberalibus* (*Ep.* 88). The choice of books to introduce to the non-professional reader is of itself significant, in that it reflects what was considered useful in Seneca's message at the beginning of the fifteenth century. In his Introduction to the translation of *De Clementia*, Cartagena shows how appropriate the book continued to be for the guidance of princes. Looking for words to translate the Latin word *clementia*, he refers to 'epiqueia', an obscure word, but much bandied about in the royal chambers, which he sees as meaning 'aquello que expediente llaman en vuestro consejo' (BN 6962, fol. 68ᵛ).

Seneca's *De Providentia Dei*, translated as *De la providencia de Dios*, explains the disturbing fact that adversity befalls good men, a fact summed up in the Prologue as 'porqué Dios consiente venir mal a los buenos y prosíguelos con polido estilo según su costumbre' (*CL* 4). In this treatise, the discussion centres not on man but on God, who, in his infinite wisdom, puts the worthiest to the test. The argument is, of course, very much in line with the Book of Job and seen to be greatly edifying, since 'de la providencia divinal muchos son los que hablan así católicos como gentiles' (Introduction).

The translation of *De Constantia Sapientis* addresses the more worldly question 'si el varón virtuoso y perfecto se turba en algo por los injurios que le hacen o quieren hacer' (BN 6962, fol. 30ʳ). We find an equally down-to-earth approach to life in the Prologue to the translation of *De Vita Beata*, which is recommended as 'un maravilloso tratado . . . para pro común de los que en esta vida vivimos'. The book appealed to all, since the subject-matter, translated as *De la vida bienaventurada*, teaches how to achieve happiness on earth, 'este soberano bien que todos desean' (*CL* 1). As was usual, Seneca's fragment *De Otio* appears as a continuation of the *De Vita Beata*, as a fitting conclusion to the argument, since it advocates retirement from worldly affairs as the ultimate good.

Interestingly, Seneca's Epistula 88 on the liberal arts had circulated separately in Latin before it was translated as *De las siete artes liberales*. The letter itself deals with the ultimate uselessness of all seven liberal arts in attaining wisdom and virtue, arguing that 'no ponen en nuestro corazón la virtud mas aparejan para la recibir' (*CL* 2). One attraction of this particular letter may well have been its apparent support of Castile's suspicion of Italian humanism.

Of all Seneca's genuine writing, the work most cherished by the medieval reader was the collection of 124 *Epistulae Morales* which Seneca wrote towards the end of his life to his friend Lucilius. Although various Spanish translations of the *Epistulae Morales* exist, very few contain all 124 letters, as does the Escorial manuscript S.II.6. Some list only the first 88 (e.g., BN 8852), and most have only 75 letters. These, in fact, go back to an anthology which Fernán Pérez de Guzmán had translated from an Italian translation, itself probably based on an earlier French version.[18] The *Epístolas de Séneca* were always a favourite with Seneca's readers, possibly because of their form, which makes for short, colloquial pieces abounding in personal advice. One extra attraction of the letters may well have been that, alongside Stoic ethics, they give a critical appraisal of much of Epicurean thought. Indeed, the Prohemio to the translation makes a special point of mentioning that Seneca was a Stoic for whom the ultimate good is virtue: 'por lo cual mezcla entre sus dichos las sentencias de un filósofo llamado Epicuro que decía que el deleite es soberano bien'.

The letters chosen for the Anthology deal mainly with everyday issues such as how to make friends, how to avoid the crowd, and how to spurn riches and all worldly pressures and excesses in general. The *Epístolas de Séneca* were read by people from all walks of life. In a letter to his cousin, the Marqués de Santillana claims to value them second only to the Holy Scriptures. A student on his way to Salamanca was the proud possessor of a manuscript of them, and Queen Isabella had a copy in her library replete with annotations in her own hand (see plate 1). Finally, as we know from the inventory of his will, Fernando de Rojas had a printed copy in his library.[19]

The ten Senecan tragedies were also translated, but in rather truncated form. There is reason to believe that the Marqués de Santillana commissioned the translations and that these came from a Catalan version made by Antón Vilaragut. However, their value for the fifteenth-century reader did not lie in their dramatic form, but rather in their moralistic content. Wherever mention is made of them, they are praised for their moral teaching, and it is recommended that they be recited rather than staged.[20] Even so, Alonso de Cartagena warns against taking them seriously, given the dubious character of some of the *dramatis personae*, whose words for that reason 'no han autoridad de doctrina' (*CL* 5, 'Tratado de la caza'). Another dramatic composition of Seneca, the *Divi Claudii Apocolocyntosis*, was translated as *Juego de Claudio Emperador* from an Italian version made by Claudio Decembrio and presented to Pero Nuño de Guzmán, the same Seneca *aficionado* who had had a revised translation made of Seneca's *De Ira* in the mid-fifteenth century.

To complete the picture of Seneca's transmission at the time, brief consideration should also be given to what was excluded from the translations. Seneca's *De Brevitate Vitae*, *De Tranquillitate Animi*, three *Consolationes*, *De Beneficiis* and *Naturales Quaestiones* were not available in the vernacular. The non-professional reader, however, had a second-hand knowledge of them through the extensive extracts included in the translation of Mannelli's *Tabulatio*. Understandably, the seven volumes of *De Beneficiis* may well have proved too much to translate as one complete work. By contrast, the reason why the equally long *Naturales Quaestiones* was not made available to all hinges more on its content.

As a philosophy, Stoicism stressed physics and logic as much as ethics, and Seneca especially was fascinated by all natural phenomena. Nowadays the Roman philosopher's inquiries into the nature of comets, wind, sounds and earthquakes constitute nothing more than an interesting chapter in the history of science, but the fifteenth-century Church considered Seneca's speculations about the universe and the nature of God potentially dangerous. On the one hand, the Stoic concept of the *logos* was perfectly compatible with Christian teaching. On the other, Seneca's thoughts on human participation in the divine origin of creation and his equation of the wise and virtuous man with God would have seemed downright heretical. So it was altogether safer only to translate those passages of the *Naturales Quaestiones* which had earlier been selected by Bishop Luca Mannelli for general consumption.

Semi- and pseudo-Senecan works and anthologies

Cartagena's translation of Mannelli's *Tabulatio* is only a selection, judging by his concluding words: 'aquí se acaba la una copilación de algunos dichos de Séneca sacados de vuestra gran copilación de sus dichos . . .' (*CL* 5). Thus the Spanish translation is yet another step in the continuous process of selecting and rearranging the Senecan canon. The selection of the material to be translated was also a collective effort, judging by Cartagena's further remarks: 'Y no van situados por ordenación por cuanto fueron trasladados acaso según que a cada uno en leyéndola le bien pareció . . .' The glosses, too, were added collectively: 'Y añadiéronle las glosas [here Mannelli's], y algunas adiciones [Cartagena's] en los lugares donde el dicho señor rey mandó [the patron].'

There is reason to believe that King John's initial preference for Seneca was dictated by this very love for potted wisdom. In this respect, the Prologue to the translation of *De Providentia Dei* furnishes us with yet another valuable piece of information as to the why and how of these first translations. Addressing his patron, Cartagena mentions how the king's interest in Seneca was aroused by a compilation which he had translated earlier: 'Y como de algunas copilaciones nuevas de las obras de Séneca muchos en uno ayuntaron, vos pluguiesen algunos dichos, mandastes a mí que los tornare en nuestra lengua, no por la orden en que ellos estaban escrito mas como acaso vinieren' (*CL* 4).

The compilations Cartagena mentions as being fused into one are Luca Mannelli's *Tabulatio et Expositio*, which was sometimes regarded as a two-part work and translated as *El libro de las compilaciones* (cf. BN 6765 and Escorial N-II-6). Another collection Cartagena translated for John II was the anonymous *De Institutis Legalibus*, which he called *Amonestamientos y doctrinas*, a title that more aptly reflects the contents of this collection of moral precepts. Here the 112 *doctrinas*, each no more than one or two lines long, are distributed into nine chapters which, true to fashion, are accompanied by extensive marginal glosses.

Other useful information for King John's courtiers could readily be found in the excerpts from Flavius Vegetius' *Epitome Rei Militaris*, which Cartagena translated as *Dichos de Séneca en el hecho de la cavallería*, and the *Formula Vitae Honestae* which had been conflated into the canon as *De Quattuor Virtutibus*, and now appeared as *El libro de las cuatro virtudes y doctrinas*.

The *Proverbia Senecae* and the *De Moribus* were given to a very different man to translate. Around 1447 King John commissioned the jurist Pero Díaz de Toledo to render into Spanish these two related collections, which were translated as *Los proverbios de Séneca* and *Obra y tractado de las costumbres*.[21]

Pero Díaz was very much aware of his task as a transmitter of classical wisdom in the Senecan sense of the word. In his translation he practises what Seneca preaches in *Ep.* 64, 7–8: namely, that our classical heritage should be passed on larger than before ('Maior esta hereditas a me ad posteros transeat'), that much remains to be done ('multum adhuc restat operis') and that he who shall be born a thousand years hence should not be prevented from adding something further ('aliquid adhuc adiciendi').

Conscious of being a mere link in the chain of transmission, he offers his book to the king with the words 'He dado comienzo para que otros que hayan más leído suplan y enmienden y corrijan lo que más vuestro señor les administrara' (R. 319). Moreover, in a gloss to Proverbio 131 he invokes Aristotle on the same topic, saying: 'dice Aristóteles en el segundo de la Metaphysica, "los postrimeros maestros que escriben sobre algunas ciencias deben trabajar por poner alguna cosa de nuevo que sus pasados no pusieron"' (R. 147). Pero Díaz de Toledo's own contribution to the transmission of Seneca's wisdom consisted of the long commentaries which he appended to each of the proverbs, and which, in the final analysis, accounted for the work's huge popularity, as each expanded on the moral message and synthesized what other authorities had said on that particular subject. (See plate 2.)

In the same fashion as other semi- and pseudo-Senecan sentence collections, the *Proverbios* have about them the flavour of the *Reader's Digest*, with which they have much in common. The non-professional reader was not prepared to spend long hours speculating on meaning or checking out sources, but rather, was looking for short answers to problems of practical conduct. The pseudo-Senecan world was populated by people who, like the readers, had somehow to cope with unpredictable women, disloyal servants, false friends, dangerous flatterers and the greedy masses. The advice given in these collections also addresses the perplexities of life and death or the complexities of inner conflict, albeit illustrated by the most common temptations of body and mind. In this fashion Pero Díaz contributed in no small way to the general, if only superficial, education of a new class of readers.

Seneca's translated wisdom in the first half of the fifteenth century was thus reduced to a code of behaviour for the ruling classes. From *El libro de la clemencia* the nobility could learn about showing leniency to one's dependants; *El libro de la constancia* contained much good advice on impassivity in the face of offence; while *El libro contra la ira y saña* admonished them to control their anger. The futility of the liberal arts was exposed in *Las siete artes liberales*, while the achievement of happiness was analysed in *La vida bienaventurada*. Moreover, all this genuine Stoic wisdom could be read in shorter, assimilable portions, thanks to the various translations of the *Epistulae Morales*. In questions of metaphysics *El libro de la providencia de Dios* was available to the lay reader, although with certain limitations brought out in the marginal glosses. Access to the *Naturales Quaestiones* was, however, limited to Bishop Mannelli's pre-selection of 'safe' passages contained in the *Copilación por alfabeto*, which also encompassed extensive abstracts from other untranslated books by Seneca.

Interestingly, Seneca had not earned the affectionate honorific 'nuestro' on account of his genuine philosophy but because of the potted wisdom contained in the compilations of his real or imagined words. It was here, after all, that the average reader could learn how to lead a civilized life in a changing world or, as Pero Díaz puts it, 'las reglas y doctrina de todo el bueno y polido vivir de los hombres' (R. 4).

First printings

In 1482, barely ten years after the printing presses had made their appearance in Spain, Pero Díaz de Toledo's *Proverbios de Séneca* were singled out to appear in print by Antón de Centenera, a bookseller in Zamora. Then, as now, the decision must have been influenced by commercial considerations based on readers' recommendations and on proven general appeal.²² In the case of the *Proverbios*, the booksell-er's choice hit the mark squarely. Of all Seneca's genuine and apocryphal writings this collection was to be the most successful of all. In 1491 the brothers Hurus in Zaragoza brought out another edition, which was followed in 1495 by a bilingual version published in Seville by Meynardo Ungut and Estanislao Polono. In 1500, Pedro Hagenbach of Toledo brought out two more editions, after which the place of publication shifted to various towns, including Antwerp, where in 1548 Johannes Steelsius obtained the privilege of printing all Spanish translations of Seneca. The successful printing history of the *Proverbios* ends in Medina del Campo, with the combined edition of Pero Díaz's *Proverbios* and Cartagena's *Amonestamientos y doctrinas* in 1555.

The printing history of Cartagena's miscellaneous translations and that of the anthology of Seneca's letters follow a similar pattern. The selection and reduction of Cartagena's versions resulted in the publi-cation of *Los cinco libros de Séneca* by Ungut and Polono in 1491. The book was reprinted several times in the sixteenth century and, like the *Proverbios*, was taken up by the famous house of Johannes Steelsius, where it appeared for the last time in 1551. (See plates 3 and 4.) The anthology of *Epistulae Morales* was the last of the fifteenth-century Seneca translations to appear in print. It was published in Zaragoza at the expense of a certain Juan Tomás de Lumelo in 1496 and was soon taken over by Pedro Hagenbach of Toledo, who printed editions of it in 1502 and 1510. As with the *Proverbios*, the printing of the *Epístolas* was ultimately taken over by Steelsius and ended in Medina del Campo in 1555.

It is worth noting that between 1491 and 1504 the same printers had seen the potential both of the Seneca translations and of *Celestina*. In 1491 Estanislao Polono of Seville published the *Proverbios* and *Los cinco libros*, and in 1501 the third extant edition of the *Comedia de Calisto y Melibea*. In 1500 Pedro Hagenbach twice published the *Proverbios de Séneca*, as well as the second extant edition of the *Comedia de Calisto y Melibea*. In 1502 the same house printed *Las epístolas de Séneca*, which was followed by the now lost *editio princeps* of the 21-act *Tragicomedia de Calisto y Melibea* in 1504. Clearly, both Polono and Hagenbach had a fine nose for potential bestsellers, and both aimed at a readers' market with an interest in Seneca and *Celestina*.

No less important for the transmission of Seneca's ideas in print is a consideration of the printers' selections from available texts. As the first volume of *Los cinco libros de Séneca* the booksellers chose Cartagena's *De la vida bienaventurada*; *De las siete artes liberales* appears as *Libro segundo*, *Amonestamientos y doctrinas* as *Libro tercero* and the first half of *De la providencia de Dios* as *Libro cuarto*. The fifth book purports to contain the second half of *De la providencia de Dios*, but instead gives the *Copilación por alfabeto*, 'algunas declamaciones' and a curious little allegorical piece entitled 'En qué manera los poetas fingieron tres hermanas vírgines . . .'.

The title and rubric of the last book of *Los cinco libros* are most misleading. This section starts out by saying 'Aquí comienza el segundo libro de Séneca de la providencia de Dios en que se trata cómo en el sabidor no cabe injuria ni ofensa alguna.' Both statements are wrong. The book neither contains the second half of Cartagena's translation of *De Providentia Dei* nor deals with impassivity to offence, which is the subject-matter of *De Constantia Sapientis*. To this confusion is then added 'Todos estos capítulos que se siguen fueron sacados de la copilación del alfabeto en el tratado del amor.' Even this is an incorrect statement, since not all the chapters come from Mannelli's section on love. This was translated separately, and by a different hand as 'Título de la amistanza o del amigo' (BN 6962), and was never printed. One might suspect that the mistake in *Cinco libros* was made by the printers. However, various manuscripts of Seneca's collected works contain the same error (BN 8177, BN 8241, BN 17,798 and BN 11,3072).

By contrast to the printers' nonchalance in selecting their manuscripts, their choice of topics was to the point. Obviously, the late fifteenth-century buyer of books was not interested in *De la clemencia* or in *De la constancia*, books that were more suitable for the education of princes. Instead, *De la vida bienaventurada*, with its detailed analysis of what constitutes happiness on earth, and *De la providencia de Dios*, which attempts to come to grips with God's apparent injustice, were of great interest to the non-professional reader. *De las siete artes liberales*, with its implicit condemnation of the literary arts as ultimately useless in man's quest for wisdom, was appropriate to the question then being hotly debated on whether philosophy or poetry was pre-eminent,[23] while the two collections of *Amonestamientos y doctrinas* and *Copilación* would appeal to all.

The printing of the translation of the *Epistulae Morales* was less fraught with choices and errors. The printers simply selected the existing anthology which Pérez de Guzmán had commissioned to be

1. Queen Isabella owned a manuscript of *Las epístolas de Séneca*, shown here with her own commentary alongside the marginal glosses of the translator. (Escorial MS S-II-9.) (*Reproduced by permission of the Biblioteca del Real Monasterio El Escorial, Madrid.*)

rememozar el beneficio al q̃ lo re
ſcibio es mas traer a indigna ci⸗
on que a gracia.pozque pareſce
demandar inominioſamente lo
que le tu diſte. ¶Pues bien di⸗
ro ſeneca que el que dize que te
dio beneficio demanda lo.

Grand debdo es cõjuntar ſe
los corazones que ſe bien quierẽ

Dize ariſtotiles enel octauo
delas ethicas q̃ la amiſtança es
de tres maneras. La vna poz d
leyte:la otra poz pzouecho.la o
tra poz honeſto. La amiſtança
poz deleyte es quãdo vno ama
a otro poz el plazer que ha cõ̦el
pozque es donoſo:pozque es a⸗
legze:pozque dize de buenas co
ſas.E eſta amiſtança non dura
mucho:pozque aſſi como ſegũd
creſce la hedad:aſſi ſe muda las
coſas que alegzan:τ trahen pla
zer ſegund dize Ariſtotiles enel
pzimero dlas ethicas.aſſi ſe mu⸗
da eſta amiſtança.La con vnoſ
hombzes contractamos vn tiẽ⸗
po:τ los queremos bien:τ ama
mos ſu compañia pozque haue⸗
mos plazer τ gaſajado conelloſ
que otro tiẽpo los tenemos por
locos:τ nos apartamos d ſu cõ
pañia como de compañia de lo⸗
cos. Otra amiſtança ay q̃ ſe di⸗
ze poz pzouecho.E eſta es q̃ cõ⸗
tracto contigo τ te amo poz el p
uecho que he de ti:τ ſi viene tiẽ⸗
po q̃ ceſſe eſte pzouecho ceſſa lue
go eſta amiſtaça pues ceſſo por

lo que eramos amigos. Otra a
miſtança ay que ſe llama hone⸗
ſto.E eſta es la verdadera ami
ſtança que es poz virtud:que yo
te amo τ te quiero bien. pozque
eres honeſto τ virtuoſo. E eſta
no puede ſer ſino entre buenos:
τ virtuoſos:τ eſta dura todo ti
empo:τ dura en pzoſperidad: τ
aduerſidad: τ mejoz en aduerſi⸗
dad que en pzoſperidad. lo que
las pzimeras dos no fazen τ ha
un no dizẽ:E entre las otras co
ſas que la philoſophia dezia bo
ecio ſegund eſcriue eñl tercero d
conſolacion pozq̃ la aduerſa foz
tuna apzouechaua mas q̃ la pſ⸗
pera era pozque la pzoſpera tra
ya le engañado creyendo q̃ to⸗
dos eran ſus amigos quãtos ſe
le moſtrauan poz amigos:la ad
uerſa diſcernio τ aparto los ver
daderos amigos dlos fengidoſ
La en tiempo d aduerſidad no
quedan conel hõbze los amigoſ
que le ſiguẽ poz el pzouecho que
del eſperauan:nin poz el deleyte
τ plazer que conel hauian: mas
ſolamente los que eran ſus ami
gos poz lo honeſto: τ poz la vir
tud.onde dixo el verſificadoz q̃n
do fueres bienauenturado mu⸗
chos amigos contaras:ſi los ti
empos fuerẽ anublados ſolo te
quedaras.E eſtos amigos ſon
vna anima en dos cuerpos:es
vn no querer:τ vn querer de am
bos a dos alegza ſe el vno dl bi⸗
en del otro:τ el otro del bien dl
otro.E el daño q̃ viene a qualq̃
b v

2. A page from Pero Díaz de Toledo's *Proverbios de Séneca* (Zaragoza, 1491),
showing how the translator's glosses dominate the text. (*Reproduced by permission of
the Biblioteca Nacional, Madrid.*)

3. Title-page of BN, INC. 661, of *Los cinco libros de Séneca* (Seville, 1491), clearly a very heavily used copy of the book. (*Reproduced by permission of the Biblioteca Nacional, Madrid.*)

Libro quinto.

dozes dixierõ así. La saña es vna (breue locura). Ca es
semeiãte aella por quãto el õbre sañudo no es podero
so dese regir oluidalo q̃ le pertenesçe. No se le miembra
delos pariêtes. psigue cõ grãd porfia lo q̃ comêço No
ētiéde razõ. ni oye cõseio. E es muy mouido τ aguija /
do de ymaginaçiones vanas. E no esta abile para co/
nosçer: q̃l es lo razonable τ lo iusto. E paresçe la saña a
la cayda delos edifiçios los q̃les q̃ndo cabé q̃brãtã aq̃l
lo sobre q̃ cabé τ q̃branse ellos sobre ello.

Enel tractado delas buenas costũbres.

Esquiuaras la crueldad τ la seruidora dela crueldad
que es la saña.

Que cosa es la saña. τ dõde nasçe.

Eneste libro.

Quieres q̃ te prueue q̃ la saña no nasçe dela iniuria q̃
nos bazé. puar te lo he así. Çierto es q̃ nos ésañamos
contra los q̃ nos (ban de iniuriar) avnq̃ no nos ayã in
iuriado. Mas puedes tu respõder el que nos ba de ba
zer iniuria enel pensamiento nos daña. τ ya nos baze
iniuria el que la quiere bazer. E quieres que te prueue
que la saña no es cobdiçia de prueua. así te lo prouare.
Veemos q̃ õbres de muy poco poder se ésaña otra los
muy poderosos τ no cobdiçiã dar les pena. ca no espe
ran delo poder bazer. Pero aesto puedese respõder.

**Breue locu
ra.**
porq̃ no es con
tinuada segund
se escriue enel ca
pitulo desuso é
la glosa sobre:
sobre la parte.
no ay diferençia
τ seneca aprue /
ua esto. E da ra
zõ porque es lo
cura. Conuiene
a saber porque
los sañudos no
son poderosos
dese regir τ dez
an la hermosura
dlas costunbres
τ no curan delos
parientes ni de
los amigos ni d̃
los cuñados co
mo si no se men
basse delos pa/
rétescos en que
son cõiuntos cõ
ellos: τ la saña
sola mente pien
sa de proseguir
lo que comen /
ço. τ esta rebelde

enello τ encienese con ligeras causas τ no acata acõseio ni arazon τ menospreçia la egualdad
τ la iustiçia. τ conpara la seneca ala cayda delos edifiçios. la qual destruyo lo que bailla enel
los quebrantase sobre la madera τ piedras sobre que cayeron.

Ban de iniuriar.

Arguye seneca que la saña no nasçe dela iniuria. porque nos ésañamos contra aquellos que
pensamos que nos ban de iniuriar τ bazer mal. E aesto argumento responde que ay tenemos
enel coraçon reçebido la iniuria que nos ban de bazer como si ya fuese becha. E poiende la sa
ña nasçe dela iniuria concebida enel coraçon del que es iniuriado. o lo cuyda ser adelante. Ca
ya reçebimos la iniuria en nuestras ymaginaçiones. τ esto es lo que dize: ya nos baze iniuria
el que la quiere bazer.

4. A page from Cartagena's translation of Luca Mannelli's *Tabulatio et Expositio
Senecae*, printed as Book 5 of *Los cinco libros de Séneca* (Seville, 1491). Note how
printers copied the manuscript lay-out of gloss and text. (*Reproduced by permission
of the Biblioteca Nacional, Madrid.*)

quexemos z amamos las cosas

virtuosas z honestas. por esa :

mesma via amamos desea

mos queremos z buscamos

la amistad. E asi commo la

soledat es aborrescable o se

gund otra letra dize la sole

5. A manuscript page from the 'Título de la amistanza y del amigo', showing the 'cordon sanitaire' of its glosses. (BN, MS 6962.) (*Reproduced by permission of the Biblioteca Nacional, Madrid.*)

translated from the Italian. They left the Prohemio intact but took out the sporadic and irrelevant glosses. At the end they added an 'Introducción siquier summa de filosofía moral', which is Leonardo Bruni's Introduction to his translation of Aristotle's *Ethics*, the same work that had aroused Cartagena's criticism fifty years earlier. The *Summa* analyses the parts of moral philosophy and the division of the virtues, concluding fittingly with the words 'y pues en la vida a cada cual ciertamente nos es proposada la felicidad, y della tenemos una codicia por natura en nosotros engendrada . . . buenos seamos y de virtudes usemos' (Anth., fol. 83r). Thus we see how, well into the sixteenth century, Seneca's *ars vivendi* kept its appeal for the man in the street.

The fact that Steelsius secured the monopoly to print *Proverbios*, *Cinco libros* and *Epístolas de Séneca* for four years in the mid-sixteenth century, and that no sooner had his privilege run out, than the firm of Ghemart and de Millis in Medina del Campo took it over, shows how much of a bestseller the translated Seneca was considered to be. The printers' confidence in the books was based on the knowledge that the name Seneca had become a household word or that, put another way, Seneca had become a tradition created by many generations of readers and transmitters.

These, of course, were not restricted to the compilers and translators of his words of wisdom alone. With the spread of literacy in the fifteenth century, artistic creativity also increased among lay readers. As is to be expected, Fernán Pérez de Guzmán's *Coplas de vicios y virtudes* and Santillana's own *Proverbios*, as well as his *Bías contra fortuna*, are replete with Senecan maxims and Stoic philosophy. Alfonso de Madrigal's *Tratado como al ome es necesario amar* owes its aphorisms to the *Amonestamientos y doctrinas*; Lope de Barrientos' *Tratado de caso y fortuna* and Alfonso de la Torre's *Visión delectable* borrow extensively from Martin of Braga's *Formula Vitae Honestae*; while Rodrigo Sánchez de Arévalo and Diego de Valera appropriate much of *De Beneficiis* and *De Clementia* in their political writings (Blüher 1983: 165–211).

However, in these early samples of literary transmission the Senecan quotations often lack coherence or meaningful relation to the text. A departure from this purely mechanical treatment of a classical author is Juan de Lucena's *Diálogo de Vita Beata*, a free translation of Fazio's *De Vitae Felicitate*. Lucena's adaptation centres around a fictitious debate on how best to achieve happiness in this world, a dialogue which is guided by none other than Alonso de Cartagena. In fact, the latter's argument is based on the glosses to his translation of *De Vita Beata*, and, although the discourse is devoid of direct Senecan quotations, the Roman philosopher's presence is implied both by the title and by the various opinions advanced by the speakers.

Finally, there is *Celestina*, composed at the end of a century now wide awake to its classical heritage. The author of Act I, as well as Fernando de Rojas and the first readers of the 16-act *Comedia* were saturated with 'fontecicas de filosofía' available to them in multiple copies of manuscripts and early editions. Thus the *Comedia de Calisto y Melibea* could be seen as a lay reader's response to an information explosion that had taken place in the course of the fifteenth century.

Many of the quotations from and allusions to Seneca that occur in the literary compositions of the fifteenth century come, of course, from a variety of second-hand sources. For instance, one particularly rich depository of Senecan wisdom is the *Floresta de Philósophos*,[24] where one-third of the 3227 maxims have their origins in Cartagena's translations (Blüher 1983: 167). Other important sources include the *Libro de los ejemplos por A.B.C.*, the *Bocados de Oro*, the *Visión delectable* (Blüher 1983: 157–61) and the Latin *Margarita poética* (see below, Ch. 5, n. 12). And then there was the little-studied *vademecum*, a copybook in which the educated reader would jot down appropriate sayings to use in his own speech and writing as the occasion demanded. Whatever the method of assembling the material, each author gave new meaning to the Senecan *dictum* '. . . hoc semper novum erit, usus et inventorum ab aliis scientia ac dispositio' (*Ep.* 64, 8), translated as 'siempre esta cosa será nueva, conviene saber el uso y la ciencia de las cosas falladas por otras y la disposición' (Anth. 55, fol. 56r).

Clearly, what Seneca anticipated with these words was an endless and successive building of and onto the edifice of moral philosophy. And so it happened: generation after generation read, commented, copied and quoted what seemed most appropriate at the time, while a powerful *vox populi* promoted literary, political and moral preferences and prejudices. In the end, all these elements resulted in an all-encompassing consensus on Seneca's ethics, nowadays commonly referred to as 'the Senecan tradition'.

2

Senecan commentary as a frame of reference

Translation in the fifteenth century meant much more than rendering a text from one language into another. It was the translators' responsibility to transmit the text in such a way that it remained or became morally and dogmatically acceptable. To achieve this they added extensive prologues, introductions and rubrics and surrounded the text with glosses which were meant to guard the unwary reader against heresy and misunderstanding. Commentary thus became a means to educate the layman and to prepare future generations of readers for the 'right' reception of the classics.[1]

The fifteenth-century translators had the double task of adapting the old *scientia* to the new readers' level of comprehension while making pagan wisdom amenable to interpretation in accordance with the demands of the Church.[2] Judging by Cartagena's preface to *De la providencia de Dios*, there were two areas where the non-professional reader needed guidance. These were in acquiring a knowledge of classical history and mythology, and in the ability to distinguish between pagan wisdom and Catholic doctrine. However, the commentaries reveal much more to the modern reader. They bespeak a general ignorance and intellectual naivety in the first half of the fifteenth century; they uncover areas of confusion and possible heresy in the untutored mind; and, most importantly, they emphasize the matters that most preoccupied the fifteenth-century reader.

As far as *Celestina* is concerned, an acquaintance with both genuine and apocryphal Senecan thought is indispensable for an interpretation of the text.[3] But equally important for an understanding of the originality of the book is the need to be aware of the fifteenth-century intellectual frame of reference, as it is defined by the commentaries to Seneca's translated work.[4]

The topics singled out for clarification in the glosses represent typical concerns of the fifteenth-century reader. They also prove to have much in common with the themes and concerns of the *Comedia de*

Calisto y Melibea. The conflicts that come to the fore both in the Senecan commentaries and in the plot of Rojas' story are generally concerned with heretical thought, psychological analysis and social behaviour. In matters of religion, we have the questions of the relation between man and God, of fate versus free will and of death and suicide. In the area of personal happiness the old question of the *Summum Bonum* crops up time and again together with an analysis of pleasure, sorrow and anger. Finally, on the topic of human relations, both the Senecan commentators and the authors of *Celestina* focus on man's attitude to his equals and inferiors, that is to say, to friends, women and servants.

The fifteenth-century layman obviously wanted to know more about himself and his world, but in his quest for knowledge he found that Christian theology emphasized life after death over that on earth. For that reason the reader turned to the pagan philosophers, who, untouched by divine revelation, concentrated on this life. This point Cartagena concedes in the Introduction to his translation of *De Vita Beata*: 'Y como ellos no tenían aquella clara lumbre de Dios y la visión divinal que en el siglo venidero esperamos, buscábanlo acá en esta vida mortal.' As a result, he says, 'dieron algunas buenas doctrinas que a esto no poco aprovechan, si son bien y a buen fin entendidas' (*CL* 1).

Cartagena's method

For his translations of Seneca's philosophy Cartagena followed the scholastic pattern of dividing the subject-matter into chapters, each headed by a rubric which summarized its contents. In the text itself he then underlined dubious words or sentences, which he clarified or refuted at length in the margin.

In the Introduction to his translation of *De Providentia* Cartagena explains his *modus operandi* to the layman in the following words:

Y aunque el tratado estaba continuo sin alguna partición, partirlo he en capítulos porque mejor y más cierto podáis hallar lo que notar vos pluguiere. Y por cuanto en algunos lugares estaba oscuro por tañer historias antiguas que no son conocidas, señalélo en los márgenes, contando brevemente cuánto bastaba a la declaración de la letra. Y así mismo donde sentí, perdóneme Séneca, alguna conclusión que contradijese a los santos doctores, contradíjela luego, porque no le dejemos con ella pasar, y el que lo oyese no fuese engañado. Ca en tanto es de dar favor a las escrituras de los gentiles en cuanto de la católica verdad no desvían. (*CL* 4)

Although much of Stoic thought was incorporated in Christian belief, there were a few points where the Church openly had to voice its disapproval. Cartagena's glosses speak of a concern lest the non-professional reader embrace some heretical thought together with Seneca's practical wisdom.

On the relationship of man and God, for instance, the layman would read in the second chapter of *De la providencia de Dios*:

Entre los buenos varones y los dioses amistad hay puesta y establecida entre ellos por la virtud. Y aunque digo amistad, bien pudiera decir parentesco o semejanza. Ca del buen varón a Dios no hay diferencia sino en tiempo.

Here Cartagena deems it necessary to intervene. The marginal gloss to 'en tiempo' adds: 'Dice esto porque Dios es perdurable y el hombre es temporal, pero otras diferencias hay infinitas que no dice aquí Séneca, y entre lo infinito y finito no hay proporción, porende no es de aceptar este dicho así gruesamente como suena' (*CL* 4, 2). This heretical thought is not further touched upon in *De la providencia de Dios*, as the discussion centres around the question of why God allows evil to come to virtuous men. In his *Epistulae Morales*, however, Seneca often talks about how man, in his quest for wisdom and perfection, approximates and ultimately equals God. Ironically, the popular *Epistulae Morales* were not translated by Cartagena; nor do the sporadic glosses to the anonymous translations question the moral implications of Seneca's thought. It is quite possible then, that some of the heresies expressed in *Celestina*, such as Calisto's likening Melibea to God, could be traced back to Seneca's unchecked teaching in the *Epístolas de Séneca*.

Another controversial point in Seneca's writing was the question of fate. As is to be expected, the book *De Providentia Dei* offers enough scope for commenting on this issue. Where Cartagena translates 'Y la luenga orden de las cosas que llamamos hado dispone y ordena todos los hechos privados y particulares y públicos', he underlines 'luenga orden', glossing it as follows: '. . . y es de parar mientes que lo que dice aquí del hado no se ha de entender generalmente. Ca las cosas que pertenecen al libre albedrío del todo son libres y no reciben necesidad' (*CL* 4, 12).

The most careful explanation of the Church's official stance in this matter is to be found in a gloss to the book *De las siete artes liberales* (*Ep.* 88). In chapter 5, which deals with astrology, Cartagena not only takes issue with the concept of Fate, but also expresses the wish to ban the word *hado* from the Spanish vocabulary altogether. In his gloss he strongly reminds the reader of human will-power – 'el varón sabidor señor será de las estrellas' – and of God's divine providence as defined by Boethius: 'que el hado es una disposición que está en las cosas movibles por la cual la providencia de Dios y divinal las ayunta y pone en sus órdenes'. Considered in this light, Cartagena concedes that there might be something resembling Fate, but he would rather not use the word 'que por ocasión de los vocablos no venga algún error en el hecho' (*CL* 2, 5). This error had caused the Church endless problems: not only did it account for man's fatalistic attitudes to his life and actions, it also made him a slave of Fortune, as the many statements in *Celestina* illustrate only too plainly.[5]

Where Cartagena disagrees with Seneca most is, of course, on the question of taking one's own life. The fact that suicide is mentioned in the commentaries so frequently points to the real danger that a superficial reader could take Seneca's approval of the act to heart under certain circumstances. For that reason, Cartagena voices his strong disapproval whenever Seneca condones suicide, as in the case of the venerated Cato: 'aunque Séneca esto habla hermosamente, ello es gran error. Ca matar a si mismo no es de loar ni es acto de fortaleza, ni de virtud. Así según la verdad católica como según la doctrina de los filósofos, antes es acto de flaqueza y reprovado' (*De la providencia de Dios, CL* 4, 3). Again, in a gloss to Seneca's eulogy of Cato in chapter 10 Cartagena concludes: 'y en todo ello es de loar salvo en lo de la muerte que erró mucho' (*ibid.* 10). In *De la vida bienaventurada*, too, there are allusions to heroic decisions to end one's life, but whatever the circumstances, Cartagena maintains 'esta conclusión no es de tener' (*CL* 1, 18) – a doctrine he repeats in the next chapter with the words 'procurando el hombre mismo la muerte . . . no es de tener . . .' (*ibid.* 19).

There were other points in Seneca's teaching which, although not outrightly heretical, were capable of bearing such an interpretation. These concerned the perception of the *summum bonum*, 'este soberano bien que todos desean' (*De la vida bienaventurada*, Introduction, *CL* 1). The Church frowned on Seneca's explanation of the happy life, although Stoic thinking here could be adapted to Catholic belief. Cartagena rightly points out that 'los sabidores antiguos . . . usaron en esto de diversa manera de hablar', but he agrees neither with Aristotle's term *felicitas* ('felicidad') nor with Seneca's wavering between *summum bonum* ('soberano bien') and *vita beata* ('bienaventuranza'). If in the end he reluctantly settles for translating Seneca's *De Vita Beata* as *De la vida bienaventurada*, he is at pains to explain in the margin that the adjective 'bienaventurado' as pertaining to man 'no conviene a otro salvo a aquel que es perfecto en virtud'. By contrast, 'el hombre que ha muchas prosperidades y bienandanzas temporales en esta vida podemos le decir venturoso' (*ibid.*). It is possible that the authors of *Celestina*, aware of the philosophical distinction between *bienaventurado* and *venturoso*, gave an ironic twist to the frequent adjective *bienaventurado* with which they describe the characters' shortlived fulfilments. Indeed, *venturoso* would have been the more fitting word to designate their state of mind and affairs.

Obviously, the Church's efforts to counteract the pagan interpretation of the word 'bienaventuranza' had failed in the face of a fifteenth-century quest for happiness, which the laity all too readily conceived in terms of worldly delights. It is interesting to note in this context that Rojas' father-in-law was accused of heresy on precisely these grounds. The main accusation against Alvaro de Montalbán was 'que dijo y afirmó que acá hubiese el bien, que en la otra vida no sabía si había nada'.[6]

In fact, Christian thinking as expressed in Cartagena's glosses rules out any possibility of happiness on earth, because of man's own imperfections; 'ca algunos males hay que no podemos en alguna manera escusar, como es ignorancia en la parte del entendimiento y la desordenada afección y movimiento en la parte del cuerpo' (*CL* 1, 26). With this commentary Cartagena seems to sum up what preoccupied fifteenth-century lay readers most. In their quest for happiness they sought to acquire wisdom in fields that had hitherto been the prerogative of the clergy, but at the same time, being men and women who lived in the world, they were well aware of the afflictions that beset body and mind. And here, linked to the question of the *summum bonum*, perhaps the most controversial issue was the problem of pleasure, since the unschooled reader of Seneca might well confuse Epicurean and Stoic teaching in this matter.

At the time Seneca was seen both as a spokesman for the Stoics and as a source of much Epicurean thought, as the Prohemio to *Las Epístolas de Séneca* makes clear. As a matter of fact, Seneca agrees with Epicurus on many points, in that, on his own admission, he often appropriates valuable ideas from the other camp: 'ca yo algunas veces suelo entrar en los campos de los otros, no como quien huye mas como espía' (Anth. 2, fol. 3r).

The Church, albeit in agreement with Seneca's teaching on virtues and vices, viewed Epicurus with great suspicion because of the pre-eminence his school gave to the principle of pleasure.[7] It would be wrong to say that Seneca was opposed to pleasure: the difference between Stoics and Epicureans was rather one of priority. While pleasure was an end in itself for the Epicureans, for the Stoics virtue remained the guiding principle in their quest for the happy life. Even so, Seneca has no quarrel with Epicurus about the quality of this pleasure, and in fact feels it necessary to defend him: 'ca yo te juro por Hércules que casta y limpia era la delectación de Epicuro. Y ellos no curan como lo entendía Epicuro, mas en oyendo nombre de deleite, vuelan para allá buscando quien ayude y dé autoridad a sus deshonestos placeres' (*CL* 1, 12). Indeed, the arguments in *Celestina* are at times purely Epicurean for no other reason than that the protagonists rely on a philosopher who sanctions their hedonistic pursuits.[8]

Just as the proper interpretation of Seneca's concept of pleasure caused problems to transmitters and recipients alike, its pendant, sorrow and grief, was also a topic that needed clarification. Judging by the many glosses that accompany Seneca's words of wisdom in this respect, sorrow was an experience with which the fifteenth century was only too familiar. However, when the average readers turned to Seneca for consolation they found that the Roman philosopher was a tough taskmaster. Contrary to twentieth-century opinion, which holds that expressing grief is good for the soul, Seneca considers excessive grieving to be yet another *affectus* which needs to be checked. Cartagena could not agree more. To Seneca's sentence 'Bien es que sepas que no es cosa natural quebrantar hombre su corazón con llantos' Cartagena comments: 'entristecer sin medida y llorar sin templamiento no es cosa natural' (*CL* 5, 'Tratado de la lágrima'). In the same extracts from the *Consolatio ad Marciam*, Cartagena uses Seneca's statement that 'toda es llorosa nuestra vida' as sufficient reason to save one's tears, 'que toda la vida humanal es llena de daños y de adversidades por las cuales las lágrimas se derraman'. Both Seneca and Cartagena suspect that many tears are shed only for show. Commenting on Seneca's sentence 'lloran algunos porque se lo vean', Cartagena first describes women's propensity to cry only when being watched, but then he comes to the more general conclusion 'y esto se hace porque los que lloran quieren contentar a los que los otean y creen que los que los miran han por feo no llorar a la muerte de los parientes' (*ibid.*).

Keeping in mind the average reader's familiarity with Seneca's thinking on sorrow through translation and commentary, Calisto's 'dolor' after Melibea's rebuke in Act I could well be seen as a mockery of the kind of sorrow to which the Stoics take exception, in the same manner as Melibea's despair moments before her suicide and Pleberio's lament could be taken as a *contra-exemplum* to Stoic thinking on excessive grief.

If giving in to pleasure and sorrow were two *affectus* that obstructed man's path to wisdom and happiness, there was one affliction which Seneca rates worse than any other, and that is anger. In his *De Ira* Seneca describes the devastating effects on body and mind that this type of loss of control causes. Seneca's *De Ira* was extensively excerpted in the *Copilación*, which is where Cartagena's glosses occur. The collection's 'Tratado de la ira' opens with the words 'pone Séneca cuántos males hace la saña'. Cartagena then explains this: 'porque la saña es de esquivar más que todas las otras pasiones por muchos males que hace al hombre turbio y rabioso y presuroso y doloroso y codicioso de armas y deseoso de derramar sangre humanal . . .' (*CL* 5).

In choosing the next passage which deals with 'Qué cosa es la saña y dónde nace', the compiler hit upon one of Seneca's sharpest insights into human psychology: that anger is often the result not of a real wrong, but of an occurrence perceived as such. Where Seneca says 'cierto es que nos ensañamos contra los que nos han de injuriar aunque no nos hayan injuriado', Cartagena comments '. . . y porende la saña nace de la injuria concebida en el corazón del que es injuriado, o la cuida ser adelante. Ca ya recibimos la injuria en nuestras imaginaciones' (*CL* 5, 'Tratado de las buenas costumbres'). As we shall see, the many instances of anger in *Celestina* have much in common with Seneca's text and Cartagena's commentary. While Calisto's behaviour in front of his servants is that of an 'angry young man', Melibea's fury is nothing more than a fit of rage. Although anger is particularly harmful to the ruler, this affliction is not confined to the privileged classes. On the contrary, Elicia explodes with anger against the Melibeas of this world, Areusa bursts out in an angry accusation of mistresses' treatment of servants, while Sempronio and Parmeno are so enraged by Celestina that they become 'deseosos de derramar sangre humanal'. Each angry action in *Celestina* has far-reaching consequences, because no passion affects other human beings to the extent that anger does. This again fits in completely with Seneca's thinking on man and society.

For Seneca, man is never an isolated being but essentially a member of a community. Consequently, his errors will always involve others, as Seneca so aptly says in *De Vita Beata* 1, 4, translated as 'ca no hay alguno que yerre para sí sólo mas yerra él y da causa y autoridad a otro para que yerre' (*CL* 1, 2). In the 'Tratado de la obediencia' the *Copilación* paraphrases a passage from *De Ira* with the words 'mucho es dañosa a los servidores la saña' (*CL* 5,), to which Cartagena adds 'cuando los servidores se ensañan no obedecen a los señores y con su rebeldía los señores son inducidos a saña y con la saña dan pena y hacen daño a los servidores'. In the section 'De los siervos' the *Copilación* extracts a passage from Book 4 of *De Beneficiis*, in which Seneca explains how 'los siervos pueden hacer gracia a sus señores'. Cartagena elaborates on 'gracia' to explain not only what special services beyond the call of duty servants can perform, but also in what way masters can benefit them. In the case of a servant, '. . . le cría como a hijo en tal caso bien parece que le hace gracia'. The servant benefits his master in turn, 'si tiene cuidado del señor y de sus provechos y de su honra'.

Generally, Seneca sides with the servants, commiserating with their sad lot, their lack of freedom and the maltreatment they suffer. Cartagena agrees. In the 'Tratado de la miseria y trabajo', taken from *De Brevitate Vitae*, he writes a long gloss on 'los servidores de los señores que están ocupados en su servicio' and explains their misery 'porque han de comer cuando no han hambre y no pueden beber cuando han sed, y duermen al albedrío ajeno' (*CL* 5). On the other hand, masters are also warned against the greed of their servants. In chapter 3 of *Amonestamientos y doctrinas*, number 23 states: 'con muy gran peligro guardamos lo que muchos desean' (*CL* 3, 3). Cartagena explains this with an example: 'y vemos lo por experiencia, que aunque los servidores sean muy leales siempre se acostumbró poner el dinero so llave, porque es cosa que suelen mucho codiciar los hombres'. The gloss then expands on greed and the *vulgus*, concluding 'Y aunque en dinero pusimos ejemplo, debemos entender en todas las otras cosas que son muy deseadas' (*CL* 3, 3).

Related to the task of governing others is the delicate question of giving or withholding rewards. As is well known, this is a frequent point of friction between the servants in *Celestina*, and in turn becomes a conflict of interests, misunderstanding, anger and death. Cartagena himself calls attention to the problem in *De la vida bienaventurada*. Where Seneca says 'Y paréceme que en diciendo yo donación alzaste las orejas cuidando que querría dar algo', Cartagena comments, with underlining in the margin, '*Nota bene hoc dictum*, cómo y a quien da el virtuoso de lo suyo' (*CL* 1, 22).

Judging by the many extracts from *De Beneficiis* that are brought together in the *Copilación* and by the many accompanying glosses, the art of giving was an important concern in the fifteenth century. In excerpting Book 2 of *De Beneficiis*, the *Copilación*, in the 'Tratado de la razón' discusses 'Qué es lo que se da y a quién y cómo y porqué y dónde', on which Cartagena comments 'ca la obra moral no sería virtuosa si no se guardase en ellas las circunstancias que se deben catar'. Here he distinguishes two important considerations: 'la una es el estado de la persona de quien da, la otra es el estado de la persona a quien da' (*CL* 5).

In the 'Tratado del trabajo', which contains excerpts from *De Tranquillitate Animi*, we find many a thought on work and reward. Where the translated text reads 'Todo trabajo algún fin acata y por algo se hace y no andarían con tanta diligencia estos locos y vanos negociando', the gloss explains '. . . la causa de su trabajo y movimiento es galardón que esperan del trabajo'. Interestingly, the passage in Seneca's treatise talks not of material reward but of success as the desired result of one's labour: 'si aut non successit aut successus pudet' (*De Tranq.* 12, 1). Cartagena, however, warns that many end up disillusioned because they are not rewarded or, if they are, will never be content 'porque aunque alcanzan aquel galardón de su trabajo que esperan, porque no han del aquel provecho que cuidaban, y así queda burlada su voluntad con la vanidad y poquedad de aquel galardón' (*CL* 5). In this context, Parmeno and Sempronio's disappointment and anger at not being rewarded by their master after standing watch outside Melibea's door springs to mind.

When to give is another problem inherent in bestowing gifts. Time and opportunity, two crucial conditions in the proper management of others, is of special importance here, as the *Copilación* brings out: 'que en el don principalmente es de considerar el juicio del dador'. He chooses the first book of *De Beneficiis* to emphasize the importance of timing, as a belated gift loses in quality, while a gift bestowed immediately has obvious advantages for both the giver and the recipient. Cartagena here remarks 'quiere decir que pequeño beneficio dado aína y préstamente es más pacible que un beneficio de gran valor cuando el que lo dió pensó mucho si lo daría o no. Y diolo tarde y perezosamente. Y éste que esto hace no sabe bien hacer ni para sí es bueno' (*CL* 5).

To underline the similarities between Seneca and *Celestina* here would be superfluous. The question of the 'galardones' is not only fundamental to the development of the plot; it also illustrates only too clearly Calisto's ill-chosen and ill-timed rewarding of services received: 'no sabe bien hacer ni para sí es bueno'.

Another theme that Seneca and *Celestina* have in common is women. But here we should state from the start that the anti-feminist view of women presented by the translations is based entirely on pseudo-Senecan texts. Seneca himself, though aware of the weaker sex's susceptibility to the *affectus*, is full of understanding and sympathy for this class of dependants. His love for his wife Paulina is well known from Epistula 104; the *Consolatio ad Helviam* speaks of sympathy for his mother; while the *Consolatio ad Marciam* voices the opinion that women as much as men can and must show fortitude in suffering.

The hostility towards women expressed in the various collections of *sententiae* is therefore mostly a product of the compiler's imagination and representative of medieval and clerical misogyny. However, credit should be given to Cartagena, who, in his gloss to 'doctrina' number 6 of chapter 3 of the *Amonestamientos y doctrinas* – 'entonces es buena la mujer cuando es claramente mala' – strongly contradicts this condemnation: 'No dice bien Séneca con su reverencia hablando', he says, 'ca este dicho quiere concluir que todas las mujeres son malas, lo cual es falso.' After mentioning various women that were famous for their virtue, he finishes with 'esta conclusión [i.e. Seneca's] no es verdadera y de más de ser falsa, es peligrosa. Ca oyendo decir la mujer que todas fueron y son malas, aína declinará a ser mala' (*CL* 3, 3). He then calls his readers' attention to a longer gloss which he has already inserted in 'El tratado de las mujeres' of the *Copilación*. The passage in question comes from Seneca's tragedy *Hippolytus* and is introduced by the compiler with the following words: 'dice Hipolito que las mujeres son causa poco menos de todos los males'. This he illustrates with a dialogue in which Hipolito cites various women as examples of atrocious deeds. The nurse, however, defends her sex by refusing to blame all women for the 'maleficio de pocas', a defence in turn taken up by Cartagena. In a long gloss he not only accuses the Holy Scriptures, Solomon, historians and chroniclers of this unfair assessment of women; he even goes as far as to say that 'por cierto de mucho de lo que de ellas se cuenta, fue la causa principal de los hombres'. In another context Cartagena again expresses his disagreement with the text. This time the verdict comes from the *Controversiae* of Seneca the Elder, a collection of oratorical samples translated at the end of the

Copilación. In the 'Tratado de la castidad', the compiler had lit upon 'no es asaz casta aquella de cuya castidad se duda' (*CL* 5). Cartagena spotted the contradiction to genuine Senecan thinking, according to which the truth rarely resides in public opinion. In an extensive gloss he starts out by saying 'muy duro suena esta letra como yace', but then he explains the provenance of this sentence, adding that Seneca here speaks under a different guise: 'y así no lo dijo por doctrina para vivir mas solamente para enseñar cómo alegue el abogado'. Cartagena then takes this opportunity to warn his readers against taking everything in the *Copilación* as coming straight from the horse's mouth: 'porende quien en esta *Copilación* leyere mucho debe catar de qué lugares son las doctrinas aquí puestas. Ca todos los dichos de Séneca no son de igual autoridad.' Even so, these pseudo-Senecan, anti-feminist sayings were taken seriously at the time, as they fitted so well into the medieval misogynistic tradition, as witness Sempronio's diatribe against women: 'Conséjate con Séneca y verás en qué las tiene' (S. 52; M. 25).

In the matter of a man's relation to his friends, classical thinking was transmitted untainted. The classics considered friendship the most important link between humans, more important than love or family relationship. The various schools of philosophy had made friendship a major point of discussion, analysing who needed friends and why, what to expect of them, and, last but not least, the moral implications of real friendship. However, there was one point where philosophers could not agree, and that was on the purpose of friendship. While Aristotle admitted a certain usefulness and Epicurus pointed to the pleasurableness of the relationship, the Stoics advocated a complete disinterest in seeking and keeping friends. Since virtue was for them the *conditio sine qua non* of all man's deeds and relations, they subordinated pleasure and gain to their overriding principle of virtue and reason. For Seneca, difference of class such as that separating masters and servants was no obstacle to real friendship; and the absence of self-interest demanded self-abnegation to the point of self-sacrifice.

Judging by the choice of excerpts and *sententiae* in Seneca's translated work, the question of friendship was uppermost in the mind of the fifteenth-century reader. Thus the glosses to Seneca's words discuss the question from many angles, including Stoic, Aristotelian and Epicurean points of view. To complicate matters, the classics often equated *amor* and *amicitia*, which was confusing for the untutored mind. In fact, one of the Tratados in the *Copilación* bears the title 'Del amor y amistad' and gives excerpts from Epistula 2, in which Seneca invites Lucilius to be his friend. The topic gives Cartagena ample scope for clearing up a possible confusion between the disinterested love which is friendship and 'un amor que es pasión y acto de la sensualidad humana'. In this context he deems it necessary to warn his readers against Ovid's *Ars Amatoria*, 'que aunque aquel libro se llama de la arte del amar, no es de aquello mas es de la arte para alcanzar y haber la cosa amada'. In a different gloss to the same passage, Cartagena singles out Seneca's words, 'que la verdadera amistad requiere que sean virtuosos ambos los amigos', to remind his readers of Aristotle's *Ethics* 8 on the reciprocity and virtuous nature of love in friendship. If true love is present, he says, friends will benefit from such a relation 'y tal amistad siempre aprovechan'. In the long 'Tratado de los amigos', Cartagena glosses the sentence 'y guardarse debe con toda diligencia el amigo' with the words 'Aquellas cosas se deben guardar con mayor diligencia de las cuales vienen mayores bienes . . . y de tres maneras es el bien según Aristóteles, honesto y delectable y provechoso.' After that Cartagena reverts to Seneca when he concludes: 'Y aquel Séneca tañe especialmente la dulcedumbre que siente hombre en revelar a su amigo los secretos, ca cosa natural es al hombre querer declarar por habla lo que tiene en el corazón.'

When we consider the importance given to friendship and love in the fifteenth century, it is not surprising that *Celestina* has so many 'fontecicas de filosofía' on the topic. Readers familiar with the discussion on the priority of virtue, usefulness or pleasure in friendship thus may well have smiled at Celestina's mixing and matching of Stoic, Epicurean and Aristotelian truths.

As in the case of Epicureanism, the fifteenth-century reader of Senecan commentaries would have picked up a substantial amount of Aristotelian thinking. For that reason, the many references to Aristotle in *Celestina* may well reflect a superficial acquaintance with the Greek philosopher such as the average reader might have gathered from Senecan commentaries and from pseudo-Senecan sentence collections. For instance, the *Amonestamientos y doctrinas* includes an Aristotelian *sententia* which states: 'Aristóteles decía grave cosa y difícil es provar los amigos en las bienandanzas, mas en las grandes adversidades ligeramente se prueba' (*CL* 3, 5). This is not Stoic thinking, and in fact Seneca would frown on the concept of 'friendship in adversity', since it would be difficult under such circumstances to eliminate a certain element of 'amiguismo'. The non-professional reader, however, might take such statements as accepted moral philosophy and use them to his best advantage.

Since Cartagena in his glosses jumps from one author to another, it must have been difficult for the non-scholar to distinguish who had said what. So his commentaries probably contributed to an eclectic, popular philosophy which was considered Stoic but was in actual fact only marginally so. But then the non-professional was probably less interested in philosophical subtleties than in seeking a guide to the good life, and that purpose was served very well by the Senecan and pseudo-Senecan potted wisdom as set out in sentence collections and commentaries. Consequently, the 'sentencias dos mil' alluded to in the prefatory 'Carta a un su amigo' of *Celestina* are nothing more than an, at times, confused mixture of Aristotelian, Epicurean and Stoic thought, to which the average reader could readily relate from his own reading of Seneca and, more especially, of the commentaries.

Pero Díaz de Toledo's method

The book that seemed to have all the answers to the fifteenth century's question of how to live well was undoubtedly Pero Díaz de Toledo's *Proverbios de Séneca*.

Generally speaking, Pero Díaz avoids philosophical speculation, preferring concrete examples as a means of helping the average reader find a *modus vivendi*. As against Cartagena's intellectual approach and critical inquiry into the validity of Seneca's teaching, Pero Díaz seldom contradicts authority. His aim is to clarify, not to dispute. Proverbio 264 sums up his own attitude to philosophy with the words 'disputando mucho la verdad se pierde' (R. 223). In the gloss, he distinguishes between 'filosofía natural y todas las ciencias matemáticas' on the one hand and 'filosofía moral y la retórica' on the other. In science, he claims, discussion helps to uncover the truth, while the opposite is true of rhetoric and moral philosophy, since 'no se puede dar tan buena razón por una parte que casi no se dé otra tan buena razón por la contraria'. He then invokes Aristotle's Prologue to the *Ethics* in support of his view that 'en las ciencias que tratan de los actos y costumbres de los hombres, que son así como la filosofía moral y la retórica, no conviene mucho disputar porque no ha por sí razones ciertas y necesarias mas probables y persuasibles y no mucho ciertas' (R. 224). The dubious nature of rhetoric is further explained in a gloss to Proverbio 272, where Pero Díaz cites Aristotle and Cicero on the question whether the *ars oratoria* might not do more harm than good, 'por los malos ministros de ella' (R. 231). Thus rhetoric practised by non-virtuous orators is immoral and dangerous, a point which the authors of *Celestina* may well have wanted to bring out.[9] The pedantic and often false reasoning which characterizes the dialogues in *Celestina* seems to justify only too well Pero Díaz's remark that 'disputando la verdad se pierde'. So it would not seem improbable that the authors of *Celestina* were intent on writing a parody of rhetorical practices to illustrate the pernicious effect of the *ars oratoria* and, at the same time, on ridiculing the speech patterns of the semi-educated classes.

As in *Celestina*, one of the topics most discussed in Pero Díaz's commentaries is that of Fortune and worldly goods. For instance, commenting on Proverbio 111, 'de la ganancia de los hombres fue habida la fortuna por diosa', Pero Díaz explains that Boethius had already recorded how 'algunos de los gentiles . . . escribieron que la fortuna fuese una señora so cuyo mando y senorío estaban todas las riquezas y bienes temporales' (R. 128). But Pero Díaz is disinclined to follow Boethius' further discussion on the difference between 'caso y fortuna y providencia', because, he says, 'es larga y profunda materia y requeriría largo hablar' (R. 130). Instead, he prefers to go into the nature of the goods that fortune can bestow, and here he cites just about every authority that ever wrote on the subject. As in other questions, Aristotle and Boethius lead the discussion on Fortune's 'bienes'. In the very first proverbio, which reads 'agena cosa es todo lo que deseando viene', Pero Díaz explains the difference between Aristotelian 'bienes interiores' and 'bienes exteriores', the latter being 'linaje, hermosura, riquezas y todos los bienes de fortuna y éstos son agenos de nos' (R. 25) – an enumeration which entirely fits Sempronio's summary of Calisto's attributes (S. 53; M. 27). Then, commenting on Proverbio 14 that 'el avariento él mismo es causa de su miseria y trabajo', he refers again to the first proverbio to elaborate 'los bienes de fortuna en especial las riquezas son agenos de nos y para eso las debemos procurar para servirnos de ellos' (R. 35) – a goal very much in accord with the attitude to worldly goods expressed in *Celestina*.[10]

The mistaken idea that money buys happiness is also discussed at length in the glosses. Commenting on the question 'en cuáles debería hombre poner su bienaventuranza por que por aquellas trabajase con toda voluntad', Pero Díaz warns 'Y algunos dijeron que la bienaventuranza estaba en tener mucho dinero.' Other glosses aim at illustrating that riches and possessions are more a hindrance than a help in achieving happiness. In his gloss to Proverbio 286, Pero Díaz enlists the aid of the Scriptures, Vergil, Cicero, Seneca and Cassiodorus to maintain that 'el rico no posee las riquezas mas las riquezas poseen a él' (R. 242), while in another gloss he mentions the much-cherished adage 'que grandes riquezas son, dice Séneca, la pobreza alegre' (R. 259).

Even more than Cartagena's marginal glosses, Pero Díaz's running commentary gives the non-professional reader a complete synopsis of what the various authorities have to say about a particular issue. At the same time, the diverse and sometimes contradictory opinions listed in short succession in these glosses contribute to a superficial pseudo-knowledge which the unthinking reader might flaunt at the drop of a hat. For instance, the question of anger is treated at length in the *Proverbios*: anger as perceived by Aristotle, Cato and Seneca; anger in combination with truth, reason or love; anger as passion, vengeance, folly – in short, anger in all its manifestations. Thus the reader learns that anger, according to Aristotle, 'no se puede escusar . . . porque es natura a nos' and may wonder 'si es tan natural a nos la ira como el deleite' (R. 67) – questions that would make a Stoic wince.

Basing himself on Cato, Pero Díaz argues that 'la ira impide el corazón porque no pueda entender la verdad', while, quoting Aristotle, he can safely extend this adage to 'el amor y la ira impiden la razón' (R. 34). He combines Aristotle and Seneca in his statement that 'la ira está dispuesta de cometer y hacer locuras', and agrees with Terence that love is stronger than anger: 'la ira de los que se aman es reintegrar y reforzar el amor' (R. 179 and 68). Thus, in some ways, the glosses are like a dazzling kaleidoscope of fractured knowledge and because of their generalizations, prove to be eminently quotable and universally applicable.

Pero Díaz also has much to say on the subject of friendship – without, however, clarifying where genuine Senecan doctrine differs from Aristotelian thinking. In his gloss to Proverbio 49 (R. 56), he rightly explains that, according to Aristotle, 'la amistanza es de tres maneras, la una por deleite, la otra por provecho, la otra por lo honesto'. And, although he goes on to say that the last one is the right one, 'que es por virtud', he does not, as does Seneca, reject the first 'maneras' as wrong. On the other hand, another gloss shows legitimate agreement between Aristotle and Seneca, in that 'los que son amigos por deleite o amigos por provecho, cesando el deleite y cesando el provecho, cesa la amistanza' (R. 228). In fact, Seneca more often than not agrees with Aristotle, as in the case of conformity between friends, 'la ley de la amistanza que sea un querer y un no querer' (Proverbio 10; R. 33), a *sententia* Pero Díaz repeats in Proverbio 262 and 307.

In Pero Díaz's commentaries (as in *Celestina*'s arguments) by far the most important facet of real friendship is the pleasure of sharing and communication. Supporting Seneca's 'de ningún bien es alegre la posesión sin compañero', Pero Díaz paraphrases Aristotle's *Ethics* 8: 'que aprovecharía a ninguno tener muchos bienes si no tuviese con quien los participase y comunicase' (R. 97). Similarly, just about every authority agrees on the delight of being able to confide in a friend. Enlisting the aid of Cicero, Aristotle, Ecclesiastes, Seneca, Socrates and Valerius Maximus, Pero Díaz enthusiastically supports Proverbio 313: '¡qué cosa más dulce que tener con quien todas las cosas comuniques, a quien creas así como a ti mismo! ¡Cuántos quisieron haber tales amigos a quien ellos no lo fueron!' (R. 265).

On the topic of love the reader would also encounter a host of sententious pronouncements, but usually of an unpleasant nature. Love, more often than not, was portrayed as a hindrance: 'bien dijo Séneca que causa de ocioso cuidado es el amor'. Moreover, on the topic of love and women, Solomon is the authority on 'love as an illness' (R. 44), while woman can safely be abhorred in accordance with Aristotle's repeated claim that she is 'varón imperfecto'. For that reason, 'no es sin razón que en consejar y en obrar mal sean más prestas las mujeres que los hombres' (R. 201).

Aristotle also provides much support for Pero Díaz's commentaries on benefits, even if at times this conflicts with Stoic thinking. For Seneca, bestowing gifts should be utterly disinterested without expectation of recognition or any sort of return. Pero Díaz's attitude however, is more worldly. In fact, he also advocates self-interest when he comments on Proverbio 41, which reads 'muchos beneficios recibe el que los sabe dar' (R. 50). Supported by Solomon, he then glosses 'el que da beneficios y hace bien siempre lo da con intención de no perder lo que da, mas que por aquello le sea respondido y le sea pagado el beneficio en semejante caso o en mayor' (R. 50).

When we consider the 'galardones' bestowed in *Celestina*, by both Calisto and Melibea, we will find that they reflect Pero Díaz's ambiguous explanations rather than genuine Senecan thought. Indeed,

Calisto and Melibea's 'galardones' are the opposite of gifts, since they are nothing more than a remuneration or down-payment for badly needed services. Seen in this light, the Senecan concept of *beneficium*, translated by Cartagena and Pero Díaz as 'galardón', becomes caricatured in the hands of the authors of *Celestina*. Whether this caricature is deliberate or not is difficult to tell. After all, the authors of *Celestina* were not aware of the distinction between pseudo- and genuine Senecan thought, nor was it their purpose to unmask errors of judgement. It could well be that, in portraying the foolish actions of their characters, all they hoped to achieve was a smile on the face of their more intelligent readers who would doubtless recognize the *Proverbios* as the origin of the pedantry underlying the arguments in *Celestina*.

The 'Título de la amistanza y del amigo'

There is one pseudo-Senecan treatise which is of particular interest for the connection between Seneca and *Celestina*. This is the *Título de la amistanza y del amigo*, which defines the human condition in terms of friendship and love.

The long manuscript, consisting of 44 folios at the end of BN 6962, is a translation of Mannelli's chapters on love, and, for that reason, may well have been the text intended to be printed in the last book of *Los cinco libros de Séneca*. After all, the rubric there states: 'Todos estos capítulos que se siguen fueron sacados de la Copilación del alfabeto en el tratado del amor.' Be this as it may, it is significant that the *Título* circulated separately and that under the general heading of friendship it gathers the same old issues of love, rewards, death and grieving. The rubric to the work reads: 'En el cual se trata que aquella es verdadera amistanza cuando el amigo es amado por si mismo, y no la que es por causa de provecho de aquel que a otra ama . . . porque si alguno quiere ser amado conviénele que ame.' This last sentence, taken from Epistula 9, 6, is underlined in red and glossed as pertaining to 'el poeta Ovidio en el libro que hizo de la arte de amar'. Further paraphrasing Epistula 9, the *Título* then refutes Epicurus' opinion that happiness resides in 'las delectaciones del cuerpo' and that friendship is useful in case of illness, poverty or imprisonment (cf. *Ep.* 9, 8). Underlined in the text and repeated in the gloss are the words '. . . ca el que es amigo de otro por su propio interés o provecho, si entienda él que ésta es verdadera amistad, su pensamiento es malo'. Comparing love and friendship, the *Título* paraphrases Epistula 9, 11 with the words 'a las veces alguna amistanza que no es por virtud quiere semejar a ella como aquella amistanza que los hombres han a la hermosura de sus enamoradas, por cumplir con ellas su voluntad, pero esta tal se puede decir loca amistad'. By 'aquella amistanza' the commentator clearly means the *affectus amantium* of the corresponding passage in Epistula 9.

The underlined and glossed sentences in the text emphasize, moreover, that once friendship is started on the wrong footing everything else will go wrong. Friends chosen for the wrong reasons become cowards, 'y así los tales amigotes huyen el tiempo de la malandanza', and discord will arise: 'a las veces querer cada uno de los amigos lo que el otro quiere es causa de disencia'.

The risk of consorting with the wrong friends, underlined in another gloss, is linked with the greedy masses, since real friendship cannot be found 'salvo si te apartaras de las gentes'. Subsequently, we hear the well-known warning 'como hay algunos que mientras más deben y son obligados a otro, mayor odio y malquerencia les tienen' and 'si la cuantía es grande no solo es deudor mas aún tórnase enemigo'. Many more glosses highlight the difficult art of giving, after which the text and its corresponding commentary turn to the question of grieving. Conceding that immediate tears are only natural, the gloss then emphasizes that prolonged weeping should not become 'cosa delectable'. Regarding the loss of a child, another gloss brings out the fact that we must love our children in the knowledge that they too will die: 'y no han de durar ni estar luengo tiempo con nos'.

In another section, the glosses underline the treachery of our fellow-men, summarized 'como al hombre está aparejado continuo peligro del hombre'. In this respect, the problem lies in the fact that many look like human beings but 'tienen corazones de bestias fieras y aún peores'. Especially dangerous, then, are those that vie for the same thing, 'así como los que contienden sobre un beneficio . . .'. Thus the leitmotiv of the *Título de la amistanza y del amigo* is the implied ideal of a relationship untroubled by 'temor ni por cuidado de provecho'.

What is interesting here is the recurrence of a stock repertoire of Senecan and pseudo-Senecan pronouncements, cordoned off by a frame of marginal glosses. (See plate 5.) Very often these seem to have the final word on a particular topic – as, for example, the last gloss in the *Título*, which explains the ambiguous sentence 'sólo el sabio enseñado es amador'. In the style of an epilogue, it says:

los filósofos estoicos dicen que sólo el sabio sabe usar de las riquezas y sólo el sabio sabe sufrir la pobreza y sólo el sabio sabe dar y recibir los beneficios y gracias y de aquí decían los que non sabían que pues esto así era que sólo el sabio sabía la arte de amar y hasta qué edad las mujeres y los mancebos son de amar.

Interestingly, this fifteenth-century synopsis of the ideal man also sums up what the characters of *Celestina* are not. The masters do not know how to use their wealth; the servants cannot cope with their poverty; neither masters nor those in their service know how to give, to receive or even to be thankful; while not one of the characters 'sabe la arte de amar'.

This is not to say that *Celestina* is based on this particular *Título*, but rather that both books reflect and reproduce a general fifteenth-century preoccupation with what the wise and virtuous man is supposed to be. Thus the *Comedia de Calisto y Melibea* was nurtured by a traditional diet of 'amonestamientos y doctrinas', which suited the taste of the average reader. And, just as it is not always possible to identify a particular spice in a well-seasoned dish, so too we should not be looking for a specific origin for certain *sententiae* in *Celestina*, but should, rather, be able to spot the Senecan way of thinking that pervades the book.

After half a century of translations and commentaries, the informed reader would bring to his appreciation of the *Comedia de Calisto y Melibea* a wealth of 'fontecicas de filosofía' which, to his delight, he would see exemplified in the fictitious figures of Calisto and Melibea, Sempronio and Parmeno, Celestina and Pleberio, Areusa and Elicia.

However, the great originality of *Celestina* resides, not in the 'sentencias dos mil' or in its 'argumento', but in the fictionalization of the sententious morality of the times. This step from treatise to fiction, from moral philosophy to imaginative literature, from dialectics to dialogue – in short from 'prosa' to 'poesia' – was an unprecedented achievement.

3

The 'antiguo autor' as a reader of Seneca

The decade in which *Celestina* came into being was also 'Seneca's Incunabula Period' (Reynolds 1965: 1). This means that, through the medium of a flourishing book-trade across all of Europe, Seneca's Latin works were available to a much wider community of scholars.[1] At the same time, the Spanish printing houses were bringing out new editions of the *Proverbios de Séneca* and the *Cinco libros de Séneca*, while in 1496 a first printing of the *Epístolas de Séneca* saw the light. Thus both the scholar and the non-scholar were very familiar with Seneca at the time *Celestina* was written.

There is no doubt that the first author of *Celestina* was himself perfectly at home in Latin and that he had a first-hand knowledge of Seneca. In his fiction, however, he portrays people who go solely by the copybook and hearsay in their pretence of being well-read and knowledgeable. So it could well be true that the anonymous author meant to entertain a small circle of scholars with a parody of the half-educated readers 'que no saben latín o si lo saben no lo entienden expedidamente' (Prologue to the *Proverbios de Séneca*). The parvenu in learning has, of course, always been an easy butt for satire. Tedious name-dropping, heavy reliance on *auctoritates*, non-sequiturs, misquotation and general misconceptions all provide a rich source of innocent fun for those who know better. However, if we are to share in the fun, readers have to be able to recognize the target of the satire; this, for the first author and his friends, may well have been the potted wisdom of the Senecan *sententia*.

The author of the first act was by no means the first to weave Senecan *sententiae* into the pattern of a literary composition. But while previous literati had used their stock of quotations to give their compositions an air of elegance and erudition, the first author of *Celestina* made Seneca's words of wisdom the very core of his fiction.

In certain ways, one could compare the poetics of the *sententia* to a game of hide-and-seek which the author plays with his readers. This game can be played on many levels, depending on the level of sophistication of the players. In the case of *Celestina*, one can easily spot a general reference to the Senecan tradition based on a whole complex of *auctoritates*, every one expressing more or less the same idea. Here we see the author playing on his readers' general frame of reference, an exercise which can take the form of parody or satire. At other times, the *sententia* goes back to a more specific source, in which case it takes the form of a quotation, although even here there are different levels of identification, such as the cryptic or the fragmentary quotation or, most ingeniously, the conscious misquotation.[2]

The 'antiguo autor' of *Celestina* uses all the possibilities and gradations allowed by the rules of the game, in the knowledge that his readers had at their disposal a matching store of words of wisdom. Moreover, being a fifteenth-century author, as well as a typical reader, he had at his fingertips a readily available treasury compiled by generations of translators and commentators. Seneca could not have said it better: 'The last in line is best placed; the words lie to hand, and reshuffled, they take on a new meaning' (*Ep.* 79, 6). As such, the *sententia* is another vehicle for the transmission of ideas, another link in the chain for passing on traditional values in a new guise.

Generally speaking, recourse to Seneca's popular wisdom occurs at three crucial moments of confrontation in Act 1: between Calisto and Melibea, followed by Calisto facing his servants, Sempronio and Parmeno, and finally Celestina's persuasion of Parmeno. It is not surprising that wisdom is most needed when man faces a new and baffling situation. Each one of the three episodes is a crisis in which counsel is needed, and this the characters of the novel seek in words of wisdom from the past. It is not until the third confrontation, however, that the interlocutors engage each other in a game of one-upmanship in quoting from Seneca's wisdom. By contrast, the first two confrontations seem to prepare the field for us, the witnesses of the debate, by means of the speakers' often erroneous allusions and references to Seneca's genuine and apocryphal words of wisdom.[3] 'Fontecicas de filosofía' is what Rojas calls them, consciously reducing them to small-talk, because that is how this moral philosophy comes through: no big truths, just snippets of popular wisdom brought together in a subtle and humorous way. However, beneath it all is the fundamental leitmotiv of the story: a quest for happiness gone sour.

The first confrontation: Calisto and Melibea

Calisto's overture to Melibea cannot, by any stretch of the imagination, be termed philosophic. And yet, by referring to nature and happiness, it reflects two important concepts in Seneca's *De Vita Beata*.

The Stoics conceived of the happy life in terms of living in harmony with Nature. Nature's gifts are plentiful and easily accessible, Seneca states more than once. By contrast, the pursuit of *voluptas* needs the help of Fortune and results in a life of anxiety, suspicion and stress ('vita anxia, suspiciosa, trepida . . .', *DVB* 15, 3). In the anthology of Seneca's letters *voluptas* is translated as 'deleites y sobras' which are said invariably to bring in their train unnecessary organization, work and worry ('solicitudo . . . angustias y trabajos': (*Ep.* 119, 15; Anth. 75, fol. 70v). Among these 'deleites y sobras' Seneca emphasizes sexual pleasures, as he states early on in *De Vita Beata* 4, 4 – a passage translated as 'ca el día que se da el hombre al deleite corporal, ese dia es necesario que haya dolor y tristeza' (*CL* 1, 5). And this is the starting-point of Act 1 of *Celestina*.

Significantly, the opening scene contains four key words: nature, beauty, gifts and sorrow. In answer to Melibea's query as to how it is that Calisto has had a vision of God's greatness, he blurts out: 'En dar poder a natura que de tan perfecta hermosura te dotase y hacer a mí inmérito tanta merced . . . que mi secreto dolor manifestarte pudiese' (S. 46; M. 18).

Traditionally, the opening scene has been interpreted in terms of courtly love.[4] However, given that Rojas parodied that tradition in the love affair of Calisto and Melibea, it follows that Seneca's thinking on love and affection is applicable here too and should be seen as a corrective to the courtly love tradition.

In this way, the reader acquainted with Seneca's *De Vita Beata* would have realized that Calisto's despair as expressed to Melibea simply does not make sense. For anyone seeing Nature's harmony and beauty is filled with joy and peace: 'tiene gozo muy grande y sin turbación' (*CL* 1, 4). Thus the reader may well ask why Calisto is so unhappy. The answer is quite simple: Calisto's 'dolor' is nothing more than 'amor', which it does not take Melibea long to identify as 'ilícito amor' and 'deleite' (S. 47; M. 19). Consequently, instead of enjoying 'los bienes de natura' which by Stoic definition should lie easily to hand, Calisto with morbid pleasure anticipates the pain he will suffer afterwards: 'Me alegro con recelo del esquivo tormento, que tu ausencia me ha de causar.'

Other key words in the first confrontation are 'bienaventurado' and 'bienaventuranza', which possibly refer not only to the translated title of *De Vita Beata*, but more specifically to the translator's commentary. As we saw in chapter 2, Alonso de Cartagena, when faced with translating the word *beatus*, had warned his readers quite early on not to use the word 'bienaventurado' or 'bienaventuranza' in the sense of happiness and contentment. For this state of mind he proposed 'venturoso' or 'ventura'. By contrast, as he explains at length in the last gloss to the work, the only 'bienaventurado' is he who contemplates God after death: '. . . nuestra bienaventuranza perfecta es la fruición y visión de Dios' (*CL* 1).

Thus, when Calisto equates his 'cuerpo glorificado' with a state of divine 'bienaventuranza', the informed reader might spot both a satirical allusion to the religious practices of courtly love and the translation and gloss of *De Vita Beata*. Nor would such a reader have been at all surprised at Calisto's further heresies, such as 'Por Dios la creo, por Dios la confieso y no creo que hay otro soberano en el cielo' (S. 51; M. 24), since here he would perceive a distorted echo of Cartagena's cautionary gloss: 'Bienaventuranza perfecta es el bien no criado que es Dios.'

Calisto's pseudo-philosophizing not only sets the tone for further heresies; it also brings out the flaws in his logic. In this respect, his judgements regarding Melibea's beauty, Nature's greatness and his own happiness can be read as an ingenious illustration of error (*opinio*) as conceived in the Stoic theory of perception and knowledge. For the Stoics, knowledge is attainable and follows on a precise succession of mental exercises which start with perception through the senses. In order to make a judgement, assent (*adsensio*) has to be given to the perceived picture (*visum*). But assent, hastily and wrongly given, leads to error (*opinio*) and all error is sin (*peccatum*). The progress from assent to knowledge then becomes very complex indeed; it is a process which passes through the comparison of many 'like' and 'unlike' experiences such as sameness (*similitudo*), analogy (*proportio*), transference (*translatio*), composition (*compositio*), opposition (*transitio*) and deprivation (*deprivatio*). These mental exercises can generally be summed up as 'reason's work of comparison' (*collatio rationis*).[5]

The first author of *Celestina* was no philosopher but a literary man, and as such he wrote a witty parody of just such a *collatio rationis* when he introduced his protagonist to the reader. In fact, the opening scene could well be a parody of a pseudo-philosophic debate, which leads to ever greater non-truths. Considered in this light, Calisto's conversation with Melibea can be read as an *exemplum* of Stoic *opinio* in a Christian context.

Calisto says: 'En esto veo, Melibea, la grandeza de Dios' (*visum* and *assentio*). Melibea then asks the reason. His answer, 'en dar poder a natura . . . etc.', becomes his hastily given *opinio* based on the wrong series of 'like' and 'unlike' comparisons: 'Sin duda incomparablemente es mayor tal galardón que el servicio, sacrificio, devoción y obras pías que por este lugar alcanzar yo tengo a Dios ofrecido' (*comparatio*). '¿Quién vido en esta vida cuerpo glorificado de ningún hombre, como agora el mío?' (*similitudo*). 'Por cierto los gloriosos santos, que se deleitan en la visión divina, no gozan más que yo agora en el acatamiento tuyo' (*proportio*); 'Mas ¡oh triste! que en esto diferimos' (*translatio*); 'que ellos puramente se glorifican sin temor de caer de tal bienaventuranza, y yo, mixto' (*transitio*); 'me alegro con recelo del esquivo tormento, que tu ausencia me ha de causar' (*deprivatio*). He then ends his dubious *collatio rationis* with the heretical conclusion: 'Téngolo [i.e. el premio] por tanto en verdad que, si Dios me diese en el cielo la silla sobre sus santos, no lo ternía por tanta felicidad.' His parting words, again, prove how one error (*opinio*) leads to another: 'Iré como aquel contra quien solamente la adversa fortuna pone su estudio con odio cruel' (S. 47; M. 19). Here as well Calisto falls short of that essential condition of the happy life: disdain of the vicissitudes of Fortune. Thus the short dialogue at the beginning of the book demonstrates as clearly as may be how ill equipped the protagonist is to aspire to any sort of 'bienaventuranza'.

For such a happy life one needs to be at one with Nature ('conveniens naturae suae'), possess a sound mind ('sana mens'), be courageous and energetic ('fortis ac vehemens') and to use rather than to serve Fortune ('usura fortunae muneribus non servitura', *DVB* 3, 3). If not, one becomes a slave, and of all types of servitude subservience to pleasure is the worst all, as the translation goes on to say: 'Ves tú agora cuán mala y cuán dañosa servidumbre es aquella en que sirve aquel de quien se enseñorean todos los deleites y las tristezas' (*CL* 1, 5).

The ensuing scene, in which Calisto confronts his servant Sempronio, then sets out to illustrate, in word and deed, how much a slave to his passions the master is. But first we should give brief consideration to the name which the author has chosen for his unwise protagonist.

The name Calisto

Modern critics have related the name Calisto to the Greek *kalistos* meaning 'most beautiful'. Fifteenth-century readers, however, had a much more recent source at hand: namely, Seneca's Epistula 47 (Anth. 48), in which the Roman philosopher deals exclusively with the difficult relationship of masters and slaves.

After condemning the cruel treatment meted out to slaves in Rome, Seneca here reminds the reader that, in the final analysis, slaves are human beings too. But, more importantly, he says, let us not forget that one day we ourselves may become slaves to former slaves turned masters. Then, as an example of the vicissitudes of servitude, Seneca recounts the anecdote of a slave called Callistus who refused to let his former master enter his house, 'aquel señor había vendido a Calisto mas Calisto le vendió a él en muchas maneras' (Anth. 48, fol. 50r). The message here is that Fortune can reverse the order of things when we least expect it. However, even more important is the thought that servitude is a very fortuitous and relative state. What matters is freedom of mind, and very few can honestly lay claim to that. The worst sort of servitude, however, is that which is voluntary ('nulla servitus turpior est quam voluntaria', *Ep.* 47, 17).

Thus the name Calisto means much more than 'most beautiful'; it contains a host of secondary meanings suggested by the context of its source. Calisto the master, blinded by passion, becomes a slave: a slave to his afflictions in the first place, then, in quick succession, to Melibea, to his servants and to Celestina. In other words, Calisto forgets that he is the master, he forgets the Stoic principle never to be 'siervo de otro, mas señor de ti mismo' (Anth. 35, fol. 34r). Consequently, instead of being wise, he becomes a fool, 'un loco enamorado', in reproof of whom *Celestina* was written (S. 44; M. 15).[6]

The second confrontation: masters and servants

If, in the course of the first encounter, Calisto showed himself a slave to his passions, the second confrontation puts him into the category of fools who do not know how to rule themselves let alone others. In fact, his very first words upon entering the house can be read as an exemplary case of how not to treat one's servant:

Calisto: '¡Sempronio, Sempronio! Sempronio! ¿Dónde está este maldito? . . .
¡Así los diablos te ganen! . . . ¡Anda, anda, malvado, abre la cámara
y endereza la cama! . . . ¡Vete de ahí! ¡No me hables! . . . ¡Ve con el
diablo! . . .' (S. 47; M. 19–20)

His harsh words are entirely in line with Epistula 47, in which
Seneca accuses masters of ill-treating their slaves, condemning particularly the practice of forbidding them to speak. Seneca then mentions the consequences of imposing silence on slaves: '. . . y si no
guardan el silencio ellos lo comprarán caramente: y de aquí viene que
ellos dicen mal de sus señores detrás dellos, porque ante ellos no osan
hablar'. Rojas was very much aware of this letter when he developed
the servants' characters. In fact in Act 9 Areusa's accusation against
modern mistresses voices the self-same complaint (see below, p. 72).
However, in Act 1 no further reference is made to Seneca's Epistula 47
except through the servants' famous asides, where they speak ill of
their master behind his back.

What the author of the first act wanted to bring out in the first place
was Calisto's madness. Sempronio's exclamation after his master's
unreasonable commands is a first confirmation of what the reader has
suspected all along, namely that Calisto is subject to a sudden affliction: '¡Oh desventura, oh súbito mal! ¿Cuál fue tan contrario
acontecimiento, que así tan presto robó el alegría de este hombre, y lo
peor es, junto con ella el seso?' The servant is perplexed by this
unexpected turn of events, not knowing whether to stay or to leave his
master alone. The ensuing conversation then deals with topics which
go back to a whole complex of *auctoritates*.

The problem of how to console a person in distress, whether to treat
him harshly or rather to humour his affliction, whether to leave him
alone or stay with him and, most importantly, how to deal with
grieving and pain generally were questions of moral philosophy only
too well known to the contemporary reader. The new reader's familiarity with these and other points was not, of course, the fruit of
intellectual debate, but rather the result of that great short-cut to Stoic
philosophy, the Senecan *sententia*, which pervaded anthologies and
sentence collections. Thus Sempronio's deliberations as to how to deal
with his master's sudden grief echo the speech of a typical reader who
has got his knowledge at second hand. For instance, his decision to let
his master rant and rave a little ('quiérole dejar un poco desbrave,
madure . . .', S. 48; M. 20) reflects a wisdom contained in the
'Tratado de la consolación a Helvia' of the *Copilación*. The gloss to this

extract from Seneca's treatise moreover seeks support in Aristotle's *Ethics* 9, which warns that the stricken friend could easily be upset by consoling words:

> y en lugar de le amansar la tristeza acreciéntasele por el enojo que ha del otro en no dolerse de su mal, y esto es lo que dice Séneca, que cuando el dolor es nuevo y grande, no cumple luego consolar con palabras hasta que se vaya algún tanto amansando.   (*CL* 5)

Similarly, the words 'oído he decir', which preface his home-made *sentencia* 'es peligro abrir o apremiar las postemas duras, porque más se enconan', could well allude to the same *Tratado*, in which hasty words of consolation are compared to administering medicine too hastily, as they could cause a 'rompimiento y renovación de la llaga'.

Searching for more counsel from the classics, Sempronio then remembers another 'fontecica de filosofía': 'dejemos llorar al que dolor tiene, que las lágrimas y sospiros mucho desenconan el corazón dolorido'. Here he alludes to a number of authorities quoted in the glosses to the *Proverbios de Séneca*, notably number 19, 'De él que ama redemirá su malenconía con lágrimas' (R. 37), which the gloss substantiates by quoting Solomon and Aristotle. Proverbio 163 has another appropriate saying on the subject of sorrow and tears, 'Trabajoso dolor es el que no tiene voz en el tormento', which is again paraphrased in the gloss as 'ha algun alivio de su dolor quejándose y dando voces del dolor que padece' (R. 165).

So far, the superficial reader would have agreed wholeheartedly with Sempronio's deliberations on sorrow and tears, all the more so as they are backed up by well-known authorities. However, both Sempronio's 'fontecicas', like those contained in the glosses, are lifted out of context and therefore might be only half-truths or even non-truths if seen in a wider context. The more educated reader, on the other hand, whose knowledge went beyond the isolated *sentencia*, would have spotted the fallacy in the servant's words of wisdom. For instance, in Epistula 99 (Anth. 47) Seneca concedes that at first tears are inevitable and might help to ease the pain somewhat – a statement translated as 'las lágrimas salen a las veces a malgrado del hombre y tiemplan el corazón y sosiéganle' (Anth. 47, fol. 48r). Nevertheless, he condemns any show of sorrow as dangerously akin to pleasure, hence the premise of this letter, 'aún en plañir y llorar hay especie de locura' ('quasdam etiam lacrimarum ineptias esse', *Ep.* 99, 1). After stating that many shed tears only when they have an audience, the letter then takes the Epicurean Metrodorus to task on the subject of mixing pleasure and sorrow (*Ep.* 99, 25): 'dijo que algún deleite hay en la tristeza y en tener duelo y que aquella debe hombre abrazar'. Seneca then refutes this idea with the emphatic statement 'esto nos no podemos decir que somos estóicos' (fol. 49r). Indeed, Calisto's 'deleites y tristezas' are entirely Epicurean and, as such, a vivid illustration of the unwise man in a Senecan reading of the text.

Seneca's letters give further clues as to the background of Sempronio's dilemma. For instance, the translation of Epistula 10 carries the Spanish rubric 'Donde escribe Séneca ser peligrosa la soledad al indiscreto y poco sabido porque trae muchos malos pensamientos lo que no hace así en el sabio' (Anth. 10, fol. 9r). The text then elaborates on these 'malos pensamientos' as being dangerous to himself and others, the main risk being a heightening of the *affectus*, such as greed, fear, anger and lust. Thus the reader acquainted with the complete text of the Anthology would have recognized Calisto's ranting and raving as the sign of an unwise man who has given in to his *affecti* and whose affliction will probably increase if he is left by himself.

In true Epicurean fashion, Calisto is enjoying every minute of his 'dolor' and asks for his lute to emphasize his state of mind. But his instrument is out of tune and, for once, he voices a true Stoic principle when he exclaims: '¿Cómo sentirá el armonía aquel que consigo está tan discorde; aquel en quien la voluntad a la razón no obedece?' (S. 48; M. 21). Although Seneca teaches that the wise man is free and subject to none, he makes one exception when it comes to reason. Reason should be obeyed at all times: 'te subice ratione', he says (*Ep.* 37, 4). Only if man submits to reason will he be able to rule others; or, in the words of the translator, 'Tú regirás a muchos si la razón rige a ti' (Anth. 38, fol. 35r). From this it follows that, in disobeying reason, Calisto has ceased to be the master; so, instead of heeding the advice given in the source of his 'fontecica', he puts himself at the mercy of his servant, unwittingly proving the gloss to Proverbio 170: 'El hombre que había de ser señor es hecho siervo pues sirve a sus deleites y afecciones desordenadas' (R. 169).

Meanwhile, Sempronio does not need any further confirmation of his master's state of mind: 'No me engaño yo, que loco está este mi amo' (S. 49; M. 22), he mutters, and, after listening a little longer to Calisto's nonsense, he concludes: 'no basta loco, sino hereje'. As if on cue, his master produces the blasphemy 'Melibeo soy, y a Melibea adoro, y en Melibea creo y a Melibea amo' at which Sempronio realizes what the matter is, 'bien sé de qué pie coxqueas. Yo te sanaré' (S. 50; M. 23).

Then, challenging Calisto's sceptical belief that there is no cure for this ill, Sempronio gives the first direct quotation from Seneca, although it is slightly adapted to the occasion. His assurance that 'el comienzo de la salud es conocer hombre la dolencia del enfermo' stems from Epistula 28, which reads: 'Initium est salutis notitia peccati' (*Ep.* 28, 9).

The Latin scholar must have been aware of the substitution of 'sin' for 'illness', mentally re-translating 'enfermo' into 'peccatum'. By restoring the general sense in this way, the informed reader would have perceived the moral implication of this altered quotation, and have applied it to the hidden intent of the new text. Obviously, Calisto is sick, for this type of love is nothing more than an illness and a disturbance, as Sempronio so aptly says soon after: '¡el amor . . . es necesaria turbación en el amante!'. *Conturbatio, affectus* and *morbus* are equivalent terms with which the Romans translate the controversial Greek word *pathos*. And *pathos* as illness is the sign under which the love affair will develop. Melibea suffers from the same illness; Celestina is summoned as her doctor, and the medicine prescribed is love's consummation. So, Sempronio's promise to cure his master has the double connotation of love as sickness and of the servant taking charge.[7]

In answer to Sempronio, Calisto also quotes Seneca with the words '¿Cuál consejo puede regir lo que en sí no tiene orden ni consejo?' (S. 50; M. 23) – a *sententia* which has its origin in Epistula 40: 'Quomodo autem regere potest, quae regi non potest?' (*Ep.* 40, 4). With this quotation the orientation of the argument changes radically. Leaving the well-trodden path of love as an affliction of the mind, the author now passes on to the theme of speech as an indicator of that same vulnerable psyche. Calisto's exclamation stems from Epistula 40, which deals with the connection between speech and reason, a topic closely related to Seneca's teaching on Nature, simplicity and truth. The meaning of the Latin sentence is 'how can that speech govern others which cannot itself be governed?', the subject being *ratio* in the general sense of the spoken word. The translator of the letters, too, makes 'language' the subject: 'cómo governará a otros aquel hablar que en sí mismo no es gobernado ni regido' (Anth. 41, fol. 35r).

As when Calisto earlier pontificated on the anarchy that results if reason does not govern will, the same thought, now expressed in terms of reason and speech, serves as an unwitting self-denunciation of the speaker in question. But there is more to this *sententia* than its ironic application to the speaker's own muddled mind. The paragraph from which the quotation is taken addresses the pernicious practice of spicing one's speech with jargon. Those readers who had the capacity for textual recall, here might have remembered the words that precede the quotation. In it Seneca explains that speech which aims at the truth should be unadorned and plain ('inconposita esse debet et simplex') in contrast to rhetorical ('popularis'), which aims to move the masses ('turba') and attract fools' ears ('inconsultas aures').[8]

For Seneca, verbosity and jargon are yet more manifestations of that same *affectus* that plagues mankind in so many forms and disguises. In Epistula 40, in particular, he singles out the lawyer's inclination to overwhelm his audience with words. But, he goes on to say, even if such a lawyer is overcome by emotion ('affectus impotens sui'), he should refrain from heaping up his words beyond what the ear can stand. Seneca, therefore, urges his friend Lucilius to avoid this ill: 'Eo autem magis te deterreo ab isto morbo' (*Ep.* 40, 13).

Mental disturbance and illness are two terms which Sempronio has used to describe his master's affliction moments before. Calisto's rhetorical question, '¿Cuál consejo puede regir lo que en sí no tiene orden ni consejo?', thus implicitly defines the very language the characters are using as yet another manifestation of that same *affectus* and *morbus*. Many of Seneca's *sententiae* are quoted out of context or are only partially true, others are not followed up by the speakers, while others, as we shall see, are quoted back to front. What is striking here is that both master and servant indulge in the same populist speech. But then the 'oratio popularis' in the sense of untruthful speech is not restricted to Calisto and Sempronio. All the characters in *Celestina* will manipulate and assail their opponents with words of wisdom which they either do not comprehend or twist to suit their own devious ends.

Thus reminded by Calisto's quotation of Seneca's stance on language, truth and concision, the educated reader would have smiled at Calisto's longwinded eulogy of Melibea's body and Sempronio's laconic question, '¿Has dicho?', followed by the master's answer, 'Cuan brevemente pude' (S. 55; M. 29). Similarly, Sempronio's warning, 'Haz tú lo que bien digo y no lo que mal hago' (S. 51; M. 24), seems to contradict Seneca's teaching on language and truth.

Sempronio's words then herald his long disquisition on woman's imperfections, for which he invokes Aristotle, Solomon, Seneca and a certain 'Bernardo' (S. 52; M. 25–6), authorities frequently quoted in the glosses to Seneca's apocryphal work. And still, the medieval notion of women as imperfect beings, expressed in Sempronio's conclusion that Calisto is 'más digno' than Melibea simply because she is 'imperfecta' (S. 55; M. 29), was not spread by Seneca himself. For the Roman philosopher had taught that women, albeit the weaker sex, could and should nonetheless aspire to the same heights of perfection as men. Thus, yet again, Sempronio's words flow from apocryphal sources, notably the *Proverbios*, where the Aristotelian 'imperfección de la flaca mujer' is a favourite topic of discussion.

The next reference to Sempronio's store of pseudo-knowledge is a blatant error, so blatant that even the credulous reader of the time would have winced at these 'words of wisdom'. Speaking of Calisto's superiority as man, Sempronio lists all the gifts that nature has heaped on him: beauty, grace, stature, strength and agility. On top of that, he continues, Fortune has given him a sufficiency of worldly goods, and this, Sempronio claims, is important 'porque sin los bienes de fuera, de los cuales la fortuna es señora, a ninguno acaece en esta vida ser bienaventurado' (S. 53; M. 27). The first half of the statement may be correct, but the second half is patently wrong, as any superficial reader of *De Vita Beata* would know. Even the commentaries to the *Proverbios* contradict such an obvious non-truth. Proverbio 202 elucidates the controversy among the 'antiguos' as to what constitutes happiness with the words 'Y algunos dijeron que la bienaventuranza estaba en tener mucho dinero' (R. 188), a notion which is duly refuted by pointing to Aristotle and Boethius. But, since what some people say fits Sempronio's purpose, he tries this on his master, and with good results. The servant's mention of material goods produces the reward of a brocade waistcoat, on which Sempronio comments: 'Prospérate Dios por éste (y por muchas más, que me darás) . . . sin merced, imposible es obrarse bien ninguna cosa' (S. 55; M. 30). With these words he announces yet another theme, of equal importance for both Seneca and the authors of *Celestina*: the difficult art of giving and receiving.

Ironically, the 'galardones' in *Celestina* are anything but gifts. They are payments in exchange for service, parodying Seneca's many ideas in *De Beneficiis*. But this book was not available in the vernacular; instead, extracts and commentaries 'translated' Seneca's thought into fifteenth-century notions of payment in exchange for goods received.

At first, the gift bestowed on Sempronio is seen as a 'merced' in anticipation of the promised work of 'piedad'. But soon the word 'galardón' crops up in connection with Calisto's apprehension about giving the right amount at the right time to the right person (S. 65; M. 42). Indeed, the master's ill-chosen rewards, matched by the ever-increasing greed of his servants, are central to the development of the plot.

Thus, from the very beginning of Act I the seeds for this conflict have been sown, a potential which Rojas is to develop to the full. Material reward, interest and gain are the motive behind Sempronio's subsequent visit to Celestina, his master being left to face the virtuous servant Parmeno alone.

Parmeno, though young, is another pseudo-philosopher saturated with Senecan and pseudo-Senecan wisdom. But this servant's mind is muddled and his knowledge shaky, as becomes painfully clear in his confrontation with Celestina. However, faced with his weak master, he easily assumes the role of the loyal servant, acting out what he has picked up from his multiple readings. Parmeno's detailed description of Celestina's occupation and reputation as a 'puta vieja' (S. 59–62; M. 34–9), followed by his master's annoyance at his revelations, sounds like an illustration of *El tratado del loor* of the *Copilación*, where it says: 'Cómo un servidor conseja a su señor, que no cometa un gran maleficio, por la difamación que dende saldrá. Y el señor responde mal, y el servidor replica verdaderamente demostrando en qué está el verdadero loor' (*CL* 5).

Now Calisto was familiar with the same *Copilación* and could answer in kind. As master he would, of course, have been more interested in reading about gifts, particularly those involving the rewarding of servants. Thus, in the section 'De los siervos' (taken from *De Beneficiis* 3, 18–21) he would have learned 'que los siervos pueden hacer gracia a sus señores y cuándo acaece esto'. The passage in question analyses the difference between 'servicio' as 'voluntad de siervos' and 'gracia' as 'voluntad de amigo'. Cartagena's marginal gloss then explains: '. . . si el siervo allende de lo que es tendido y obligado tiene cuidado del señor, y de sus provechos y de su honra, en tal caso bien se puede decir que hace gracia el siervo al señor. El tal siervo puédese llamar amigo.'

Interestingly enough, Calisto expresses his gratitude to Parmeno in identical terms: 'asaz soy de ti avisado; téngotelo en gracia . . . por tal amigo a ti me concedo' (S. 62–3; M. 39). As if to tell his master that they are on the same wavelength, Parmeno, in turn, alludes to the same gloss, exclaiming: '¿Cuándo me viste, señor, envidiar o por

ningún interés ni resabio tu provecho estorcer?' This short exchange
between master and servant illustrates how both are cast in the same
mould. They have the same superficial knowledge of predigested
words of wisdom and, therefore, are liable to quote them back to front.

Calisto's explanation, 'Yo temo y el temor reduce la memoria y a la
providencia despierta' (ibid.), is just such a 'misquotation'. The Latin
text reads: 'timoris enim tormentum memoria reducit, providentia
anticipat' (Ep. 5, 9). The meaning is that memory recalls past horrors
and foresight anticipates those of the future, 'memoria' and
'providentia' being the subject and not the object of the two verbs.
The Spanish anthology comes closer to an accurate translation where
it says: 'ca la remembranza de lo pasado nos atormenta, y el temor de
lo que está por venir hace que nos proveamos antes de tiempo' (Anth.
5, fol. 5r).

The most interesting aspect of Calisto's misquotation is perhaps the
context in which this sententia occurs in Seneca's Epistula 5, where he
repeats what he has argued in De Vita Beata: namely, that the wise man
lives according to nature, and therefore does not lust after anything
unnecessary. After stating that, to achieve its object, greed (cupiditas)
generates hope coupled with apprehension of failure, Seneca explains
the connection between hope and fear with the metaphor of prisoner
and guard, translated as: 'Así como una cadena tiene al preso y al que
le guarda.' As before, the context of the (mis)quotation underlines and
explains Calisto's state of mind; as soon as the master surrendered to
his cupiditas he became chained to an ever-increasing number of affecti,
such as fear, hope and apprehension. The image of the chain thus
appears hidden in Calisto's quotation; it is a metaphor which Rojas
will develop in all its consequences. Meanwhile, other readers equally
acquainted with Seneca's letters would spot the error in the quotation
and thus identify the speaker's deficient knowledge. Such is the
potential of the poetics of quotation: the original content and context
of the quotation act as a sub-text in the new setting and as such can
reveal the author's implicit meaning.

Parmeno's last protestation sums up his concern for his master:
'Oyeme y el afecto no te ensorde ni la esperanza del deleite te ciegue'
(S. 63; M. 40) – a clear allusion to Seneca's general stance on the
nature of the affectus. Here one might compare Parmeno's words to the
Copilación's gloss to the 'Tratado de lo que es provechoso': 'la afección
desordenada y la pasión recia turba el juicio y hace a los hombres
desear y pedir aquellas cosas que le son empecibles y dañosas' (CL 5).

But Parmeno's words may equally well allude to that other short-cut to moral philosophy, the *Proverbios de Séneca*. There the gloss to Proverbio 78 lists love and hatred as harmful to the mind: '. . . como dice Aristóteles en el segundo de los Retóricos que el amor y la malquerencia conturban el juicio' (R. 83). Another gloss, this one to Proverbio 94, leans on Cato to elucidate that 'El aquejo y arrebatamiento embarga o impide el consejo' (R. 107). Parmeno thus refers to a wide range of sources which, as in the case of Sempronio, have come to him second-hand. Both master and servants are portrayed as typical *Reader's Digest* subscribers, who not only read but also reproduce the style of this sort of processed knowledge.

The third confrontation: Celestina and Parmeno

The last confrontation in Act 1 presents the go-between as a virtuoso in influencing others through the skilful manipulation of her words. Indeed, her persuasion of Parmeno brings out her superior rhetorical talents in sharp contrast to the servant's pitiful attempts to defend himself. Celestina and Parmeno vie with each other in quoting *exempla* and *sententiae* – in the case of the experienced woman to defeat her opponent, in the case of the young servant to express what his poverty of mind cannot put into words.

The verbal skirmish between Celestina and Parmeno reads like nothing quite so much as a vivid example of Seneca's teaching on the use and abuse of quotations for polemical purposes. The interspersing of one's speech with the sayings of others he derisively calls 'captare flosculos' (*Ep.* 33, 7). 'Ex commentario sapere' is how he terms this notebook knowledge further on, thus condemning a pseudo-philosophy of which he would, with time, become the most quoted authority. But, as if to justify his own tendency to borrow from others, Seneca does concede that using maxims has its good side too. In this connection, he particularly recommends Epicurus' words of wisdom, because they are so unexpected ('inexpectata') and noteworthy ('mirum est'), coming, as he claims, from an effeminate man.

With this parenthesis Seneca underlines another important aspect of the poetics of the *sententia*: namely, the way in which the unexpectedness of a maxim enhances the impact of its new application. According to Seneca, another reason for quoting from apparently opposing schools is the fact that some truths are universal: 'publicae sunt et maxime nostrae' (*Ep.* 33, 2). Thus, many *sententiae* can be traced to various sources, many have become proverbs, many have changed their words but not their content, and even more have been applied to the achievement of opposite ends. This last usage of classical wisdom, of course, prevails in Celestina's speech when dealing with Parmeno.

Confronted with the interfering servant in Calisto's house, Celestina reassures Sempronio that she can cope with him. Her tactics, she explains, will be to let Parmeno share in the gain: 'demosle parte, que los bienes, si no son comunicados, no son bienes' (S. 64; M. 41). Interestingly, here she bases herself on Aristotle, as quoted in the gloss to Proverbio 86: 'ca, como dice Aristóteles en el octavo de las *Ethicas*, que aprovecharía a ninguno tener muchos bienes si no tuviese con quien los participase y comunicase' (R. 97). In turn, these words are an explanation of a famous Senecan *sententia*, with which the gloss starts: 'como dice Séneca, de ningún bien es alegre la posesión sin compañero'. This sentence, taken from Epistula 6, 4 and combined with Aristotle's words from *Ethics* 8, was no doubt popular in the fifteenth century, for Proverbio 217 repeats the double quotation, this time to elucidate the nature of friend and foe (R. 195). Thus hashed and re-hashed, these *sententiae* will be used by Celestina in much the same way as other compilers had amassed maxims 'según que a cada uno en leyendo le bien pareció' (*CL* 5, final statement of Cartagena's *Copilación*).

As Celestina's offensive gains momentum, so Parmeno's reliance on his copybook increases. Thus, his Aristotelian exposition of 'acto' and 'potencia' comes dangerously close to the typical syllogism so abhorred by Seneca. There can be no wonder at Celestina's comment, '¡Como que no se te entiende!' (S. 67; M. 45), when she decides to talk plainly for a change. But her revelations about Parmeno's mother ('que tan puta vieja era tu madre como yo') and her commiseration with his wanderings ever since he left her house, soon take her back to their common source of knowledge: 'Que, como Séneca dice, los peregrinos tienen muchas posadas y pocas amistades' (S. 68; M. 47). This line heralds the largest quotation of Act 1, lifted almost word for word from Epistula 2, 2–3.

As we have seen when dealing with previous textual resemblances, the conspicuous quotation can hide a whole complex of meanings. But on this particular occasion we have reason to be more than suspicious, because Celestina, most unusually, gives the source of her quotation. Could this be to make Parmeno aware that she knows Seneca as well as he does? Or are we here faced with a mockery of all those half-educated 'namedroppers' desirous of showing off their newly acquired knowledge?

This particular quotation cites Seneca's words with only minor alterations. However, rather than dismiss the author's changes as carelessness or even as a mistake, we should wonder whether there might not have been an ulterior motive involved. The letter from which the long quotation is taken warns against the pernicious effects of reading too many books, drawing a parallel between the restless traveller and the voracious reader. Too many sources of wisdom, he says, make for a scatterbrain ('vagum et instabile'). This being the main point of the argument, Seneca starts his comparison with 'nusquam est qui ubique est' ('being everywhere means being nowhere'), which is followed by 'vitam in peregrinatione exigentibus hoc evenit, ut multa hospitia habeant, nullas amicitias' (*Ep.* 2, 2). But Celestina reverses the order in her quotation: 'Que, como Séneca dice, los peregrinos tienen muchas posadas y pocas amistades, porque en breve tiempo con ninguno [no] pueden firmar amistad. Y el que está en muchos cabos, [no] está en ninguno' (S. 68; M. 47).

Why the reversal of the first two sentences? Because, for Celestina, what matters most is the parallel with pilgrims devoid of friends, since her quotation follows closely on her commiseration with Parmeno's uprooted existence: 'has por tantas partes vagado y peregrinado, que ni has habido provecho ni ganado deudo ni amistad'. Of secondary importance in Celestina's debate is the sentence 'nusquam est qui ubique est'. For the reader, however, this last statement is most revealing, as it alludes to Parmeno's restless wandering and, implicitly, his unstable mind ('vagum et instabile'). As the debate goes on, it becomes clear that Parmeno's voracious reading will get him nowhere: 'nusquam est'. He completely loses himself in his own *sententiae*.

Celestina, of course, leaves out the reference to this approach to learning (which, incidentally, is her own) but wholeheartedly adopts Seneca's analogies on how too much food causes indigestion, how change of medicine hampers healing and how frequent transplanting stunts growth. Then, again, the author leaves it to his readers mentally to supply the last clause of the paragraph: 'distringit librorum multitudo' (*Ep.* 2, 3) – a *sententia* which Celestina tactfully omits. Thus, in this apparently conspicuous quotation the author communicates a whole subtext of meanings precisely by this set of omissions.

As far as the content and context of this quotation in relation to the original paragraph are concerned, he again leaves it to his readers to discover the discrepancy: Celestina's purpose in quoting Epistula 2 was to make Parmeno settle for one doctrine alone – in fact, her own, which contradicts the doctrine proposed by Seneca in this context. Here, Celestina's purpose is to gain profit from an association with Sempronio, while Seneca's wisdom of the day for this letter was the Epicurean adage 'honesta res est laeta paupertas' (*Ep.* 2, 6), which Parmeno quotes in retaliation.

Celestina's next doctrine is the well-known Stoic principle of 'vivir a su ley' which, coming from her, sounds more like 'everybody for himself' – a far cry indeed from Seneca's message. The law of which the Stoics spoke was the law of Nature. In effect, *De Vita Beata* 3, 3 describes Nature as the sole guide of the wise and free man – 'porende aquella vida es bienaventurada que conviene y concuerda con su natura' (*CL* 1, 3) – while Epistula 45, 9 defines the happy man as 'el cual sigue a la natura por maestra, y se rige y ordena según la ley de natura' (Anth. 33, fol. 30r). In Seneca's canon this invariably amounts to living the simple life: 'Gran riqueza es pobreza bien ordenada según la ley de natura', he says, quoting Epicurus in Epistula 4, 10 (Anth. 4, fol. 4r); or 'amengua y abaja tu riqueza porque no es a nos necesario ninguna destas cosas y tornemos nos a la ley de natura' (Anth. 25, fol. 24r = *Ep.* 25, 4).

Celestina's words, 'Pues aquellos no deben menos hacer . . . sino vivir a su ley' (S. 69; M. 48), in fact go back to Epistula 20, 2: 'ad legem suam quisque vivat', translated as 'que cada uno viva a su ley' (Anth. 20, fol. 18r). However, Celestina's quotation leaves out the second half of the *sententia*, which continues: 'ne orationi vita dissentiat' ('y que su vida no sea desacordante de sus palabras'). Again, the dissonance between Seneca's moral teaching and its application in *Celestina* is beautifully orchestrated by the author. Moreover, by inviting his readers mentally to supply the missing part of this fragmentary quotation, the author offers them a clue as to the real meaning of Celestina's words and deeds.

Now Parmeno manages to put the ball back into Celestina's court with the correct quotation from Epistula 2, when replying to all this 'tengo por honesta cosa la pobreza alegre' (S. 69; M. 49). Not satisfied with this sentence alone, he then proceeds to indulge in one-upmanship by enlarging his quotation: 'Y aún más te digo, que no los que poco tienen son pobres; mas los que mucho desean', which is an exact translation of Seneca's preceding sentence, 'non qui parum habet sed qui plus cupit pauper est' (*Ep.* 2, 6).

To conclude, and as if to show off a little more, Parmeno then quotes in quick succession from various books. His admission, 'riqueza deseo', is preceded by the maxim 'pero quien torpemente sube a lo alto, más aína cae que subió'. Interestingly, he prophesies his own downfall with this textual borrowing from *Amonestamientos y doctrinas* (*CL* 3, 3, no. 2). His expressed desire to live without envy or fear goes back in turn to his favourite *De Vita Beata*: 'potest beatus dici qui nec cupit nec timet' (*DVB* 5, 1); but, significantly, he forgets the crucial words that finish this sentence: 'beneficio rationis', translated as 'con tanto que lo haga en la fuerza y ejercicio de la razón' (*CL* 1, 6). Instead he paraphrases Seneca's pithy words with the long-winded sentence 'Querría pasar la vida sin envidia, los yermos y aspereza sin temor, el sueño sin sobresalto, las injurias con respuesta, las fuerzas sin denuesto, las premias sin resistencia.' Celestina herself has to laugh at his verbosity – '¡Oh hijo! Bien dicen que la prudencia no puede ser sino en los viejos: y tú mucho mozo eres' (S. 69; M. 49) – only to retaliate with the proverbial wisdom 'la fortuna ayuda a los osados', which, among other *auctoritates*, alludes to Seneca's 'audentes iuvat fortuna' (*Ep.* 94, 28).

Celestina now switches her line of attack to the complicated topic of friendship, skilfully working it into a discussion on love. Her question '¿Y no sabes que has menester amigos para los conservar?' (S. 70; M. 49) points to both the *Copilación* and the Anthology of Seneca's letters. The controversial point of whether anybody needs friends was taken up in the 'Tratado de los amigos' of the *Copilación*, where it says: 'dice Séneca que los hombres, aunque sean constituídos en grandes dignidades, han menester amigos' (*CL* 5). Epistula 3, which analyses the difference between true and false friendship, has the Spanish rubric '. . . como debe cualquier escoger el amigo y saberle guardar' (Anth. 3, fol. 3r), while Epistula 9 appears in the Anthology under the rubric 'como el sabio por ser contento de lo que tiene . . . dice que no ha menester amigos' (Anth. 9, fol. 7r), an Epicurean notion which is contradicted in the text.

Celestina's next 'fontecica', 'en los infortunios el remedio es a los amigos', is an Epicurean stance which Seneca condemns in the same letter on friendship on the grounds of its utilitarian motive (*Ep.* 9, 8).

However, since Celestina's reasons for persuading Parmeno to become Sempronio's friend are purely 'por utilidad y provecho', she here needs a better authority than Epicurus to support her, and that she finds in Aristotle as elucidated in Pero Díaz's glosses to the

Proverbios. Celestina's rhetorical question '¡Y a dónde puedes ganar mejor este deudo, que donde las tres maneras de amistad concurren, conviene a saber, por bien y provecho y deleite' has its origin in Proverbio 49, 'gran deudo es conjuntarse los corazones que se bien quieren'; this is explained by the gloss 'Escribe Aristóteles en el octavo de la *Ethica* que la amistanza es de tres maneras: la una por deleite, la otra por provecho, la otra por lo honesto' (R. 55). Although Celestina's words reflect an Aristotelian wisdom, the author of Act I does not here refer to Aristotle's text nor to the popular compendium of his *Ethics*, where the three 'maneras' are called 'especias' and translated as 'honesta, utile y delectable'.[9] As is the case with Epicureanism, Aristotelian thought expressed in *Celestina* has its source in the commentaries to Seneca's translated work, in this particular case in the gloss to Proverbio 49.

Celestina's words and subsequent explanation concerning the benefits of friendship also allude to other Senecan and pseudo-Senecan texts, and wherever commentaries are provided they quote both Seneca and Aristotle in the same breath, sometimes combining the two, often confusing the issue, but always referring to these three categories: 'deleite', 'provecho', 'virtud'.[10]

The reason why Celestina inverts Pero Díaz's order is that 'por deleite' would be her trump card, especially after the mention of Areusa, Parmeno's unrequited love. But Parmeno still resists: 'Mi fe, madre, no creo a nadie.' To this Celestina replies with 'Extremo es creer a todos y yerro no creer a ninguno', a near-textual quotation from Epistula 3, 4: 'utrumque enim vitium est, et omnibus credere et nulli'. Significantly, Epistula 3 deals with true and false friendship and how one must pass judgement before and not after forming a friendship – a condition Parmeno should have remembered but did not. Instead, with Areusa's name ringing in his ears, he can hardly believe his good fortune. At the same time, just as with Calisto moments before, hope and fear go hand in hand: 'Digo que te creo, pero no me atrevo.' For that, Celestina has another maxim ready: 'De enfermo corazón es no poder sufrir el bien' (S. 70; M. 50). This, again, is a slightly altered textual reference to Epistula 5, 6: 'infirmi animi est pati non posse divitias'.

The Latin scholar would have spotted the translation of 'divitias' into the ambiguous concept of 'bien', readily grasping why the author had again substituted the particular for the general. Desperately,

Parmeno then ransacks his memory for more maxims with which to fend off Celestina's eloquence; '¡Oh Celestina! Oído he a mis mayores que un ejemplo de lujuria o avaricia mucho mal hace' – a textual borrowing from Epistula 7, 7, 'Unum exemplum luxuriae aut avaritiae multum mali facit.'

This letter introduces a different subject, that of the pernicious results stemming from consorting with the crowd. As we know from Rojas' continuation, this will become yet another crucial theme in *Celestina*. For the moment, however, Epistula 7 points the reader of Act 1 in the right direction. With his quotation Parmeno unwittingly prophesies his fatal association with Sempronio. But Parmeno only vaguely remembers this letter and does not heed its import. Subsequently, and almost as an indication of Parmeno's muddled recollections, the author then deliberately makes him commit an error in the second half of his sentence: 'y que con aquellos debe hombre conversar, que le hagan mejor, y aquellos dejar a quien él mejores piensa hacer' (S. 71; M. 50).[11] Parmeno here misquotes from the next paragraph of the same letter: 'Cum his versare qui te meliorem facturi sunt. Illos admitte quos tu potes facere meliores'.

The mistake in Parmeno's quotation is conscious, since the author wanted his readers to see Parmeno as one of those who do not think for themselves but quote the wisdom of others. Had he not prefaced his defence 'Oído he a mis mayores'? Celestina has spotted his mistake and says 'Sin prudencia hablas, que de ninguna cosa es alegre posesión sin compañia' – a partial quotation of Seneca's favourite sentence: 'nullius boni sine socio iucunda possessio est' (*Ep.* 6, 4). Significantly, in Celestina's version 'nullius boni' is translated as 'ninguna cosa', leaving out the virtue of the 'cosa'. Moreover, the letter refers to sharing knowledge and not 'deleite'.

Subsequently, her humorous analysis of how 'El deleite es con los amigos' is in answer to Parmeno's general statement 'si hombre vencido del deleite va contra la virtud, no se atreva a la honestad' (S. 71; M. 51) – a Stoic principle he has probably retained from reading *De Vita Beata* 14 and 15, which appear translated as chapters 13 and 14 of *De la vida bienaventurada*. This allusion has not escaped Celestina, who, therefore, concludes her analysis with '¡Alahé, alahé! La que las sabe las tañe. Este es el deleite; que lo al, mejor lo hacen los asnos en el prado.' With these words she, too, refers to *De Vita Beata* 9, 4, translated in chapter 10 of *De la vida bienaventurada* as 'Para qué me nombras deleite como gran bien . . . E aun lo sienten mejor los animales brutos y las bestias fieras.' Here again, 'lo al' in Celestina's words alludes to a purely sexual activity; Seneca, however, had the pleasure of the stomach in mind, while Cartagena referred to 'deleite' in general.[12]

Parmeno has taken the hint and for the last time relies on *De Vita Beata* for his answer: 'No querría, madre, me convidases a consejo con amonestación de deleite, como hicieron los que, careciendo de razonable fundamento, opinando hicieron sectas envueltas en dulce veneno para captar y tomar las voluntades de los flacos y con polvos de sabroso afecto cegaron los ojos de la razón' (S. 71; M. 51).

This could be an allusion to *De Vita Beata* 12–13, which takes Epicurus to task and which is translated as 'en oyendo nombre de deleite vuelan para allá buscando quien ayude y dé autoridad a sus deshonestos placeres . . . no digo lo que muchos dicen, que la secta y doctrina de Epicuro es maestra de maldades, mas digo esto, que no cumpla al hombre mozo oirla' (*CL* 1, 12–13).

Since Parmeno's knowledge of Stoicism is purely theoretical, he does not apply these words of wisdom to his own circumstances. Therefore Celestina is quite right in quizzing him on the meaning of these words: '¿Qué es razón, loco? ¿Qué es afecto, asnillo?'; coming to the conclusion that he lacks the 'discreción', 'prudencia' and 'experiencia' to have anything to say on the subject. With that, she threatens to leave Parmeno out of the business altogether. Naturally, Parmeno is perplexed and tries out a last 'fontecica': 'Yerro es no creer y culpa creerlo todo' (S. 71; M. 50) – an adaptation of Epistula 3, 4 on choosing friends, which, if he had remembered better, would have prevented him from entering into a friendship with Sempronio.

With Parmeno's quotation, the author leaves the topic of friendship, gradually steering the reader's attention back to the theme of gifts. Spotting *sententiae* here was the more difficult in the fifteenth century as Seneca's *De Beneficiis* had not then been translated, although excerpts were readily available in the *Copilación*.

For Seneca, one of the many and diverse errors of the unwise man is his ignorance in matters of giving and receiving: 'Beneficia nec dare scimus nec accipere', he states in the first paragraph of *De Beneficiis*. Of the seven books of *De Beneficiis*, the first three seem to have been of particular interest in the fifteenth century. Book 1 looks at the nature of a gift, Book 2 discusses the way in which a gift should be bestowed, and Book 3 debates whether a gift should be returned in any way, taking into consideration the legal aspect of the question. This part of the treatise, in particular, would have attracted students of law, as it considers ingratitude one of the most common of crimes, and yet one for which no redress exists in law. It is to this third book of *De Beneficiis* that Celestina refers when she says: '¿Y cuándo me pagarás tú esto? Nunca, pues a los padres y a los maestros no puede ser hecho servicio igualmente' (S. 71–2; M. 51). Since Celestina's words go back to a passage that was not known in translation, the quotation was obviously aimed at the Latin scholar and student of law.

In actual fact, Celestina's words echo *De Beneficiis* 3, 34, in which Seneca discusses the question of gifts bestowed by parents and teachers. While nothing should ever be given with a view to restitution, Seneca says, parents and teachers especially must have no expectation of this, as the father's gift of life and the teacher's gift of knowledge are difficult to return in kind. Moreover, he adds, the teacher's gift of knowledge comes later in life, and therefore one has to distinguish that which is first in time from that which is first in importance. The author of Act 1 clearly had this passage in mind when he made Celestina exclaim: '¿Y cuándo me pagarás tú esto?' Seeing herself as a surrogate parent and teacher to Parmeno, she then answers her own rhetorical question with: 'Nunca, pues a los padres y a los maestros no puede ser hecho servicio igualmente.'

Act 1 closes with another allusion to Seneca's thinking on rewards, but this time to Book 2, which deals with when and how to give. This particular question was more familiar, thanks to the many excerpts from this book in the *Copilación* and *Proverbios*. When Celestina acknowledges Calisto's 'dádiva pobre' with the words 'Y sin duda la presta dádiva su efecto ha doblado, porque la que tarda, el prometimiento muestra negar y arrepentirse del don prometido' (S. 73; M. 53), her *auctoritas* is Proverbio 78, 'dos veces da al pobre limosna quien se la da prestamente' (R. 173); while the second half of her sentence sends the reader to the *Copilación*, which, under the rubric 'con qué razón se deben dar los beneficios', states: 'ca no es gracioso aquel beneficio que tarda mucho entre las manos del que lo da, ni el que parece ser dado de malamente. E así lo dan como se lo tomasen por fuerza' (cf. *De Ben.* 2, 1, 2).

With this, Rojas chose to close Act 1 even if the original fragment continued the dialogue with the master's anxious questioning of his servants: 'Hermanos míos, cient monedas di a la madre, ¿hice bien?' (S. 74; M. 55).

At this point, Rojas knew how to continue the story. He had recognized the frame of reference of both the author and his fiction, he had spotted the provenance and subtext of the 'fontecicas de filosofía' and he had grasped the potential of the quotation.

4

Fernando de Rojas continues the story: the *Comedia de Calisto y Melibea*

If Senecan thinking pervaded the genesis of *Celestina*, we can also follow a steady Senecan thread through the continuation of the story, since Seneca's authority is present both in the wealth of new quotations and in the development of the plot.

In the prefatory letter in which Rojas talks about the merits of the first act, he particularly praises the 'principal historia o ficción toda junta' from which such enjoyable 'fontecicas de filosofía' emerged (S. 36; M. 3). 'Ficción' and 'fontecica' are thus two constituent elements in *Celestina*, even if the philosophy remains subordinate to the overall story at all times. Nevertheless, the fiction of Rojas' 'Comedia' feeds on these words of wisdom and, as in a master/servant relationship, depends on them. Thus, to some extent the quotations in the first act supplied Rojas with the raw material of his continuation.

Later on, in the Prologue to the completed work, Rojas explains the potential of the quotation as follows: 'toda palabra del hombre sciente está preñada'. As if to justify the word *preñada* he then describes what he means: 'de muy hinchada y llena quiere reventar [*sic*], echando de sí tan crecidos ramos y hojas, que del menor pimpollo se sacaría harto fruto entre personas discretas' (S. 40; M. 9).

This is a pregnant statement in itself. The metaphor of the bursting bud which grows into abundant foliage and fruit is full of further implications. The image of the fruit refers to the moral message, while the additional clause, 'entre personas discretas', reveals that this rich harvest is not for everybody. The metaphor of the 'crecidos ramos y hojas' in turn points to the powerful ramifications of the isolated thought, which, in the hand of the poet, then blossoms into a work of art, a 'ficción toda junta'.

At first glance, the possible ways in which to continue the fragment seem limitless. The plot itself was rudimentary, the only characters with a definite profile were Calisto, the two servants and Celestina.

Melibea and Elicia's presence was minimal, while Areusa and 'el plebérico corazón', presumably Melibea's father, were wide open.

Still, Rojas was not entirely free in his choice, since he meant to continue the sketch according to the unspoken message of its 'fontecicas de filosofía'. Thus, we see that the name Calisto drew his attention to Epistula 47 on masters and slaves, which then gave him many further ideas for the development of both the plot and the main characters. The first author's allusions to Epistula 9, which show how passion and false friendship are both motivated by greed ('codicia'), then made him equate the master's love affair and the servants' ill-fated friendship, while simultaneously following the lead of the quotations taken from Epistula 7 insofar as they concern the fateful results of a close association with the 'vulgus'.

Similarly, the several allusions to *De Beneficiis* gave him a clue as to what would result from the rewards which Calisto distributes so unwisely, while the mention of sorrow and tears at the beginning of Act 1 directed him to Epistula 99 for a fitting conclusion to the *Comedia*.

In addition, his own reading of *De Ira* gave him an idea for the characters' actions and reactions, while he relied heavily on the *Proverbios*, *Cinco libros* and *Epístolas* for many new *sententiae*.

In certain respects, Rojas was less discriminating in choosing his quotations than the first author. While the latter had used his first-hand knowledge of Seneca to make fun of the new readers' copybook acquaintance with moral philosophy, Rojas seems to be closer to his readers in his own reliance on second-hand sources. Thus, in the *Comedia* the gap between the author and his target narrows and inevitably results in a diminished satirical impact. Be this as it may, Rojas wrote in the same critical vein as the first author, exposing the weaknesses of masters and servants in their misguided search for the *summum bonum*. And here *Las epístolas de Séneca* proved to be Rojas' main frame of reference.[1]

Servitude

Epistula 47 is listed as number 48 in the Anthology under the rubric 'como los que tienen siervos deben ser graciosos y no crueles con ellos, ca por el contrario permite Dios a veces que sean los señores siervos de aquellos que mal trataron . . .' (Anth. 48, fol. 49r).

Here, surrounding the name Calisto, Rojas would have found a clue as to how to develop all the other characters. Seneca's challenge to show him a man 'que no sea siervo . . . de lujuria, otro de avaricia, otro de miedo y temor, otro de pompa y ufana' of course implies that nobody fits the bill (Anth. 48 fol. 49v).

In accordance with this roll-call, Rojas develops Calisto as 'siervo de lujuria', Celestina as a slave to her own 'avaricia'; 'miedo y temor' become the typical vices of the cowardly servants, while Pleberio pays a bitter price for having been 'siervo de pompa y ufana'.

The character who best fits Seneca's description of a slave is Calisto, the master, judging by the examples Seneca adduces: 'Tu hallarás que algún alto hombre fue siervo de una vieja, algún hombre rico sirve a una mala mujer . . .' (fol. 50v), which is a free translation of 'dabo consularem aniculae servientem, dabo ancillulae divitem . . .' (Ep. 47, 17). However, for Seneca the worst form of slavery is a voluntary subservience; this is summed up as 'nulla servitus turpior est quam voluntaria'. Here again the translator takes some liberties with the text when he paraphrases this maxim as 'no hay servidumbre tan deshonrada ni tan vergonzosa como aquel que es siervo de su voluntad y apetito' (ibid.).

In many ways, the speech and actions of the protagonists of Celestina are a vivid example of this state of affairs. Celestina describes Melibea's surrender in general terms as 'hácense siervas de quien eran señoras, dejan el mando y son mandadas' (S. 83; M. 68), while Calisto and Melibea repeatedly profess to be each other's slave (see S. 164, 171, 190; M. 189, 199, 228). Masters in their own household, they forget that most important Stoic principle never to be 'siervo de otro mas señor de ti mismo' and that 'la mayor potencia y señoría es ser señor de si mismo' (Anth. 35 fol. 34r).

The words 'cativo' and 'siervo', of course, belong to the courtly love vocabulary. However, when we examine the use and context of the words in Celestina, we realize that they also refer to the lovers' dependence on Celestina, Celestina's relation to the servants and Areusa's condemnation of the serving-maid's status.

Quite early on, the still loyal Parmeno, seeing the great danger of his master's dependence on Celestina, exclaims: 'y lo [que] peor es, hacerte su cativo'. When Calisto then asks '¿Cómo loco, su cativo?' the servant answers: 'Porque a quien dices el secreto das tu libertad' (S. 76; M. 58). Celestina is caught in the same way as Calisto, as witness her words to Parmeno and Sempronio moments before her death: 'No pienses que soy tu cativa por saber mis secretos y mi vida pasada' (S.

182; M. 215). Meanwhile, Melibea is 'cativa' to both Calisto and Celestina, to go by Lucrecia's assessment of the situation: 'El seso tiene perdido mi señora, gran mal es éste. Cautivádola ha esta hechicera' (S. 157; M. 180). Finally, just before her suicide, Melibea confesses that she has lost all her freedom when she invokes God with the words: 'Ves mi poco poder ves cuán cativa tengo mi libertad' (S. 228; M. 257). These words in turn parallel Calisto's state of mind as diagnosed early on by Parmeno: 'perdiste el nombre de libre cuando cautivaste tu voluntad' (S. 77; M. 59).

In contrast to these unfree fools, Areusa has consciously broken out of the vicious circle of servitude. Confronted by Melibea's submissive maid Lucrecia in Act 9, Areusa bursts forth into a long list of accusations and condemnations of 'estas señoras que ahora se usan'. The vivid description of the cruel treatment servants have to endure at the hands of their mistresses is all of Rojas' invention. He bases himself, however, on Seneca's Epistula 47, and especially on its conclusion. Areusa's exclamation 'Denostadas, maltratadas las traen, continuo sojuzgadas, que hablar delante [de] ellas no osan' points to Seneca's words 'Y los desaventurados siervos están ante ellos en pie y no osan hablar, y si alguna palabra dicen luego son heridos y denostados como canes' (Anth. 48 fol. 49v). Moreover, Areusa's words at the beginning and end of her accusation reflect a true Stoic principle of freedom when she says: 'Por esto me vivo sobre mí, desde que me sé conocer. Que jamás me precié de llamar[me] de otrie, sino mía' (S. 149; M. 167). How different this sounds from Melibea's state of mind as reported by Celestina to Calisto: 'que es más tuya que de si misma' (S. 164; M. 189). Areusa's rage at modern mistresses then concludes with the Stoic assertion 'Por esto, madre, he querido más vivir en mi pequeña casa, exenta y señora, que no en sus ricos palacios, sojuzgada y cativa' (S. 150; M. 168).

Rojas was inspired by Epistula 47 in other respects too. As we saw in chapter 3, Seneca elaborates on the consequences of imposing absolute silence on slaves with the words '. . . y si no guardan el silencio ellos lo comprarán caramente, y de aquí viene que ellos dicen mal de sus señores detras dellos, porque ante ellos no osan hablar' (Anth. 48, fol. 49v). Indeed, gossiping and whispered asides are salient features of the servants' behaviour. This has not escaped the attention of Calisto, who more than once expresses his annoyance at their constant whispering behind his back: 'vosotros susurráis, como soléis; para hacerme mala obra y enojo. Por mi amor, que calléis.' When the servants keep whispering, he explodes: 'no hay cierto tan malservido hombre como yo, manteniendo mozos adevinos, rezongadores, enemigos de mi bien' (S. 113; M. 112). This, again, is entirely in line with the letter on masters and slaves, which concludes 'tantos enemigos tenemos cuantos siervos habemos' – a point which was to become proverbial (cf. Proverbio 311).

True and false friendship

The first author dedicated a major part of the dialogue to a discussion of friendship. But, although he inserted quite a few 'fontecicas de filosofía' on the topic, he left more unsaid. Instead, he illustrated the unspoken message through the portrayal of its advocate, Celestina. Her very occupation as a witch and go-between makes a mockery of friendship and love and for that reason alone invalidates her words. As we saw in previous chapters, the first author gave an important clue on how to develop the theme of friendship and love in Celestina's persuasion of Parmeno, by hinting at the rubric of Epistula 9 with the words 'Y no sabes que has menester amigos para los conservar' (S. 70; M. 49).

In this particular letter, Seneca resolves the important question of why one needs friends, through a whole series of 'why not's, weighing all the pros and cons against one another. After a brief discussion on why even the wise man (and not the rich man, as in Celestina's argument) needs friends, Seneca briefly touches upon the question of how to make friends.

The philosopher here equates real friendship with real love, and the answer is so simple that one maxim suffices: 'si vis amari, ama' (*Ep.* 9, 6). The much quoted *sententia* is not Seneca's but borrowed from Hecaton, as Seneca states here: 'Hecaton ait: "Ego tibi monstrabo amatorium sine medicamento, sine herba, sine ullius veneficae carmine: si vis amari, ama." ' The translator of the anthology misread Hecaton as Cato, but otherwise the message is the same: 'Catón dijo yo te mostraré una manera de hacer amigo sin arte de medicina y sin confación de hierbas y sin encantamiento, si tú quieres ser amado ama' (Anth. 9, fol. 7v). Rojas caught on to 'how not' to enter into a friendship and developed Celestina's character in keeping with the mistaken notion that medicine, herbs and witchcraft are the only way of making friends and finding love.

The letter's detailed analysis of the wrong reasons for entering into friendship gives Rojas ample scope for developing a different side to Celestina's character. In many ways she is the *contra-exemplum* of a true commitment. She repeatedly assures Parmeno that she has come to him as a friend and begs him to be hers in the same way as his mother had been: 'Pues séme tú, como ella, amigo verdadero' (S. 125; M. 130). Her tearful reminiscences of her associate seem a running commentary on Seneca's condemnation of such a friendship: '¿Y tuve yo en este mundo otra tal amiga, otra tal compañera, tal aliviadora de mis trabajos y fatigas?' she moans (S. 122; M. 126). Later on she remembers how both of them were caught and sentenced: 'juntas nos prendieron y acusaron, juntas nos dieron la pena . . .' (S. 123; M. 128). Celestina's fond memories come close to an Epicurean friendship, which Seneca finds too limiting, as witness his words in Epistula 9: 'no pero así como Epicuro decía que el sabio tenga quien esté cerca del porque si él fuese enfermo que lo visitase, y si fuese preso o en pobreza que lo socorriese'. The letter then goes on to say: 'porque aquel que por su utilidad y a fin de su provecho usa de la amistad y para esto quiere los amigos, no usa della virtuosamente' (Anth. 9, fol. 8r).

As in other respects, Seneca here distinguishes between short-term and long-term good: 'éstas son las amistades que la gente llama temporales porque aquel que es recibido por amigo a fin de utilidad y provecho tanto será placible cuánto será útil y provechoso'. The distinction between short-lived and enduring good does not refer to friendship and love alone; it generally separates good from bad, virtue from evil. In *Celestina* this philosophical point is illustrated not in so many words, but through the very action of the story. The character's untruthful motivations are brought out by the hurry with which Celestina brings Sempronio and Parmeno together, the speedy matchmaking between Parmeno and Areusa and the quick dispatch of the 'negocio' once an agreement has been reached. It also helps to explain the short-lived happiness of Calisto and Melibea's consummated love and the quick succession in which all involved in the 'negocio' meet their death.

Just as Hecaton's maxim equated true love and disinterested friendship, Seneca condemns carnal love and false friendship on similar grounds. In Epistula 9, 11 he draws a parallel between the two:

Y así aquella amistad de la cual nos habemos ya hablado no es amistad mas mercadantia (*negotiatio*) que siempre reguarda a la utilidad y ganancia que él podrá haber del amigo. Sin duda esta tal amistad tiene imagen y semejanza al loco amor de los enamorados (*affectus amantium*), así que el hombre lo puede llamar amistad loca y flaca (*insanam amicitiam*).

In this last sentence the mercenary nature of such a friendship is brought out by the word 'negotiatio', which is reflected in the word 'negocio', by which Celestina refers to Calisto and Melibea's love affair. Still more striking is the way in which in Seneca's text such a 'negotiatio' is compared to the infatuation of lovers, the 'affectus amantium', translated as 'el loco amor de los enamorados'.

Although Seneca concedes that the lover may not love 'lucri causa, ambitionis aut gloriae' ('por causa de ganancia ni de codicia de honor o gloria'), he nevertheless makes the point that the lover is driven by another type of 'codicia': 'aquel amor . . . inflama y enciende el corazón con codicia de hermosura ('in cupiditatem formae') con esperanza de común amor' ('mutuae caritatis').[2] Indeed, 'codicia' is the exact translation of 'cupiditas', the origin not only of profit, honour and glory but also of possessive and self-seeking love. 'Codicia' is, too, the common denominator of the main characters' search for happiness in *Celestina*, be this by means of profit (Celestina and the servants), honour and glory (Pleberio) or love (Calisto and Melibea, Parmeno and Areusa).

In Act 7 Celestina renews her attempts to forge a friendship between the two servants. Speaking of Sempronio, she assures Parmeno that he is ready for a reconciliation: 'Quiere tu amistad. Crecería vuestro provecho, dándoos el uno al otro la mano' (S. 120; M. 123). She then adduces the much quoted words 'Y pues sabe que es menester que ames si quieres ser amado', referring not only to the useful friendship with Sempronio but also to what she has in store for Parmeno as a reward: Areusa's love. Once Celestina leaves the topic of friendship to enter upon that of love, the action in Act 7 again illustrates how closely related are Parmeno's friendship and love.

The scene in which Celestina visits Areusa with Parmeno in tow could, in itself, be an *exemplum* of Seneca's ideas on profit, beauty, nature, love and friendship. First, Celestina answers Areusa's inquiry regarding who is visiting her at such a late hour with the words 'Quien nunca da paso, que no piense en tu provecho . . . una enamorada tuya . . .' (S. 126; M. 132) Then Celestina praises Areusa's physical beauty: 'Por hermosa te tenía hasta agora, viendo lo que todos podían ver; pero agora te digo que no hay en la ciudad tres cuerpos tales como el tuyo, en cuanto yo conozco' (S. 127; M. 133). Finally, persuading Areusa to consent to Parmeno's love, she invokes Nature: 'Ninguna cosa hay criada al mundo supérflua ni que acordada razón no proveyese de ella natura. Mira que es pecado fatigar y dar pena a los hombres, pudiéndolos remediar' (S. 127; M. 134).

Bringing Nature into the picture here is entirely in keeping with Epistula 9, which closes with a consideration of the wise man's friendship as a 'movimiento natural'. However, the notion that nothing superfluous exists in Nature and that her gifts should be shared without trouble or pain goes back to Seneca's Epistula 4, where he says: 'muy presto y a la mano se halla aquello que la natura quiere y ligeramente se puede haber; nunca hombre trabaja ni afana ni suda sino por cosas supérfluas y demasiadas' (Anth. 4, fol. 4v).

And so, manipulating Seneca's philosophy, Celestina achieves her ends when finally she brings Parmeno and Areusa together. At that moment her words to Areusa are the final proof that Seneca's 'amor por codicia de hermosura' and 'amistad por utilidad y provecho' can be combined in one single act. Celestina reassures Areusa that Parmeno 'se huelga mucho con tu amistad . . . y asimismo . . . me promete de aquí adelante ser muy amigo de Sempronio y venir en todo lo que quisiere contra su amo en un negocio, que traemos entre manos' (S. 131; M. 139). From then on events take their inevitable course: love affair and false friendship are related errors in Seneca's philosophy, as they are in *Celestina*, pointing up that error is sinful and sin leads to death.

Associating with the crowd

When Parmeno rejected the very possibility of becoming Sempronio's friend in Act 1, he quoted Seneca on the topic of consorting with the crowd. The first quotation was 'un ejemplo de lujuria o avaricia mucho mal hace' (S. 71; M. 50), which he remembered correctly; the other, 'con aquellos debe hombre conversar que le hagan mejor, y aquellos dejar [instead of 'admitir'] a quien él mejores piensa hacer', is a lengthy *sententia* which he gets wrong.[3] Rojas spotted the error, but also the provenance of the quotations. These, he knew, came from Epistula 7, in which Seneca warns his friend Lucilius never to mix with the crowd. 'Tú me demandas qué es aquello que tú debes esquivar sobre todas las cosas', he starts out. The answer is 'rumor y ruido de la muchedumbre de la gente' (Anth. 7, fol. 6r). By 'gente' Seneca means the mob, variously designated in Latin as *turba*, *multi*, *populus*, *plures* or *multitudo*. He sees the main danger of the crowd as their vicious habits:

'sin duda la muchedumbre es muy contraria a los que se desean corregir y enmendar de sus vicios, porque imposible es que de los vicios de los otros no se nos lleguen y apeguen algunos en alguna manera'. Most susceptible to their bad influence, Seneca feels, are the young and naive, who for that reason should avoid close contact with them: 'él que es flaco y aún no bien afirmado en la virtud se debe alongar del pueblo, porque de ligero se junta hombre a la gran compañía' (*ibid.*).

There is no doubt that the first author meant to portray Parmeno as an earnest young man striving for the virtuous and happy life as taught by Seneca. But he is young and inexperienced and is driven into the arms of the mob almost against his will. As we have noted in chapter 3, the parallel between the master and his servant is striking. Inexperienced in love and life, they make fools of themselves by not being aware of the ramifications of their own *sententiae*. Words of wisdom are not taken to heart, despite the admonition which closes Epistula 7: 'Estas sentencias debes tú fincar en el tu corazón porque desprecies los deleites que vienen del consentimiento de los muchos' (Anth. 7, fol. 6v).

Rojas was well aware of the importance of this letter for the development of the plot. Both Calisto's and Parmeno's association with the Celestinesque underworld will have fatal consequences, not only for themselves but also for others. Indeed, had it not been for Calisto's mixing his world with that of Celestina there would not have been any story. In many of the letters Seneca returns to the danger of associating with the masses, whose aims are so different from one's own: 'gente desemejable y deseosa de diversas cosas' he calls them in Epistula 32 (Anth. 35, fol. 33v). Stay clear of the crowds: 'Que te partes y desvíes de la gente', he warns in Epistula 25, 7 (Anth. 25, fol. 24v); do not try to ingratiate yourself with the mob, whose favour is earned in devious ways: 'la gracia y el favor del cual se gana por mala arte', he warns in Epistula 29, 11 (Anth. 29, fol. 27v) and, most importantly, do not enter into friendship with them: '. . . no puede hombre con la viciosa y mala gente haber amistad . . .' (*ibid.*). This, of course, is the mistake Parmeno makes when he finally consents to Sempronio's friendship, in spite of his own words of wisdom on the topic. But then having misquoted Seneca's *sententia*, it is hardly surprising that he is ignorant of its source and content. Had he been a Latin scholar like Rojas, he would have known that the paragraph from which the quotation was taken explains the many ramifications of one bad example: if the friend is lecherous, he will weaken us; if the neighbour is rich, he will arouse our greed; if the companion is slanderous, we will catch that disease too.

Carnal love, a desire for riches and slander, will become three typical vices in which Parmeno indulges as he follows the example of Sempronio and Celestina. Parmeno's misquotation of Seneca's words of wisdom illustrates in word and deed how little he has taken to heart the 'fontecicas de filosofía' with which he adorns his speech. The servant is equally well read, and equally ignorant of *De Vita Beata*, which nevertheless provided him with quite a few lines in his first confrontation with Celestina. Likewise, he is forgetful of the very premise on which the treatise is built: namely, that a happy life has nothing to do with the example of others. Let us not be like 'el ganado ovejuno', the translation starts out: that is to say, the many 'que se guían por la común opinión del pueblo, y piensan que es lo mejor aquello que muchos siguen' (*CL* 1, 1). Rather, he says, let us look for that which will bring us 'la bienaventuranza verdadera, no cual es lo que place al pueblo, que es muy mal conocedor de la verdad'.

Confident that his readers will at least remember the beginning of *De Vita Beata*, Rojas makes Parmeno renounce these very words of wisdom, when, at the end of Act 2, the servant in despair opts to follow the lead of the majority. His dramatic monologue is a tragic example of 'la común opinión de la gente': '¡Oh desdichado de mi! Por ser leal padezco mal; otros se ganan por malos; yo me pierdo por bueno. El mundo es tal. Quiero irme al hilo de la gente' (S. 78; M. 61).[4]

Clearly, to follow the crowd was a well-worn road to 'malaventuranza' and most readers would have known, then and there, where Parmeno's decision would lead. However, for him, as for so many who have sold their souls, things at first seem to look up, as witness Parmeno's speedy introduction to Areusa's bed. In striking contrast to his despair at the end of Act 2, we find Parmeno jubilant in Act 8 shortly after he has taken his leave of Areusa: '¡Oh placer singular! ¡Oh singular alegría! ¿Cuál hombre es ni ha sido más bienaventurado que yo? ¿Cuál más dichoso y bienandante? ¡Que un tan excelente don sea por mí poseído y cuan presto pedido tan presto alcanzado!' (S. 135; M. 146). Unfortunately, the admission of the speed with which everything was concluded points to the short-term nature of the 'good' he has just enjoyed and, implicitly, to its unhappy ending. From now on, Parmeno belongs firmly to the *vulgus* and, as such, becomes a danger to his master.

The next letter on the topic of the *vulgus* is Epistula 14, which primarily analyses man's behaviour in the face of danger. Although he starts out by pointing to silent enemies, such as poverty and ill-health, which creep up on one, Seneca talks more about the overt violence of an overpowering force, 'ex aliena potentia' ('fuerza demás poderosa'). Interestingly enough, this force consists as much in the violence inflicted by the tyrant as in the harm that comes from the mob. One way to avoid getting entangled with the latter, Seneca says, is to prove that one is different from them. Not only should our desires and aspirations be dissimilar to theirs, but our possessions should also leave them indifferent: '. . . que no hayamos cosa que gran utilidad y provecho pueda hacer a otro' (Anth. 14, fol. 13r). Rojas exploited these words of wisdom to the full by portraying the servants' animosity to their master exclusively in terms of that same 'codicia' which underlies their enforced friendship. Seneca's analysis of the mob's potential criminality may well have given Rojas additional ideas for the action of his fiction. Murder is seldom committed out of a thirst for blood, Seneca says in this letter, but rather because of a desire for another's belongings: 'lleva poca ropa sobre tí y serás seguro porque o no son ningunos o son muy pocos los que matan por haber sangre, mas por les robar lo que tienen, no porque mal los quieren mas por lo que llevan' (Anth. 14, fol. 13r).

Another Senecan precept is never to incur the mob's scorn: 'acerca desto según los antiguos debemos esquivar tres cosas: enemistad, envidia y menosprecio'. Seneca then subtly adds that such reactions are entirely of our own making: 'quiero decir que nos debemos guardar que por nuestra culpa no seamos malquistos ni que otros hayan envidia de nos y que no seamos despreciados de la gente'.

The first author has already brought out Sempronio's disdain for his master's unseemly behaviour. Rojas continues, and emphasizes this attitude by making Parmeno join in the *sotto voce* condemnation of his master's silliness – but then it must have been painful for the erstwhile loyal servant to see Calisto so dependent on Celestina's help and advice. In this instance, the master is himself a *contra-exemplum* of the wise man's behaviour in the presence of the *vulgus*. This is summed up in the words 'saberse hombre en tal manera templar y contener que no cayamos en desprecio y vileza . . . y que no mostremos poder ser vencidos y avisados por viles' (*ibid.*).

The servants' scorn is not limited to their master; soon Celestina, too, becomes the object of their hostility. This is another completely predictable outcome of the master's unwise actions. Here, however, the servants' animosity towards Celestina is not by reason of Calisto's love affair or of his possessions *per se*, but rather because of the golden chain he has given to Celestina.

The reward immediately arouses the servants' jealousy, and they decide to take the chain by force. 'Sobre dinero no hay amistad' is their justification, a maxim which is questioned in Epistula 19, 12: 'Quid ergo? Beneficia non parant amicitias?'

The letter which provided this ambiguous *fontecica* jumps in typical Senecan fashion from one topic to another. But then in real life too man's actions and motivations are intricately interwoven, a circumstance which Seneca in his moral philosophy and Rojas in his 'dulce ficción' brings out in such a masterly way.

The interactions of recipients of gifts are analysed at length in Book 2 of *De Beneficiis*, where, in chapter 27, Seneca explains the self-perpetuating nature of greed: 'maiora cupimus, quo maiora venerunt' (*De Ben.* 2, 27, 3; see also *Ep.* 73, 119, etc.). Far worse, however, is the effect on others of an ill-placed gift, as it creates jealousy. 'Some may say', Seneca warns, 'this he gave me, but to him he gave more, and an earlier reward to yet somebody else' (*De Ben.* 2, 28, 1).

In his continuation of the story, Rojas illustrates this pernicious side-effect in the growing envy of Sempronio and Parmeno as they see Calisto heap rewards on Celestina. Their annoyance is expressed first in their whispered commentaries on her angling for her just reward in Act 5, and then becomes overt jealousy when she receives the golden chain in Act 11. Their resulting rage, followed by their assault on and murder of Celestina in Act 12, is thus the logical outcome of *galardones* that were ill given and ill received.

Rojas' dramatic portrayal of the inevitable succession of events speaks not of a deep pessimism on the part of the author, but rather of a real understanding of man's deepest motivations. He had no doubt gained this insight from direct observation, but also from a thorough knowledge of Seneca's psychological analysis of mankind. Rather than blame the world or even Celestina for the fatal outcome of the love story, Rojas makes Calisto solely responsible. The perilous art of giving and receiving thus becomes yet another crucial theme in the continuation of the work.

Just as Seneca had declared at the beginning of *De Beneficiis* (1, 4, 2) that benefits constitute the chief bond of human society ('maxime humanam societatem alligat'), so Rojas will make Calisto's gifts an important link between the main characters of his fiction. The exchange of gifts takes place not only between the master and his servants, but also between Melibea and Calisto (in the form of Melibea's present of her sash) and between Pleberio and Melibea (as parent to child). By contrast, the *galardones* that change hands between Calisto and Celestina are not *beneficia* at all, but rather payments in return for a service or a deposit on account. From the very beginning of *De Beneficiis* Seneca disqualifies this type of exchange as a gift on the grounds that gifts should be given for the sake of giving. Anything given with an eye to restitution is 'lucrum', he says in *De Beneficiis* 1, 2, 3. Most important of all, however, is Seneca's warning that benefits should not be bestowed on the mob: 'nec in vulgum effundenda sunt' (*De Ben.* 1, 2, 1).

The reversal of day and night

One detail which had caught Rojas' imagination when reading Act 1 was how Calisto, rebuked by Melibea, had shut out the day and taken to his bed. At first glance, this seems a mere illustration of the master's defeatism. Seen in the Senecan context of the story, however, Calisto's desire to take to his bed in bright daylight means much more than the despair of a love-stricken youth. It goes against Nature, and that, of course, is a sure road to lasting unhappiness. Rojas takes up this seemingly insignificant detail of the first act by making master and servant an *exemplum* of such an unnatural life-style. Act 8, in fact, starts out with Parmeno awaking in Areusa's bed and wondering what time it is. When he realizes that it is bright daylight, he hastily takes his leave with the excuse 'porque es ya mediodía' (S. 134; M. 145). As in other circumstances, Parmeno here precedes his master, for later on in the same act Calisto also wakes up when it is 'tarde para levantar'. As in Parmeno's case, the night is gone and 'aún harta parte del día' (S. 140; M. 152).

For Seneca, such a reversal of sleeping and waking hours epitomizes the decadent life-style of many of his contemporaries. The Stoic's stance in these matters is summed up in the rubric to the translation of Epistula 122 in unequivocal terms: 'donde repre[he]nde Séneca los dormidores y que hacen de la noche día por entender en vicios vergonzosos' (Anth. 70, fol. 66v). The antidote, as usual, is to follow Nature and not desire.

So, Parmeno's and Calisto's explicit mention of the time of day might well refer to the content of this letter, where Seneca goes into more detail: 'y es de blasmar y reprehender el que tanto duerme y está en la cama que el sol es ya levantado y él se despierta al mediodía . . . y así son cativos y mezquinos como las aves de la noche' ('nocturnae aves', *Ep.* 122, 3). Interestingly enough, Seneca then mentions how the debaucheries of the night are followed by rich banquets, but, as the Spanish translation puts it, 'esta tal no es fiesta de hombre vivo mas oficio de hombre muerto' (*ibid.*). Banqueting was, of course, one of the most visible signs of decadence in Rome, and for Seneca an occasion to lash out against saturnalia or precious foods imported from afar to satisfy the most demanding Roman palate (cf. *Ep.* 18, 60 and 89). Ironically, just as Rojas had scaled down the physical abuse of slaves by Roman masters to the scolding of servants by fifteenth-century mistresses, and Rome's sexual excesses to the simple pleasures in Areusa's 'pequeña casa', so too the banquet in Celestina's house the day after the night before seems rather innocent and down-to-earth. The white bread, Monviedro wine, bacon, six chickens and one pigeon that Parmeno steals from Calisto's pantry are a far cry from Rome's culinary decadence. Nevertheless, the implications of both servants' and master's new life-style become painfully clear as the story unfolds.

From now on Calisto will consistently reverse day and night, confirming the artificiality of his life and love. The unnaturalness of his encounter with Melibea at her door (Act 12) is then emphasized by the dangers inherent in this late hour. Night is the time to put on heavy armour, while murderers go about and the watch makes his tireless rounds. This is the atmosphere in which Calisto, guarded by his armoured servants, is to meet his beloved. The very circumstances of this and subsequent encounters are very much in line with Seneca's description of passion in *De Vita Beata* 7, 3: 'voluptatem latitantem saepius ac tenebras captantem . . . ac loca aidilem metuentia', translated as 'al deleite hallarás que las más veces se anda escondiendo y buscando tinieblas y oscuridad . . . y en los lugares que han temor del alguacil' (*CL* 1, 7).

Fear and apprehension are, indeed, important factors in the first meeting between the two lovers, and are reinforced by the servants' readiness to fly at the slightest provocation. And all the while the servants' commentaries remind us of the constant presence of the 'gente del alguacil' (S. 176; M. 205).

The tragic dimension of the master's nocturnal adventure is brought out the following morning, when Calisto wakes up after his successful first meeting with Melibea. Again he wonders what time it is, and again the answer is 'bien de día'. Oblivious of his servants' death, the master then turns over with the request not to be woken until dinner-time. Meanwhile, of course, Sempronio and Parmeno have been publicly executed and Calisto's reputation is at risk. The master's consistent reversal of day and night thus illustrates how much his actions are contrary to the natural order of things. In this respect, Calisto's behaviour is yet another *contra-exemplum* of an important leitmotiv in Seneca's thinking, summed up in the conclusion to Epistula 122 as 'Todas las cosas son prestas y posibles a aquellos que la natura siguen, mas la vida de aquellos que usan contra natura es semejante a los que navegan agua arriba' (Anth. 70, fol. 67r).

Anger and rage

So far Rojas has been heavily indebted to the first author. The themes of masters and slaves, both in the literal and in the figurative sense, of friendship and love, of gifts bestowed on the *vulgus* and of following the order of Nature were all waiting to be developed with multiple ramifications and moral implications.

However, like all continuators, Rojas adds something uniquely his own, and that is the inclusion of anger as a contributing factor to the tragic outcome of the love affair. By bringing uncontrolled and uncontrollable rage into the picture he completes the spectrum of the many *affectus* that can take hold of mankind.[5]

While in Acts 2 and 3 Rojas has been mainly concerned with developing the unfinished action of the first act, in the fourth he begins to follow his own train of thought. This is when Celestina starts her *negocio* in earnest, with a visit to Melibea's house. At first her mission seems to go well, the small talk between the women skirting the main purpose of the visit, but as soon as Celestina mentions the name Calisto an enormous change comes over Melibea. From being agreeable and polite, answering Celestina's sententious words with short commentaries only, she all of a sudden bursts out in a barrage of abuse which seems to increase as she goes on. Clearly, Melibea is the victim of a uniquely human affliction, that of anger spilling over into rage.

In the 16-act *Comedia*, Rojas limited himself to the description of Melibea's first reaction through Celestina's report: 'en nombrando tu nombre, atajó mis palabras . . . como quien cosa de grande espanto hubiese oído, diciendo que cesase mi habla y me quitase delante, si no quería hacer a sus servidores verdugos de mi postrimería' (S. 111; M. 109). Rojas felt that Melibea's verbal abuse sufficed to make his readers recognize her reaction as that of the most rabid of all afflictions, rage. For, as Seneca says, 'turba y escurece la claridad del buen juicio más que ninguna otra cosa' (Rubio, 1961: 121).

At first Melibea refers to her state of mind as merely annoyance: '¿Aún hablas entre dientes delante mí, para acrecentar mi enojo y doblar tu pena?' However, from the start Celestina has ascribed her changed attitude to anger': 'tu presencia me turba en verla airada', she comments (S. 95; M. 87). Consequently, she decides to wait, knowing that, like a thunderstorm, a fit of anger does not last: 'Mientra viviere tu ira, más dañara mi descargo' (S. 97; M. 89). When Melibea recovers, she too recognizes the nature of her attack, justifying her fit of anger by Calisto's offensive approach and by a concern for her good name, two circumstances she feels were enough to put her out of her mind (S. 99; M. 91).

The devastating effects of anger and rage were of great concern in the fifteenth century, as witness the revised translation of Seneca's *De Ira*, which appeared in mid-century. Of course, there were short cuts to the long treatise as well – such as the *Proverbios* and *Copilación*. Here the many extracts and their glosses highlight what aspect of anger was most important to the fifteenth-century reader. For instance, the 'Tratado de la ira' of the *Copilación* stresses the angry man's bloodthirsty desire for revenge: 'codiciosa de armas y de sangre y de dar tormentos . . . y no es encendida según otra humanal codicia' (*CL* 5). The marginal gloss then takes up the element of *codicia*, warning about the intensity of such a desire: 'todas las cosas que desea codícianlas con gran ardor allende de la codicia común de los hombres'. The gloss also mentions what the extract does not say, but what Seneca adds in the first paragraph of *De Ira*: namely, that there is no redeeming feature for this sort of *codicia*: 'y no hay cosa en la saña placentera ni graciosa como en las otras pasiones. Ca en el amor y en la codicia de las otras cosas y en la delectación hay alguna cosa de placer [*sic*], mas en la saña no la ha.' The gloss, moreover, sums up what follows in *De Ira*: 'y enciéndese con ligeras causas y no acata a consejo ni a razón . . .' (*ibid.*). The ensuing 'Tratado de las buenas costumbres' starts out by saying 'esquivarás la crueldad y la servidora de la crueldad que es la saña', prior to explaining 'qué cosa es la saña y dónde nace' (*ibid.*). Here basing itself on Aristotle, it analyses this *affectus* as the reaction to a perceived and not a real wrong. On this the marginal gloss comments:

'y porende la saña nace de la injuria concebida en el corazón del que es injuriado, o la cuida ser adelante. Ca ya recibimos la injuria en nuestras imaginaciones y esto es lo que dice.' The 'Tratado' also specifies that, even given the desire, not everybody is able to wreak revenge. Hence the slightly altered definition of anger as a desire to inflict harm: 'ca Aristóteles decía así, "la saña es codicia de dolor" '.

Thus we see that rage was analysed from all angles, the conclusion being reached that it is yet another manifestation of *affectus*, or a disturbance of the mind akin to *locura, esclavitud* and *codicia*. However, for all the short duration of anger, its effects can be infinitely more harmful, since it is primarily a 'codicia de armas y de sangre'.

All these aspects of anger are present in *Celestina*. When we remember how, in the fifteenth century, anger was considered to be primarily a reaction to a perceived wrong, Melibea's sudden fit can be understood as a fit of rage. In her imagination, Calisto's approaches in her garden were offensive to her honour, and therefore she feels them to be an *injuria*. At least, this is how Rojas must have explained her irate dismissal of Calisto upon reading the opening scene. Then, when he had to develop her character, he seized upon these angry words to bring out her susceptibility to this *affectus*. Knowing, as only a fifteenth-century reader would, all the implications of *ira*, her initial reaction would have been enough to predict the outcome of the conflict. By letting herself go in such a disgraceful manner, Melibea shows how little she is in control of her feelings, and therefore, by definition, of her life. Only once is the devil mentioned in Act 4, and this is when Alisa leaves her daughter alone with Celestina. Such imprudence, according to Celestina, can only be the work of the devil: 'Por aquí anda el diablo aparejando oportunidad.' Melibea's fury, however, seems to be more the result of a complete loss of control in the Senecan sense of the word than the desired effect of Celestina's 'conjuro'. The Senecan connection with Melibea's condition is, moreover, brought out in eight textual quotations from the *Proverbios de Séneca*, with half referring to the various effects of anger (see chapter 5). Still, one question remains to be answered: what was the cause of Melibea's anger? Here the explanation is also to be found in Seneca, more particularly in Epistula 18, which sends us to Epicurus for the 'wisdom of the day'. As usual, the letter roams from one topic to another, ending on the note of anger. The Epicurean *sententia* was 'inmodica ira gignit insaniam' ('uncontrolled anger begets madness', *Ep.* 18, 14), translated as 'tormento desmesurado engendra locura'

(Anth. 18, fol. 16v). More important for the genesis of *Celestina*, however, is Seneca's elucidation. This *affectus*, he says, springs from love as well as hate and has its origin as much in jest as in serious talk. What matters is not so much the cause (*causa*) as the recipient (*animus*). He then compares cause and effect to those of a flame, which may or may not set fire to the surrounding material: if a spark falls on dry and highly inflammable material, it turns into a conflagration. According to this psychological analysis, Rojas may well have conceived Calisto's approach in the opening scene as the spark that fell on highly inflammable material. The resulting fire was kindled by a feeling of love, not anger ('ex amore nascitur'). This is how Rojas interpreted the opening scene, and this is how he portrayed Melibea in Act 4 – as a passionate, highly inflammable girl whose polite gentility was only skin deep.

Rojas then looks at Parmeno and Sempronio, two characters already firmly committed to *codicia*, and completes the vicious circle by making them 'codiciosos de armas y deseosos de derramar sangre humanal' (*CL* 5, 'Tratado de la ira').

Throughout the servants' asides we have been made aware of their increasing annoyance with Celestina. The frustration about what they perceived as an unjust distribution of rewards for their efforts then grows into anger.

In Act 12 this turns into rage, when they are confronted with Celestina, the very source of their perceived *injuria*. Initially, the purpose of their late visit to Celestina's house is not to murder but rather to frighten her into handing over the chain. However, incensed by their own account of the dangers standing watch outside Melibea's garden, their quarrelsome mood increases by the minute. Parmeno explains how 'alterados y cansados del enojo' they are, and he pretends that some food might calm their 'alteración'. He then admits that he needs somebody 'en quien vengar la ira'. Sempronio, however, assures Celestina that he will not take it out on her: 'aunque para contigo por demás es no templar la ira y todo enojo'. However, we perceive more clearly Sempronio's loss of control through his own admission, 'Por Dios, sin seso vengo, desesperado', and Celestina's reaction to his claiming the chain when she asks '¿estás en tu seso, Sempronio?' (S. 180; M. 211–12).

Obviously scared, Celestina tries to reason with Sempronio and Parmeno, a move which will have a fatal outcome. The only result of her explanations is Sempronio's accusation of *codicia* levelled against her, a verdict which, as so often is the case in *Celestina*, reflects more the mental state of the speaker than that of the person spoken to. In answer to his accusations, Celestina hits the nail on the head when she refers to the servants' 'enojo', 'codicia' and 'amenazas', finishing her defence with 'Y no pienses con tu ira maltratarme', followed by 'contra los que ciñen espada, mostrad vuestras iras; no contra mi flaca rueca' (S. 182–3; M. 215–16). The servants' uncontrollable rage needs no more verbal commentary. Once they have drawn blood they cannot stop until Celestina is dead.

Still victims of their rage, they then commit a typical error, which is entirely in keeping with Seneca's analysis of *ira*. In the same paragraph in which he describes anger as a 'deseo de armas', he warns that the harm an enraged man intends to inflict on his victim sometimes boomerangs: 'y por tal que haga mal a otro no piensa en el mal que le viene y que le puede venir, entremetiéndose por lanças'. To illustrate the fact that an act of rage can do more harm to the perpetrator than to the victim, he uses a metaphor: 'Ca así como la cosa que cae o se derriba se quebranta en aquello que hiere, asimismo la saña, cuidando hacer mal a otro, hizo peor a sí' (Rubio 1961: 122). This, of course, is how Sempronio and Parmeno come to their end. Unable to think, they jump from a high window, only to fall straight into the arms of justice and death.

Celestina's murder, in the 16-act *Comedia*, spells the beginning of the end. In quick succession, first the servants and then the masters meet their death, each being the natural outcome of a *codicia*. Even Melibea's suicide fits entirely into this ineluctable chain of cause and effect, if we read her foolish act as yet another outcome of a Senecan *codicia*.

Suicide

Melibea's death, patterned on the literary conventions of the sentimental romance, has the same Senecan subtext as Calisto's attempts to appear a courtly lover.[6] Among the many ways one can leave this life, according to Seneca, suicide enshrines man's ultimate freedom of choice. However, just as he makes a distinction between real and false friendship, true love and passion, gifts and profit, so too does Seneca tell his readers about the right and wrong reasons for taking one's own life.

In Stoic terms, Melibea's self-inflicted death is anything but a heroic act. Rather, it is motivated by self-interest and self-pity. The only regret Melibea voices when she contemplates the shattered body of her lover evokes the short-lived pleasure she has had from it all: 'i tan poco tiempo poseído el placer, tan presto venido el dolor . . .', she moans, followed by '¿cómo no gocé más del gozo?' (S. 225; M. 251). At no time does she commiserate with her beloved: her grief is entirely self-centred, bordering on rage. Equally, her impulse to follow her lover in death is indifferent to the pain she is about to inflict on her father: 'Gran sinrazón hago a sus canas . . . gran ofensa a su vejez. Gran fatiga le acarreo con mi falta, en gran soledad le dejo' (S. 228; M. 255).

Considering her state of mind, she is surprisingly lucid in the analysis of her folly. In fact, at one point she identifies her passion in Senecan terms as rage. Warning her father that no advice of his will make her desist from her mad intent, she explains: 'Porque, cuando el corazón está embargado de pasión, están cerrados los oídos al consejo y en tal tiempo las fructuosas palabras, en lugar de amansar acrecientan la saña' (S. 229; M. 257). Melibea's words echo various popular notions about the pernicious side-effects of anger, as expressed in the *Proverbios* (see numbers 19, 94, 200) and the many tratados on anger in the *Copilación*. In fact her present fit matches the angry man's reactions, described in the 'Tratado de la ira' as follows: 'la saña es una breve locura . . . no se le miembra de los parientes, prosigue con gran porfía lo que comenzó, no entiende razón ni oye consejo'. If we consider Melibea's parting words in this light, it is more than likely that Rojas meant his readers to interpret her exit as the result of yet another fit of anger, very similar to the one brought on by Celestina's mention of Calisto's name in Act 4.

When she sees the object of her short-lived pleasure shattered at the foot of her garden wall, it is only natural that she should become enraged. Indeed, she may well have perceived Calisto's premature death as a personal affront for which somebody had to pay. A natural target, then, would be not her maid, but her beloved father. Why else should she reveal to him, blow by blow, her 'no acostumbrados delitos'? (S. 229; M. 258). Could there be a morbid pleasure in inflicting such torment? Could it be that Rojas meant Melibea unconsciously to take revenge on her father for having brought her up as a 'doncella encerrada'? This psychoanalysis might seem far-fetched for a fifteenth-century author. But Rojas' astute psychological insight has nothing to do with Freud and everything to do with classical philosophy. Aristotle, Solomon, Seneca, Boethius, St Augustine and many others analysed man's motivation and its manifestation in speech and action. Rojas' question in the Prologue, '¿Quién explanará sus guerras, sus enemistades, sus envidias, sus aceleramientos y movimientos y descontentamientos?' (S. 42; M. 11), expresses a typical fifteenth-century concern to know the origin of 'otros muchos afectos diversos y variedades que de esta nuestra flaca humanidad nos provienen'. The answer, as we have seen, could be found in the *auctoritates*, whose words of wisdom were contained in the great lay encyclopaedia of the time, the glosses to the translations from the classics.

However, Rojas' great achievement consisted in satisfying this widespread thirst for knowledge with a 'dulce ficción'. In doing so he portrayed Melibea as a woman who had read the classics but who, like Parmeno and Calisto, had forgotten the message: 'Algunas consolatorias palabras te diría antes de mi agradable fin, colegidas y sacadas de aquellos antiguos libros que [tú] por más aclarar mi ingenio, me mandabas leer', she says to her father (S. 231; M. 260). Her own admission that she cannot remember these consolations because of her 'dañada memoria con la gran turbación' clearly reveals that her mind is in the grip of a severe *affectus*. It also shows how little she has profited from reading the classics; and, worse, she may well have gathered the wrong ideas on life and death from those 'antiguos libros'.

Death has always had a strange fascination for the young, and to them Seneca's teaching must have seemed new and revolutionary. For instance, in Epistula 12 Melibea would have read that nobody can stop us from taking our own life – 'ninguno es poderoso de nos tener ni hacer contra nuestra voluntad' (Anth. 12, fol. 11r) – and in Epistula 4 Seneca reminds us 'tú me dirás gran cosa es despreciar y no temer la muerte, acuérdate tú que ya muchos por muy pequeñas causas la menospreciaron y aún usaron della' (Anth. 4, fol. 4r). Seneca then gives examples of such small reasons as unrequited love, slavery or persecution, describing the ways in which a speedy death may be accomplished as 'alguno se enhorcó . . . otro se lanzó de un tejado ayuso . . . otro se metió una espada por el cuerpo'. Whatever the means, Seneca says, 'tú debes continuamente pensar que tú puedes francamente y sin miedo dejar la vida la cual algunos abrazan y se tienen a ella' (*ibid.*).

However, the discussion of suicide does not end there. Some letters, left untranslated for obvious reasons, deal with why and when to take one's life. Epistula 70 is one of them. It explains that it is not a question of dying earlier or later, but of dying well or ill. And dying well means escape from the danger of living ill: 'Bene autem mori est effugere male vivendi periculum' (*Ep.* 70, 6), an echo of which we find in Melibea's words 'Pues, ¿qué crueldad sería, padre mío, muriendo él despenado, que viviese yo penada?' (S. 230; M. 259). In such a case, Seneca says, we may look about us for an easy exit ('Cui permittit necessitas sua, circumspiciat exitum mollem', *Ep.* 70, 24), and by whatever means that please ('moriaris quemadmodum placet', *Ep.* 70, 28).

These and other words from the 'libros antiguos' which Pleberio had given Melibea to read might well have prompted her to say 'Bien se ha aderezado la manera de mi morir . . . Todo se ha hecho a mi voluntad . . .' (S. 228; M. 255). However, other dramatic statements reveal how little she has understood Seneca's teaching on suicide. Addressing herself to her father, she contradicts herself when she says 'oirás la causa desesperada de mi forzada y alegre partida' (S. 229; M. 257). According to the Stoics, nobody is forced to commit suicide; rather, according to the precepts of the same letter, life is an open space in which Nature keeps us: 'in aperto nos natura custodit' (*Ep.* 70, 24). But then, like Calisto, Melibea does not know much about Nature, reason or freedom.

Worst of all, she has not taken to heart the reverse of the coin which Seneca shows us at the end of Epistula 24. Starting out with heroic examples of self-inflicted death, he warns that death should be contemplated in the light of reason, freedom and tranquillity: 'El hombre fuerte y sabio no debe huir de la vida mas blandamente salir de ella.' By this he means that one should leave this life without making a fuss. Melibea's lengthy speech to her father from the top of her tower before she hurls herself down thus becomes yet another illustration of how not to conduct one's life and death in Senecan terms. Seneca then concisely sums up the unwise man's decision to commit suicide with the simple warning 'y sobre todas las cosas debemos esquivar aquella codicia que ya muchos han habido, conviene saber deseo de la muerte, ca algunas veces se inclina el corazón al hombre a querer morir así locamente como a otras cosas' (Anth. 24, fol. 24r).

As was the case with anger, 'codicia' is the chosen word by which the fifteenth-century translator conveys the difficult concept of this *affectus*. In Latin, the paragraph reads: 'Et ante omnia ille quoque vitetur affectus, qui multos occupavit, libido moriendi' (*Ep.* 24, 25).

Thus we see that Melibea's two main *affectus*, her anger being a *codicia de venganza* and her passion for Calisto being a *codicia de hermosura*, culminate in that ultimate *codicia*, a *libido moriendi*. In both Christian and Stoic terms, Melibea fails tragically in her quest for happiness.

Sorrow and tears

Last but not least, Rojas unmasks Pleberio's lament as yet another sample of a literary convention.[7] Once again, Seneca's position on sorrow and tears provides the unspoken commentary. Although sorrow is a natural necessity and should not be repressed, Seneca says, it should not become a spectacle, and under no circumstance should one derive pleasure from such a display, since that is nothing other than a *libido dolendi* (*Poly.* 4, 1).

In the Spanish anthology of Seneca's *Epistulae*, the letters preceding and following number 48 on masters and slaves also have something very important to say regarding Pleberio's lament and, therefore, on the conclusion of the work. Number 47 (*Ep.* 99), discusses how to mourn for the death of a child, number 49 (*Ep.* 101) speaks of providing for old age, again in connection with death, and numbers 50 and 58 (*Ep.* 107 and 63) refute the idea that there should be an order in dying. In addition, number 54 (*Ep.* 86) questions the value of planting trees for posterity.

We have had occasion to mention the Anthology's number 47 (*Ep.* 99) in connection with Calisto's sorrow at the beginning of Act 1. There, the first author only wanted to point out the hedonistic nature of the young man's affliction. Rojas may well have been alerted to Seneca's teaching on sorrow and grieving by this letter when he was looking for ways to develop the 'plebérico corazón'. Indeed, the rubric to number 47 reads like a summary of Pleberio's lament:

Donde trata Séneca de la muerte del hijo de Menilo su amigo. Demuestra cómo al sabio que mucho dura el dolor debe ser más reprehendido que aconsolado. Trata de la brevedad y poca firmeza de nuestra vida y de la presta y repentina muerte. Pone la forma de llorar honesto con piedad y no forzado.   (Anth. 47 fol. 47r)

In the body of the letter Seneca describes how his friend Menilo could not get over the loss of 'un su chiquito hijo', but that, contrary to his custom, he felt he should be harsh with the bereaved father in telling him that 'aún en plañir y llorar hay especie de locura'. With this statement he addresses those that are looking for 'duelos y plantos' and blame fortune 'así como si ella te diese justa causa de plañir'. This does not mean, he says further on, that we should be hard and unfeeling: 'ca esto sería una crueldad muy inhumana y no virtud de no sentir las muertes de sus parientes y amigos y deben atormentarse de la pérdida de su familia' (Anth. 47, fol. 48r). However, he warns that once the first tears have been shed we should not give in to a 'loco sentimiento' ('affectus', *Ep.* 99, 16). As an example, Seneca then describes those who cry their heart out as soon as they see anybody approaching: 'y en viendo que alguno viene tornan a llorar y danse golpes en la cabeza, . . . y se quieren matar y demandan a dios la muerte. Si no hay quien los vea ni les diga nada cesa el duelo'. Such exhibitionist behaviour is wrong, mainly because it is dictated not by Nature, but by following the crowd ('ad plurium exempla', *Ep.* 99, 17). This very mention of them makes Seneca lash out once again against the masses, who cannot do anything right. But worst of all, he says, 'locura es querer hombre alcanzar nombradía y fama con tristeza y duelo' (Anth. 47, fol. 48v = *Ep.* 99, 18).

The vivid description of Pleberio's loud wailing as he exhibits the broken body of his daughter reads like an *exemplum* based on this letter. The picture is completed by his wife's astonished comments: '¿Por qué son tus fuertes alaridos? . . . tus gemidos, tus voces tan altas, tus quejas no acostumbradas, tu llanto y congoja de tanto sentimiento?' (S. 231; M. 261), followed by '¿Por qué maldices tu honrada vejez? Por qué pides la muerte? Por qué arrancas tus blancos cabellos? Por qué hieres tu honrada cara?' (S. 231–2; M. 261).

True to the model, Pleberio then calls for an audience: '¡Oh gentes que venís a mi dolor! ¡oh amigos y señores, ayudadme a sentir mi pena.' His subsequent claim that he, at the age of sixty, should be in the grave instead of his twenty-year-old daughter in turn reflects the start of the Senecan letter, where the bereaved father is reminded that, although only a child, his son was a human being and therefore subject to the vicissitudes of Fortune (cf. *Ep.* 99, 8).

Once we begin to suspect that Pleberio's show of sorrow is 'al ejemplo de muchos', we also begin to wonder about the meaning of the adjective 'plebérico' with which the first author had hinted at his existence.[8] Could it be that the name had something to do with 'el pueblo que jamás se apareja ni adereza a alguno bien' (Anth. 47, fol. 48v)? Once alerted to this side of his character, we may legitimately look for more signs of his plebeian disposition.

So far, there has been no reference to Pleberio's character; Rojas has only mentioned his power and wealth. But now, through his complaints, he unmasks him as one of the world's fools who misspend their life acquiring goods and chattels in the hope of enjoying a leisurely old age.

The memory of his now redundant worldly goods makes Pleberio resent the accumulation of palaces, honours, gardens and ships. His unreasonable complaints reflect the contents of two letters that immediately follow the letter on masters and slaves in the Anthology. Number 49 (*Ep.* 101) has the title 'del ya limitado e incierto término del fin de los días y cómo la muy luenga vida es causa de grandes trabajos' (Anth. 49, fol. 50v). The point of departure is the sudden death of a rich nobleman (*eques*) whose life was cut off at the peak. Surprisingly enough, the moral here concerns the foolishness of providing for one's old age, considering how one lacks control over the day to come. Interestingly, Seneca here inserts the Vergilian line 'Insere nunc, Meliboee, piros, pone ordine vites' (*Ep.* 101, 4), only to refute such foresight as madness. The connection between the name Meliboeus and Pleberio's accumulating worldly goods points to this letter as the probable source for Melibea's name, even though the Spanish Anthology does not include the Vergilian hexameter. Also, Pleberio's regrets about having acquired buildings and honour have much to do with the ensuing explanation: 'Como son locos los que han luenga esperanza diciendo en sus corazones: yo compraré posesiones, yo haré casamiento, yo daré a usura y allegaré moneda en gran abundancia, afin que en mi vejez pueda reposar y vivir en ocio sin trabajo alguno' (Anth. 49, fol. 51r).

The father's further complaints then echo number 50 (*Ep.* 107), the next letter in the Anthology, which is introduced in the rubric as 'que muchas cosas lloramos que debemos sufrir y no mal hablar del orden del mundo como algunos que presumen emendar a Dios antes que a si mismos' (Anth. 50, fol. 51v). As if on cue, Pleberio first blames Fortune for bringing him bad luck in old age: 'no pervertieras la orden, mejor sufriera persecuciones de tus engaños en la recia y robusta edad, que no en la flaca postrimería'. Then he turns to the world: '¡oh mundo!, ¡mundo! . . . Yo pensaba en mi más tierna edad que eras y eran tus hechos regidos por alguna orden' (S. 233; M. 263). His obsession with order has already been brought out earlier, when he blamed death for her disorderly procedure: 'Turbóse la orden del morir con la tristeza que te aquejaba' (S. 232; M. 262).

The ridiculous nature of Pleberio's complaints is further exposed in number 58 (*Ep.* 63), in which the rubric announces: 'que aún en el llanto quieren ser algunos pomposos o vanagloriosos' (Anth. 58, fol. 57r). The text then has such poignant *sententiae* as 'Bien es que hombre llore, mas no que haga llanto.' Pondering on why people indulge in such 'llanto y duelo', Seneca ventures 'nosotros andamos buscando prueba y argumento del nuestro deseo y no seguimos el duelo antes lo mostramos'. Even so, he admits that he had been very upset by a friend's death, but when he started thinking about it, he had to confess that he had not thought it possible that his friend would die before him, 'y aquella era la cosa que yo más pensaba, porque él era más mozo que yo asaz, así como la muerte ordenada anduviese por orden' (Anth. 58, fol. 58r). Pleberio's great mistake so far, then, has been to count on a happy old age by relying on a certain order in life.

In this context, it is worth noting that the trees Pleberio regrets having planted are also mentioned in a Senecan letter, although the metaphor is borrowed from Vergil. The rubric to number 54 in the Anthology (*Ep.* 86) mentions Seneca's ambiguous stance on planting trees for posterity. Rather than subscribe to Vergil's moral that planting trees is a disinterested act, Seneca attacks him on the grounds that 'los árboles que hombre planta hacen sombra a él mismo' (Anth. 54, fol. 55v). The same controversy about planting trees is addressed in *De Vita Beata* 17, 2, this time, appropriately, in the context of acquiring worldly goods. Interestingly, the problem is introduced with the same series of 'why's' as in Pleberio's lament. While for Seneca a man's wealth is displayed by a show of land, lavish banquets, elegant furniture, rare wines, etc., Rojas sums up the fifteenth-century status symbols as 'torres', 'honras' and 'navíos'. Both, however, mention planting trees in this context. Pleberio's question 'Porqué planté árboles' (S. 232; M. 262) also reflects the Senecan comment in *De la vida bienaventurada*: 'porqué haces plantar y tienes árboles que no traen otro fruto salvo la sombra' (*CL* 1, 16). Obviously, the question of whether planting trees was a disinterested or even a useful act was familiar and the subject of discussion. Hence the dubious grounds of Pleberio's lament.

His last admission, 'yo no lloro triste a ella muerta, pero la causa desastrada de su morir' (S. 235; M. 265), only adds to the list of errors. To conclude both his lament and the whole sad story, he blames love: '¿Quién forzó a mi hija a morir, sino la fuerte fuerza de amor?' 'Wrong again', the informed reader may have said to himself. Nothing forced Melibea to commit suicide but her own *affectus*. But then that is probably what Pleberio meant by 'amor'. Love is 'un nombre que no te conviene', he says most appropriately. If it were love, he continues, it would cherish its servants instead of torturing or killing them: 'dulce nombre te dieron; amargos hechos haces' (S. 235; M. 266). Pleberio then mentions love's unequal *galardones*, which we identified as being the opposite of gifts in *Celestina*, and condemns love's 'inicua ley', which is so contrary to Nature. His accusation of love as being 'enemigo de amigos, amigo de enemigos' in turn reminds us of the connection between passion and false friendship, while his examples of classical victims, such as Paris, Helen, Clytemnestra and Egistus, remind us of Seneca's tragedies, which likewise illustrate the fatal effects of the 'affectus amantium' on its victims and their surroundings.[9]

Pleberio's last complaint is directed against his daughter. Unable to comprehend her lack of sympathy for her mother and her cruelty to himself, he bewails his loneliness in this valley of tears. Even this last note of solitude, in the context of his foregoing complaints, seems unnecessary and unreasonable in a Senecan context. The wise man should be sufficient to himself and not rely on others for his happiness. Pleberio's complaint at being left alone by his daughter's departure also bespeaks the true nature of his love for her. Just as Calisto and Melibea's passion for each other was possessive and self-seeking, and as Sempronio and Parmeno's friendship was based on profit and gain, so too were Pleberio's expectations of his only child.

Pleberio's lament thus becomes a most fitting epilogue to a *Comedia* which has set out to portray men's 'muchos y diversos afectos', that is to say the classical *affectus* which in Spanish translation and gloss are presented as the one and many faces of 'codicia' (*cupiditas*).

The Latin scholar would have caught on to this unifying theme and would have interpreted the *Comedia de Calisto y Melibea* as a *laus stultitiae* in the Erasmian sense of the word. But most readers were genuinely moved by the force of love and commiserated with the lonely old father. And so Rojas, 'muy importunado' and 'contra su voluntad', decides to prolong the love story and call it a tragicomedy. He does not say why he was against it, but his reluctance may well have something to do with the loss of the message which he had so skilfully hidden in the text of his narrative.

5

Res et verba in Seneca, Petrarch and Rojas

Nowhere in Seneca's canon is the futility of bookish knowledge discussed more consistently than in his Epistula 88. In addition, the fact that this particular letter was circulating as a separate book in the Middle Ages tells us something about the medieval preoccupation with learning. When we then consider that Epistula 88 was not only translated as *El libro de Séneca de las siete artes liberales*, but also appeared in print as the second book of *Cinco libros*, we have reason to examine the treatise more carefully in the light of *Celestina*'s frame of reference.

The *liberalia studia*, Seneca maintains, may be the proper pursuit of a free-born man, but they do not teach him to be free or, in the words of the translator, 'sabidor, virtuoso, alto, fuerte de gran corazón' (*CL* 2, 1). Seneca especially takes issue with the study of language and literature, arguing that wisdom is not to be found in letters, since what matters are deeds, not words ('. . . cum sapientia non sit in litteris. Res tradit, non verba', *Ep.* 88, 32). Seneca thus derides research into questions of literary history, such as why Hecuba, being younger than Helen, shows her age so badly, where exactly Ulysses roamed, and whether Penelope was as chaste as she is made out to be. In matters of music, he challenges the teaching of harmony, preferring to be enlightened on how the mind may be attuned with itself. Mathematics, according to Seneca, only teaches book-keeping; while, of course, a belief in astrology makes an easy target. Even philosophy, albeit not a liberal art, finds itself the subject of stricture if it is reduced to a squabble over syllables, conjunctions and prepositions. Such useless pursuits, Seneca maintains, make people 'molestos, verbosos, intempestivos, sibi placentes' (*Ep.* 88, 37) while ignorant of real issues, preoccupied as they are with trivia. In fact, he compares the accumulation of superfluous data to a type of excess: 'Plus scire velle quam sit satis, intemperantiae genus est' (*Ep.* 88, 36).

Readers of Seneca and of *Celestina* were very familiar with these

ideas on the ultimate futility of letters in the getting of wisdom and
happiness – all the more so as the controversy over the study of
literature or of philosophy had recently been an issue at the University
of Salamanca (see above, p. 18). One might even argue that, as a
student of law, Rojas would have been especially sceptical about the
pursuit of letters as an end in itself.

In his continuation of the story Rojas brings in another rich source
of *sententiae*, 'aquel gran orador y poeta Francisco Petrarca' (Prologue). The Italian humanist was read by the same literati as admired
Seneca.[1] This is no coincidence, as Petrarch was the most Senecan of
the Italian humanists. As we saw in chapter 1, his *De Remediis Utriusque
Fortunae*, the book from which Rojas quotes so abundantly, is modelled on the pseudo-Senecan *De Remediis Fortuitorum*. But while Seneca
was first and foremost a moralist, Petrarch was also a poet. It should
come as no surprise, then, that Rojas felt attracted to Petrarch's style,
particularly insofar as it reflected the same practical wisdom which so
appealed to the fifteenth-century reader.[2] Even so, there is a difference
between the use and purpose of the Petrarchan and of the Senecan
sententiae in *Celestina*.

As far as Petrarch is concerned, Rojas almost seems to overstate his
presence, as witness the Prologue to his finished work. Here, he not
only gives Petrarch's name as the *auctoritas* for his introductory sentence, 'omnia secundum litem fiunt', but also translates the Latin into
Spanish. Not content with this, he then quotes another entire passage
from Petrarch's *De Remediis*, which he again meticulously translates
for his readers. This preamble is followed by other lengthy translations
from the same source, consisting mostly of rather bizarre *exempla* from
natural history. Indeed, Rojas' Prologue becomes so top-heavy with
quotations that it arouses our suspicions. One is tempted to believe
that Rojas used Petrarch to illustrate the liberal arts student's obsession with quoting the poet laureate – all the more so when we examine
the type and source of the *sententiae* in question.

The Petrarchan quotations stem mainly from two sources. One is
the text of *De Remediis Utriusque Fortunae*, which, inspired as it is by
Seneca's *De Remediis Fortuitorum*, is entirely in line with Seneca's
philosophy, and the other, the more copious of the two by far, is the
Index to Petrarch's work. This is highly significant in itself. While the
first author of *Celestina* had been most careful to pick *sententiae* from
Seneca's work with context and subtext in mind, Rojas used the Index
to Petrarch's work as a handy checklist for isolated quotations.

Both Seneca and Petrarch stress the necessity of speaking the truth plainly and call our attention to the potential deviousness of language.[3] Mindful of their teaching, Rojas illustrates the limitations but also the subversive power of speech in the content and form of his dialogues. Content here should be understood as flattery, twisting the truth, feigning and lying, and form as ridiculous metaphors, high-sounding poetics, pedantic name-dropping and empty clichés.

But there is another dimension in the speech-patterns of *Celestina*, and that is Rojas' own re-creation of everyday language. He purposely sets the pedantic *sententiae* in a flow of plain language, spiced here and there with proverbial wisdom to offset the pedantry of the borrowed words of wisdom. Pervading it all, however, is Rojas' humorous treatment of all these devices, an aspect overlooked by most critics ever since Proaza suggested 'Suplico que llores discreto lector,/ El trágico fin que todos hobieron' (S. 291; M. 271).[4]

Since the action of *Celestina* is solely defined by speech-patterns based on an ingenious interplay of *sententiae* and *exempla*, I shall examine in this chapter how Rojas built up his argument through the logical sequence of speech and action in each consecutive act.

Acts 2, 3 and 4

Although it is not quite clear where Rojas' 'maldonadas razones' begin (Prologue), the opening scenes of Act 2 are still very much the first author's. Sempronio's arguments on honour and liberality are as opinionated as was his master's reasoning on Nature and beauty at the beginning of Act 1, and for that reason as wrong in their conclusions. However, while Calisto's overture to Melibea seemed a persiflage of a Stoic *collatio rationis*, Sempronio's words parody the much-abhorred practice of syllogism (cf. *Ep.* 85). The purpose of Sempronio's persuasion is to make Calisto reward Celestina (and himself) generously. Starting out from the dubious premise that honour is the greatest of all worldly goods, he supports this with a series of Aristotelian maxims in order to prove that 'es mejor el uso de las riquezas que la posesión de ellas' (S. 74; M. 56).

Apart from being an entertaining sample of an empty syllogism (cf. *Ep.* 85, 2), Sempronio's speech is also a conscious exercise in flattery, where he glorifies his master's munificence and liberality. Rojas caught on to this particular aspect in Sempronio's speech and ends Act 2 on exactly this topic. After going over previous events in the conversation between Calisto and Parmeno, he concludes the act with Calisto accusing Parmeno of feigned loyalty: 'Fingiéndote fiel, eres un terrón de lisonja . . .', he bursts out (S. 77; M. 60). Typically, the master addresses the wrong servant, for here Sempronio, not Parmeno, has consistently been the culprit.

With the theme of flattery, Rojas broaches the subject of the connection between truth in language and truth in behaviour. The topic was well known to the average reader. For instance, the 'Tratado del oir en la palabra' of the *Copilación* starts out with a reference to Seneca's Epistula 122, to expand on 'el habla de los lisonjeros y de aquellos que loan las cosas malas' (*CL* 5). This merits a long gloss on the necessity of avoiding flatterers: 'porque el son de los lisonjeros es dulce, y porende no es ligero de les quitar y echar del corazón'. Here flattery is seen as affirming the opposite of truth, as in 'que la bienaventuranza de la buena vida es hacer que use hombre libremente y a su voluntad de lo que tiene', an argument used by Sempronio at the beginning of Act 2. A similar thought is expressed in Epistula 45, 7 (Anth. 33), which warns that 'el lisonjero viene a mí en semejanza de amigo', a statement followed by another verbal world upside down such as 'la riqueza se esconde so nombre de ardideza' and 'la pereza se llama modestia y templanza, el medroso se llama sabio' (Anth. 33, fol. 30v). Indeed, Seneca calls these and other non-truths 'sophismata' and 'fallacia' (*Ep.* 45, 8), translated in the Anthology as 'sofismos' and 'engaños' – two characteristics which all along have been the hallmark not of Parmeno's but of Sempronio's speech.

In the same letter Seneca warns his friend against how much these sweet words sink into the heart: 'entran dentro en lo profundo del corazón y tanto más deleitan cuanto más dañan'. This warning is reflected in Parmeno's last beseeching words to his master: 'conocerás mis agras palabras ser mejores para matar este fuerte cáncer, que las blandas de Sempronio que lo ceban . . .' (S. 78; M. 60). Calisto, however, rejects Parmeno's advice with an impatient reply: 'Estoy yo penando y tú filosofando, no te espero más.' This is a sign for Parmeno to do exactly what his favourite philosopher condemns most: he becomes a flatterer. Following Sempronio's example, he will, from now on, colour his discourse with 'sofismos' and 'engaños' when addressing his master: 'pues a los traidores llaman discretos, a los fieles necios' (*ibid.*). Parmeno's decision to follow Sempronio's example thus completes the pair of 'malos y lisonjeros sirvientes' in apprehension of which *Celestina* was written.

In other respects as well Seneca's moral philosophy underlies the speech-patterns in Act 2. Love is diagnosed as a disease which affects one's speech and mind, a 'secreta enfermedad, según tiene mi lengua y sentido ocupados y consumidos' (S. 75; M. 57). Likewise, the first act's ideas on solitude and grief are repeated in Sempronio's admonishment. 'Que en viéndote sólo dices desvaríos de hombre sin seso', to which Calisto replies: '¿No sabes que alivia la pena llorar la causa?' (*ibid.*). Indeed, their discussion on sorrow and tears is very much in line with the first confrontation between the master and his servant, which, as we saw in chapter 3, was inspired by Seneca's Epistula 99. Even Sempronio's retort, 'Lee más adelante; vuelve la hoja', may well allude to the same letter, where, in a later passage, Seneca corrects the view that tears can be a remedy for sorrow.

The ensuing *sententia* on the folly of seeking out a reason to grieve is, according to Deyermond (D. 61), a first Petrarchan borrowing. The immediate source for Sempronio's statement '. . . buscar materia de tristeza, que es igual género de locura' (S. 75; M. 58) is *De Remediis* 2, which in turn reflects a Senecan thought expressed in Epistula 99, 1 and is translated as 'Nos andamos buscando duelos y plantos' and '. . . aún en plañir y llorar hay especie de locura' (Anth. 47, fol. 47r). The text of Petrarch's *De Remediis* 2 also produces the next quotation: 'Finge alegría y consuelo y serlo ha, que muchas veces la opinión trae las cosas donde quiera, no para que mudes la verdad, pero para moderar nuestro sentido' (D. 62). The notion that public opinion often decides the matter is a Senecan thought (cf. *DVB* 1, 5). But, while Seneca interprets this fact in a negative way, Sempronio cunningly quotes Petrarch, for whom there is some good to be had from general consensus. With these words of wisdom Sempronio leaves his master in the hands of Parmeno, who for the last time beseeches his master to come to his senses.

Parmeno, who in Act 1 had been an ardent, albeit garbled, spokesman for *De Vita Beata*, also produces a Petrarchan maxim which similarly reflects a Senecan truth. With his remark 'que un inconveniente es causa y puerta de muchos' (S. 77; M. 59) he quotes Petrarch's 'vitium unum est omnibus aditus' (D. 63). With the Petrarchan quotation, Rojas reiterates the first author's Stoic thinking on the chain of cause and effect, and this gives him the opportunity to recapitulate how one thing has led to another. Impatient with his servant's moralizing, Calisto answers with another Petrarchan *sententia* from the Index – 'el primer escalón de locura es creerse ser sciente' (S. 77; M. 60; D. 144) – which is followed by Seneca's reminder of the futility of advice when the mind is affected by grief and pain.

The appearance of the Petrarchan quotations may well mark the beginning of Rojas' continuation. With the exception of the first casual borrowing from the Index, however, the thoughts expressed in the Petrarchan *sententiae* can be traced back to various Senecan sources. And so we see Seneca and Petrarch join forces in Rojas' continuation of the story.

Act 3 also combines Senecan wisdom, a Petrarchan *sententia* and Rojas' unique blending of the two. The only Petrarchan quotation in Act 3 again rings like a proverb and is used to reinforce Celestina's confidence in the power of money. Assuaging Sempronio's doubt as to the outcome of their 'negocio', she quotes *De Remediis* 1 on 'no hay lugar tan alto que un asno cargado de oro no le suba' (S. 82; M. 68; D. 59). On the other hand, Celestina's pronouncement 'Digo que la mujer o ama mucho a aquel de quien es requerida o le tiene gran odio' (S. 83; M. 68) echoes the pseudo-Senecan Proverbio 6, 'la mujer ama o aborrece; no hay tercera cosa' (R. 29), a verdict which is repeated in the gloss to Proverbio 96 (R. 111). All in all, however, the quotations and reminiscences begin to lose some of their intellectual dimension and ramifications. As Rojas' style becomes more col-loquial, the narrative gathers momentum and the characters begin to speak more for themselves.

Perhaps the great achievement of Act 3 is the creation of the old go-between in the guise of solicitor and witch. The combination is surprising and almost a contradiction. On the one hand, Celestina's self-description reflects the dubious lawyer's practice of making a show of zeal to impress the client: 'es necesario que el buen procurador ponga de su casa algun trabajo, algunas fingidas razones, algunos sofísticos actos . . . y así verná cada uno a él con su pleito y a Celestina con sus amores' (S. 81; M. 65). Here Rojas, the student of law, is speaking his own language, portraying Celestina as a practical busi-ness woman whose main asset is her ability with language. It may, therefore, seem surprising that Rojas concludes by portraying her as a witch in league with the devil.

It is quite possible that to begin with Rojas followed the first author's view of Celestina as a woman of six 'oficios', the last one being 'un poquito hechicera' (S. 60; M. 36). Although the first author obviously took great delight in describing her apothecary's repertoire in detail, he finishes, in the words of Parmeno, with 'Y todo era burla y mentira' (S. 62; M. 39). As Rojas' continuation was taking shape, he may well have realized the potential of verbal magic. The 'conjuro' which finishes Act 3 thus seems an addition which Rojas himself put in at an early stage (cf. M. 77, 79, 88).

Then there was another incentive to stress Celestina's supernatural powers, and that was the very example of Seneca's own poetic practice when it came to writing fiction. A belief in magic is, of course, strictly taboo in Stoic thinking, yet in his tragedies (e.g., *Medea*) Seneca introduces witchcraft as an acceptable part of the plot. Seen in this light, Rojas' emphasis on Celestina's diabolical powers does not represent contradiction of the Senecan content of his story, but, rather, the use of poetic licence to capture the imagination of his readers. And in this he succeeded: his creation of Celestina appealed to many who related her image to real-life experience. As such Celestina's witchcraft was as 'real' as her other *oficios*, but, more than that, magic in *Celestina* gave the story that extra dimension of mystery lacking in the practical advice contained in the Stoic message.[5]

Finally, with Celestina's visit to Melibea in Act 4 Rojas gives free rein to his own creative powers. All this notwithstanding, the episode is full of *sententiae*, taken both from Petrarch and from Seneca, and, as we saw, much indebted to Seneca's *De Ira*.

The action starts out with Celestina's understandable fear in approaching Pleberio's house. As usual, Seneca's wisdom is needed and provided, this time in the form of a maxim on deliberation and foresight. With the words 'Porque aquellas cosas que bien no son pensadas, aunque algunas veces hayan buen fin, comunmente crían desvariados efectos' (S. 86; M. 75), Celestina is quoting Proverbio 59: 'Ca las cosas que no son bien pensadas, aunque algunas veces hayan buen fin, más comunmente habrán desvariados efectos' (R. 65; cf. also Proverbio 98, R. 113).

And so, armed with this Stoic truth, Celestina calls on Melibea. When the go-between is faced with the young girl, Petrarch's words of wisdom at first seem more appropriate. For instance, the old woman's complaints about old age are taken from *De Remediis*, where the debilitating effects of the passing years are described in depressing detail. Petrarch's *De Remediis* also provides Rojas with lengthy reflections on the folly of retracing one's steps and on the satisfaction of finding the inn at the end of the road. Then, by way of conclusion, Rojas borrows from the Index a *sententia* which he translates as 'Ninguno es tan viejo, que no pueda vivir un año' (S. 92; M. 82).

As Deyermond has pointed out, Rojas checked this entry against the text of *De Remediis*, where he found the second half of the sententia: 'ni tan mozo, que hoy no pudiese morir' (D. 43). The Petrarchan *sententia* does not go back to the discussion on death in the pseudo-Senecan *De Remediis Fortuitorum*, but is more likely a reference to Seneca's Epistula 12, in which old age is praised as a splendid phase in one's life. Seneca's words here, 'Conplectamur illam et amemus; plena est voluptatis, si illa scias uti' (*Ep.* 12, 4), are translated as 'la cual [mi vejez] debemos amar y abrazar, ca por cierto ella es llena de deleitación a quien bien della sabe usar' (Anth. 12, fol. 10v). To the objection that, even so, the prospect of death is hardly a pleasing one Seneca retorts that death is not reserved for the old alone, and this is followed by 'Deinde nemo tam senex est, ut improbe unum diem speret' (*Ep.* 12, 6), translated as 'No hay hombre tanto viejo que no espere de vivir un día' (Anth. 12, fol. 10v).

To those more familiar with Seneca than with Petrarch (and they included readers whose Latin was not up to the mark) the quotation may well have been a reminder of Seneca's stance on old age and happiness. For the select circle of those who knew Petrarch's Latin works, the *sententia*, of course, offered an additional thrill when they recognized Petrarch as the textual source. Be this as it may, the *sententia* is charged with meaning and premonition. Apart from fore-shadowing Pleberio's long life and Melibea's premature death, the quotation also indirectly contains a value-judgement on Celestina's moaning and groaning on the subject of old age. And so we see that Seneca and Petrarch go hand in hand, the philosopher supplying the ironical subtext, the poet adding an ironic flavour of literariness.

As far as the Petrarchan quotations are concerned, we here begin to detect a definite pattern. They either reflect solid Senecan doctrine, or are rather bizarre anecdotes. In the first category we have statements such as 'Pues sabe que no es vencido sino el que se cree serlo' (S. 96; M. 88; D. 145), 'la verdad no es necesaria abundar de muchos colores' (S. 97; M. 70; D. 145) and 'a la firme verdad el viento del vulgo no la empece' (S. 98; M. 91; D. 145). To the second category belong *exempla* from natural history, such as 'la telaraña que no muestra su fuerza sino contra los flacos animales' (S. 98; M. 90; D. 40) and the bizarre 'antico, de quien se dice que movía los árboles y piedras con su canto' (S. 99; M. 93; D. 40), or the more sentimental example of 'aquel emperador y gran músico Adriano' (*ibid.*).

Throughout, Rojas' 'gems' from the Index are matched by those

coming from Pero Díaz's *Proverbios*.[6] The *sententiae* on gifts, 'Porque
hacer beneficio es semejar a Dios' (S. 94; M. 85), go back to the Index
(D. 144) as well as to Proverbio 305 (R. 258), while 'El que puede
sanar al que padece non lo haciendo le mata' (*ibid.*) is a version of
Proverbio 301, 'El que puede sanar al que padece, non socorriendo, lo
mata' (R. 255). Meanwhile, 'Que por demás es ruego a quien no
puede haber misericordia' (S. 96; M. 88) and 'Tu mucha sospecha
echa, como suele, mis razones a la más triste parte' (S. 100; M. 94) are
textual borrowings from Proverbio 124 (R. 141) and Proverbio 7
(R. 30) respectively.

At the end of her visit to Melibea, Celestina, confident that the
storm has subsided and that all is well again, explains how during
Melibea's rage she had preferred to step back: 'que del airado es de
apartar por poco tiempo, del enemigo por mucho' (S. 101; M. 95).
This last sentence quotes Proverbio 189, 'Del irado apártate por poco
tiempo, del enemigo por largo' (R. 180). The gloss then explains the
way Seneca in the first book of *De Ira* describes how 'la ira está presta de
se volver en locura . . . así que el irado con la ira sale de seso . . .' (R.
181). These last words are echoed in turn by Melibea's own admission
that the name Calisto 'era bastante para me sacar de seso'. Another
fontecica used by Celestina to show how well she has understood
Melibea's reaction is her answer to the girl's gratitude for bearing with
her during her fit. 'Señora, sufríte con temor, porque te airaste con
razón. Porque con la ira morando poder, no es sino rayo' (*ibid.*). This
sententia comes from Proverbio 188, which reads: 'Donde con el poder
mora la ira, rayo es' (R. 151). The crucial difference between quotation and source, however, is the slight alteration in the Celestinesque
sententia. Celestina wants to sound reassuring by saying 'no es sino
rayo', while Pero Díaz warns his readers that 'el rayo no perdona cosa
y hace daño sin reparo'. The irreparable harm caused by Melibea's
outburst is nearer the truth, given that her rage will soon reach
breaking-point. And so, while Melibea's short attack of anger may
mean little more on the surface than a moment's rage, in reality it
spells her downfall and death.

Acts 5, 6 and 7

Just as the first trio of acts by Rojas' hand consisted of two slow-paced
chapters leading up to the climax of Celestina's visit to Melibea's
house, so too do we see him slow down in Acts 5 and 6, to accelerate

towards Celestina's visit to Areusa's bedroom in Act 7. As the tempo of the narrative quickens, the actual number of Senecan quotations diminishes in favour of Petrarchan *sententiae*. At the same time, however, the Senecan implications of speech and morals become more and more apparent.

The fifth act sees Celestina in a self-congratulatory mood after the succesful outcome of her conversation with Melibea. Although the go-between expresses a perfunctory gratitude for the devil's co-operation in leaving her alone with Melibea, she nonetheless attributes her success to self-control and perseverance. Her own considerable part in the achievement is then expressed by two *sententiae* of Senecan flavour. One, 'Sábete que la meitad está hecha cuando tienen buen principio las cosas' (S. 102; M. 97), reflects the proverbial maxim 'principia totius operis dimidium occupare' (*Ep*. 34, 3), translated as 'el comienzo es la mitad de la obra' (Anth. 36, fol. 34r), while the other, 'oh buena fortuna, como ayudas a los osados y a los tímidos eres contraria' (*ibid.*), might well be a version of 'audentes fortuna iuvat, piger ipse sibi obstat' (*Ep*. 94, 28; cf. also *Ep*. 64 and 67, and *Medea*, v. 159).

The Senecan introduction then alternates with a clever Petrarchan sentence on *admiratio*, uttered by Sempronio upon sighting Celestina. When the servant's curiosity about her visit to Melibea gives way to the suspicion that he may only see a small part of the coveted reward, Rojas spices the servant's indignation with a string of quotations taken from both Petrarch and Seneca. 'Oh qué mala cosa es de conocer el hombre' and 'más seguro me fuera huir de esta venenosa víbora que tomalla' are both *sententiae* taken from the Petrarchan Index (D. 55, 143), while 'Que quien con modo torpe sube en alto más presto cae que sube' (S. 104; M. 99) comes from the *Amonestamientos y doctrinas*, which reads: 'Quien por maneras torpes sube a lo alto más aína cae que subió' (*CL* 3 1, 2). This *doctrina* Rojas borrowed from the first author, who, in Act 1, had put these words in the mouth of Parmeno (S. 69; M. 48). Interestingly, Sempronio quotes the self-same *sententia* in Act 5, also predicting his own death. Sempronio's next Petrarchan quotation, 'no me maravillo que seas mudable, que sigas el camino de los muchos', is, of course, pure Seneca, as is Celestina's answer concerning sudden pleasures which cause alteration and disturb calm deliberation.

So far, all has been made up of easily recognizable maxims and plain truths, but then Rojas comes up with a very ingenious quotation. Calisto, too, has a maxim to illustrate his impatience: 'es más penoso al delincuente esperar la cruda y capital sentencia que el acto de la ya sabida muerte', he says (S. 105; M. 101).[7] This thought, condensed as a maxim in *Controversia* 3 ('mortem timere crudelius est quam mori'), is elaborated in *De Beneficiis* 2, 5, 3 as 'quod antecedit tempus, maxima venturi supplicii pars est'.

In the Senecan context the comparison is only used to explain that the gratitude for a gift will be the greater the less long it has been in the balance. Interestingly enough, this is precisely the topic of debate between Celestina and Sempronio prior to their seeing Calisto. Celestina and Sempronio had been arguing about the greater or lesser benefits that might result from breaking the good news at once or from holding back a little longer. But Rojas gives the *sententia* an extra dimension, in that with these words Calisto alludes to his own tragic end. After all, the news he is so impatiently awaiting also implicitly contains his death sentence.

With the various ramifications of Calisto's *sententia*, Act 5 comes to an end, but not before introducing the next act with yet another portentous pronouncement. Calisto urges Parmeno to open the door to 'esa honrada dueña en cuya lengua está mi vida' (S. 106; M. 101). Again, readers aware of the Senecan sub-text would readily substitute 'muerte' for 'vida', as Melibea's fateful invitation was the result of Celestina's crafty words.

Language is the main theme of Act 6. The servants' many asides, as well as Calisto's non-stop blathering and Celestina's transparent hinting at her just reward, are not only examples of untruthful speech, but also an eloquent manifestation of an unhealthy mind.

Seneca lashes out against long-windedness, jargon and maxims in several places, but nowhere more emphatically than in Epistula 114, where he equates verbal and sexual excess. As an illustration of verbal affectation, Seneca tells us how some sport old-fashioned words ('antiqua verba atque exsoleta'), others make up new words or twist them around ('fingit et ignota ac deflectit'), while others follow the latest fad in metaphors ('pro cultu habetur audax translatio ac frequens'). Another sign of this disease is indulgence in brilliant, high-sounding and poetical terms ('splendidis, sonantibus et poeticis'), and the avoidance of what is necessary and in ordinary use ('necessaria atque in usu posita', *Ep.* 114, 10–14).

All through *Celestina* the characters' speech-patterns are an example of this sort of affectation in speech, but nowhere more explicitly than in Act 6. Celestina's metaphor of the bee (S. 108; M.

105), Calisto's comparison with 'aquella Tusca Adeleta' (S. 112; M. 110), as well as his evocation of Alcibiades (S. 114; M. 113) – all three taken from the Index to Petrarch's work (D. 41, 39, 143) – added to the latter's reference to Dido and Aeneas, illustrate Seneca's thinking on excessive metaphor and contrived poetics in speech.

Seeing the many Petrarchan *sententiae* in this parody, one cannot help thinking that here perhaps Rojas consulted the Index to the poet's work merely to gather a few classical references and metaphors to highlight the characters' affectation in speech. In addition, the Petrarchan quotations are in such contrast to the ongoing action that they create a comic rather than a dramatic effect.

Meanwhile, Calisto's behaviour in this act illustrates yet another Senecan truth. The scene in which the love-stricken master passionately embraces Melibea's sash could be seen as alluding to Seneca's warning in Epistula 69 that any tangible reminder of the beloved incites amorous thoughts. The letter itself (Anth. 51) has little to do with passion or love. It talks of settling down after a hectic business career, and it is only for the sake of comparison that Seneca mentions how, just as the lover should not be reminded of the beloved by any of her possessions, so should the wise man eschew any thought of past honours and riches, because such feelings come back very quickly: 'cito rebellat affectus' (*Ep.* 69, 3). Interestingly, the early fifteenth-century compilers had singled out this particular comparison in their selections of Senecan words of wisdom. The *Copilación* starts out with this truth: 'Séneca en la Epístola 69 dice que los que quieren quitar de sí el amor que deben esquivar de ver y oir aquellas cosas por las cuales se torna en el corazón la memoria de la amada' (fol. 1r).[8]

Rojas then makes concrete the Senecan moral with the scene in which the possession of Melibea's sash results in excessive amorous speech which, in turn, inflames the lover with renewed hope of possessing Melibea herself. Calisto's adaptation of Proverbio 30, 'esa misma cosa que llaga del amor, sana la hace' (R. 44), gives another dimension to his words and actions. Ironically, by adding 'Seguro estoy' to his *sentencia* 'pues quien te dio la herida, la cura' (S. 116; M. 115), Calisto shows how ignorant he is of the psychological danger in possessing Melibea's sash. Interestingly, the gloss to this proverbio elucidates: 'no se sana si no cuanto ve hombre la cosa que ama y mientras más la ve y más contracta con ella, más crece el amor y por consiguiente, más crece la llaga'.

On this note, Rojas leaves Calisto and concentrates on Parmeno's possession of Areusa. The fact that the servant precedes his master in this pursuit inverts the traditional saying 'like master like man' and points up yet another reversal of roles in the master/servant relationship.

Act 7 describes Celestina's triumph over Parmeno, followed by the latter's love-making with Areusa. Action takes over and, as is so often the case, illustrates a typical Senecan tenet in word and deed, in this instance equating 'falsa amistad' and 'loco amor'.

In a way, this act is also a culmination of the verbal and sexual *affectus* brought out in the previous two episodes. Celestina's persuasion of Parmeno and her keenness to witness his love-making strongly remind us of Seneca's teaching on speech and morals. Celestina's reluctance to leave the scene will be developed later on in the *Tragicomedia* (p. 126). In the *Comedia* we only have a hint of the source of her behaviour: namely, paragraph 25 of Epistula 114. Here, Seneca, still on the topic of morals, delights in describing the verbal *voluptas* that corrupts speech as much as the soul. By way of a metaphor he illustrates how, when sexual excesses have debilitated the body, the mind still delights in the sight of others using limbs it can no longer use itself. 'Instead of delighting in its own pleasures', he goes on, 'it views those of others, it becomes the procurer and witness of sex' ('pro suis voluptatibus habet alienum spectaculum, sumministrator libidinum testisque', *Ep.* 114, 25). As usual, Rojas makes the metaphor concrete in this last scene, and as before he consults Petrarch's Index in search of examples to illustrate the verbal implications of such an *affectus*. Of these, the well-known maxims 'es menester que ames si quieres ser amado' and 'El cierto amigo en la cosa incierta se conoce' (S. 120–1; M. 123–4; D. 39, 43) were such well-worn truths that they should be termed platitudes.[9] In the same vein are the pronouncements on sin, love, language and Nature.

Last, but not least, the whole of Act 7 is a vivid illustration of Seneca's equation of a love based on desire and a friendship based on self-interest.

Acts 8, 9 and 10

The next three acts also start out with much speechifying, culminating in Melibea's surrender in Act 10. Here again, the Index to Petrarch's Latin works is used to furnish comparisons: 'como la hez de la taberna . . .' (S. 137; M. 148; D. 40), famous sayings such as the Terentian 'las iras de los amigos siempre suelen ser re-integración del amor' (S. 138; M. 150; D. 143), proverbial moralism such as 'en poco espacio de tiempo no cabe gran bienaventuranza' (S. 140; M. 153; D. 58) or metaphors such as 'Mucha fuerza tiene el amor . . .' (S. 147; M. 165; D. 39). Rojas could have found similar *sententiae* in Seneca's canon, or even in the *Copilación* and the *Proverbios*. However, the direct provenance of these well-known truisms is not Seneca, but Petrarch's Index.

Thus a new suspicion arises concerning the usefulness of the Italian sage. Could it be that Rojas had spotted the similarity in thought between Petrarch and Seneca and that, tired of looking for appropriate maxims in Seneca's own copious work, he had found a most appropriate short-cut to Petrarch's work in the Index? After all, Rojas was a student, and students have a liking for short-cuts, especially where they seem so effective. It could just be that the power of the *sententia* was beginning to fade in the face of the human drama that was unfolding. It is as if Rojas were so absorbed in his own story that he simply did not want to take time off to turn the pages of Seneca's collected work in search of appropriate sayings. What a temptation it would have been to have at hand a list of quotations in Petrarch's Index, quotations which so often synthesize in a few well-chosen words a whole complex of Senecan thinking!

For instance, in the case of Hecaton's maxim 'si vis amari, ama', Rojas was aware that Seneca had quoted it in one of his letters on friendship. But where? Rather than search through the letters or even the Anthology he had the ready-made sentence to hand in Petrarch's Index: 'si vis amari ama' (D. 39). The same is true of the *sententiae* on the *vulgo*: 'nunca alegre vivirás, si por voluntad de muchos te riges' and 'que cualquier cosa, que el vulgo piensa, es vanidad' (S. 145–6; M. 163; D. 145). Rojas knew that Seneca had said this somewhere in *De Vita Beata* and also in the *Epistulae*, but it also could well be found somewhere in the *Copilación*. So, rather than scan all these books, he found the potted version in the Index. This seems to explain how Petrarchan *sententiae* do not change the meaning of the *Comedia* but generally reinforce the Senecan moral, particularly where affectation in speech is concerned.

Celestina's resentment at Melibea's previous anger, expressed in an aside as 'Tú me pagarás, doña loca, la sobra de tu ira' (S. 154; M. 177), now takes us back to Seneca's *De Ira*. Here Rojas found a quotation to colour Celestina's professionalism in her statement 'más presto se curan las tiernas enfermedades en sus principios que cuando han hecho curso en la perseveración de su oficio' (S. 155; M. 177). This is an almost textual quotation from *De Ira* 2, 18, 2, which reads: 'facile est enim teneros adhuc animos componere, difficulter reciduntur vitia quae nobiscum creverunt'.

In keeping with the Senecan stance on vice as an illness of the mind, Rojas translates 'vitia' as 'enfermedades'. He had made a similar 'mistake' in a previous quotation from Epistula 34, 3, by translating 'pars magna bonitatis est velle fieri bonum' as 'gran parte de la salud es desearla'. Here, too, Rojas consciously changed 'bonitas' into 'salud', knowing full well that Melibea's health has little connection with being good. In fact, Melibea's speech illustrates that she neither is virtuous nor has any wish to be so. Her conscious lies to her mother with which the act closes make this perfectly clear. But most readers would not have had to wait for the end to realize how Celestina's untruthful speech is matched by Melibea's. Their conversation is full of inflated metaphors and platitudes. Melibea's comparing Celestina's healing powers to the great Alexander, King of Macedonia, who in a dream had seen 'en la boca del dragón la saludable raíz con que sanó a su criado Tolomeo del bocado de la víbora' (S. 155; M. 177; D. 143), is nothing short of ridiculous. The fact that Melibea's 'poetics' come straight out of the Index lends a comic note to her words. On the other hand, Celestina's moralizing in the form of *sententiae* taken from *De Remediis* only reflects the most pedestrian truths, such as 'lo duro con duro se ablanda' (D. 61), 'pocas veces lo molesto sin molesto se cura', or 'un clavo con otro se expele' (S. 158; M. 181; D. 61). Then, Rojas inserts 'nunca peligro sin peligro se vence', which comes from both the Petrarchan Index (D. 144) and the Senecan Proverbio 244: 'no se vence peligro sin peligro' (R. 209). Celestina's down-to-earth truths then alternate with her well-known poetic quotations from *De Remediis* on the 'amor dulce' (D. 58), which, given the context, should not be taken too seriously either.

Finally, Melibea's complete capitulation is portrayed in the lies she tells her mother when questioned about Celestina's second visit. The daughter's explanation, 'por venderme un poquito de solimán', does not, however, match Celestina's excuse about supplying more thread. Be that as it may, the mother prefers to believe the story of Melibea, who now pretends to be the obedient daughter. Alisa's warning that Celestina has a bad reputation then produces Melibea's feigned protestation: '¿De ésas es? ¡Nunca más! ¡Bien huelgo, señora, de ser avisada por saber de quien me tengo de guardar!' (S. 162; M. 186).

With these lies Rojas completes Melibea's portrait as a person whose speech and actions do not jibe. At the same time he illustrates the moral of Epistula 34, from which he has taken the 'misquotation' on health and virtue. This letter contains the well-known adage 'opera verbis concordent' (*Ep.* 34, 4), translated as 'que los tus hechos se acuerden con los tus dichos'. This admonition is then followed by the reminder that 'aquel corazón no es justo ni recto que sus dichos desacuerdan de sus hechos' (Anth. 36, fol. 33r), which is a translation of the concise 'cuius acta discordant'.

Acts *11, 12, 13 and 14*

With Melibea's surrender to Celestina's blandishments, the pace of events quickens and action follows speech more closely. Many words are exchanged in Acts 11 and 12 – words that generate murderous actions and fatal decisions on the part of the servants. Likewise, Acts 13 and 14 are full of words that incite amorous actions with equally fatal results for the masters.

In both cases the greed to possess is the motive behind speech and action: the possession of Celestina's gold chain in the case of the servants, possession of Melibea's body in the case of the master. Interestingly enough, the object of desire in both cases is regarded as a just reward for suffering.[10] So 'codicia' and 'galardón' are the main points of discussion, followed by action as the *Comedia* comes to its logical conclusion.

In these four climactic acts Seneca and Petrarch still fulfil the same function as before. Seneca's philosophy on gifts, nature, language and, of course, the all-encompassing *affectus* pervades the action, to which Petrarch supplies an embellishment in the form of *sententiae* and classical references.

The force of language is brought out at the beginning of Act 11, this time as a reminder to Calisto of the danger of gossip: 'Por Dios, que huyas de ser traído en lenguas' (S. 163; M. 187), Sempronio warns his master. More dangerous to his well-being, however, are Celestina's ensnaring words. This first point is brought out by the short exchange between Calisto and Celestina upon the latter's return: '¿En qué está mi vida?' Calisto asks; 'en mi lengua', Celestina answers. The master's paralysing dependence on the go-between's words is emphasized again in Parmeno's commentary: 'está colgado de la boca de la vieja, sordo y mudo y ciego, hecho personaje sin son' (S. 164; M. 190).

Obviously the master has lost that precious gift of language in the sense of *logos*, meaning both speech and reason. As a result he loses all sense of value and, blinded by desire, acts foolishly. In comparison to the 'galardón' which Celestina is about to bestow on him, he qualifies the gold chain as 'cadenilla' and 'liviano galardón'. With his unreasonable speech and actions he then puts in motion a whole series of tragic events.[11]

To reinforce the wrongheadedness of Calisto's gift, Rojas now alludes to a passage in *De Beneficiis* 2, 15, 3 by having Celestina comment: 'Como todo don o dádiva se juzgue grande o chica respecto del que lo da, no quiero traer a consecuencia mi poco merecer, ante quien sobra en cualidad y en cuantidad' (S. 165; M. 190). The Senecan paragraph states that when contemplating a gift, one should give consideration to the means of both the giver and the receiver. Some gifts are too small for the benefactor, and others may be too great for the beneficiary – hence the importance of careful deliberation in these matters: 'aestimanda est eius persona, cui damus; quaedam enim minora sunt, quam ut exire a magnis viris debeant, quaedam accipiente maiora sunt'.[12] Again, the subtext of the allusion, and not the asides of the servants, themselves blinded by their greed to lay claim to the chain, supplies the real comment.

Petrarch's contribution to Act 11 is one quotation, taken from the *Index*, on how good fortune is more difficult to suffer than bad fortune. This again is entirely in keeping with Seneca's thinking, according to which the challenge of meeting adversity is to be preferred to sinking into a life of complacent pleasure (See *Ep.* 64 and 67).

Significantly, Act 12 starts with Calisto's concern about the time of day. And he has reason to be worried whether it is ten or eleven o'clock at night, as he is to meet Melibea at her door at midnight. From his parting words in the previous act, we gather that Calisto has been sleeping the better part of the day so as to make up for the preceding sleepless night, and also in order to fortify himself for the one to come (S. 167; M. 194).

The night's dangers ultimately seal the servants' friendship, which makes Sempronio exclaim: '¡cuán alegre y provechosa es la conformidad en los compañeros!' (S. 170; M. 198), a statement which reflects the Senecan attitude to friendship as expressed in Proverbio 307. Ironically, the final alliance between the servants is based on fear and cowardice, two *affecti* which Rojas is at pains to bring out in their speech.

Similar *affecti* determine the lovers' first conversation as well. They are beset by suspicion and doubt about each other's sincerity, fearing a trap or, worse, a fatal betrayal. Melibea's feigned protestations, followed by Calisto's loud despair gradually resolve themselves in a mutual profession to be each other's slave. Meanwhile Petrarch lends an extra artificiality to Melibea's speech. Worried about losing her reputation, she reminds Calisto 'y pues sabes que tanto mayor es el yerro cuanto mayor es el que yerra' (S. 174; M. 203; D. 59) and, commenting on her parents' waking up, 'no hay tan manso animal que un amor o temor de sus hijos no asperece' (S. 177; M. 208; D. 40). The sayings come from Petrarch's *De Remediis* and Index respectively, and both, therefore, should be seen as poetics rather than truth. Meanwhile Seneca provides the reader with the satisfaction of seeing through the lovers' hollow words.

In this respect, the gravest error is committed by Calisto, who upon returning home fails to reward his servants in any tangible way. Instead, he only gives them words of thanks with the promise of a reward: 'Hijos, en mucho cargo os soy. Rogad a Dios por salud, que yo os galardonaré más complidamente vuestro buen servicio. Id con Dios a reposar' (S. 178; M. 210).

Left empty-handed by their master, the servants decide to claim their just reward from Celestina. Their affliction is then illustrated in word and deed, first in their lies about the dangers endured while standing watch over their master's affairs, and then by accusing Celestina of the greed which is so apparent in their own behaviour. Again, the verbal comment on the nature of greed comes from Petrarch, where he says: 'Así que adquiriendo crece la codicia y la pobreza codiciando, y ninguna cosa hace pobre al avariento sino la riqueza' (D. 59). These are all thoughts that go back to Seneca's many pronouncements regarding poverty, riches and greed.[13] However, none of Seneca's statements sums up the idea in quite as poignant a way as the *sententiae* that Rojas found in Petrarch's prose work.

The next pair of acts now deals with the master's *codicia*, which, set against his servants' death, acquires an extra dimension of uncaring selfishness. Act 13 starts out with the query as to the time of day, and, although the master is informed that it is 'bien de día', he turns over with the command 'déjame dormir hasta que sea hora de comer' (S. 185; M. 221). Thus the master sleeps on while his servants are publicly executed. When the news finally reaches him, he openly admits that he is less perturbed by his servants' unexpected death than by the consequences this might have for his unfinished business. Again, Petrarch's Index is used to illustrate how afflicted the master is in speech and mind. Petrarch's Stoic wisdom on the fall of the great (D. 143) and on adversity (D. 39) consoles him on the one hand and, on the other, leads him to the (Epicurean) decision 'que más me va en conseguir la ganancia de la gloria que espero, que en la pérdida de morir los que murieron' (S. 188; M. 225).

And so Rojas leads us into Act 14, which in its original form was as short as the 'breve deleite' the lovers were to enjoy. The abrupt ending of Calisto and Melibea's love in the *Comedia* is not fortuitous but, on the contrary, is very much in accord with *De Vita Beata*'s verdict on passion: 'At voluptas tunc, cum maxime delectat, extinguitur' (*DVB* 7, 4), translated as 'mas el deleite cuando más deleita entonces se acaba' (*CL* 1, 8).

Petrarch's only contribution here is Melibea's expression of regret at not having enjoyed her short-lived pleasure more: 'Jamás conocéis vuestros bienes sino cuando de ellos carecéis' (S. 225, M. 252; D. 58), she quotes from Petrarch. Otherwise, Rojas traces the many ways in which the lovers' *affectus* finds its final expression. Melibea asserts once again that she is Calisto's 'sierva' and 'cativa'. Calisto's haste to descend her garden wall is expressed in Melibea's warning, 'no vengas con tanta presura', countered by Calisto's passionate words, 'mora en mi persona tanta turbación de placer, que me hace no sentir todo el gozo que poseo' (S. 190; M. 228). In turn, Melibea's protestations at his tempestuous approach seem feigned: 'no quieras perderme por tan breve deleite y en tan poco espacio'. But Calisto is in pursuit of just reward in payment for lifelong (*sic*) suffering. Thus his lie, 'por conseguir esta merced toda mi vida he gastado', is accompanied by action made explicit by verbal references to Melibea's 'lindas y delicadas carnes'. When Melibea for the last time implores him to stop, he identifies his actions with '¿Para qué, señora? ¿Para qué no esté queda mi pasión?'

After the event Melibea feigns regret at having lost her virginity, but the conventionality of her words is unmasked by the new servant, Sosia, who has overheard everything and comments: 'Todas sabéis esa oración despues que no puede dejar de ser hecho. ¡Y el bobo de Calisto, que se lo escucha!' (S. 192; M. 230). A commentary is also provided to Calisto's subsequent fall by the new servants, as they gather their master's shattered brains: 'Coge, Sosia, esos sesos de esos cantos, júntalos con la cabeza del desdichado amo nuestro' (S. 224; M. 250).

With these words, Rojas makes concrete a powerful Stoic truth. For Seneca slavery to the *affectus* is spiritual death, while for Rojas it is the physical end of his characters' lives. The Senecan *affectus*, so manifest in speech and actions, has made them quite literally 'lose their heads'. The only one now left to follow in this inexorable chain of cause and effect is Melibea.

Acts 20 and 21

In the last two acts the dialogue pattern is broken. Both Melibea in her *apologia* and Pleberio in his *planctus* speak in monologue. Nevertheless, there is a difference. Action still follows speech in Melibea's soliloquy, since her last words, 'Pon tú en cobro este cuerpo que baja' (S. 231; M. 260), are accompanied by her fall from the tower. Pleberio's lament, by contrast, is as static as his closing *sententia*, which evokes a quiet valley of tears. The language itself is very different in the last two acts as well. Melibea's speech is uninterrupted by *sententiae* or proverbs; in fact, her discourse flows quite naturally on the current of Senecan thinking. Pleberio's lament, however patterned on the traditional elegiac form, is interrupted by many Petrarchan quotations. As on previous occasions, these reflect Senecan truths on Fortune's instability, the world's deceits and the unfairness of love's laws. Other *sententiae* refer to classical examples of bereaved fathers such as Paulus Emilius, Pericles, Xenophon and Anaxagoras (S. 234; M. 264), all taken from Petrarch (D. 40, 42, 83). In itself this is not a surprising occurrence. However, their sheer quantity gives one pause to wonder. Could it be that Rojas was overdoing it for the same reason that he was to overstate Petrarch's presence in the Prologue? Other examples, this time referring to love's victims, comprise Paris and Helen, 'Hipermestra' (Clytemnestra?) and Egistus, names taken from Seneca's tragedies or possibly just from Proverbio 40, which uses these characters to illustrate the maxim 'Dos veces muere el que por voluntad de otro muere' (R. 50). Indeed, in the light of these all too well-known examples from classical literature, Pleberio's use of Latin in his closing words, 'in haec lachrymarum valle', sounds like that same affectation in speech which Rojas had consistently brought out in his characters' dialogue.

Thus the speech patterns in *Celestina* fulfil a special function. Since there is no narrator to supply background information, the reader has to deduce each speaker's characteristics for himself through his unaided reading of the dialogue alone. From the artificiality of Pleberio's discourse in the last act, crowned by his pedantic show of Latin in his closing words, as well as his mistaken naming of 'Hipermestra', we might deduce that, like Melibea and Calisto, he needs the sayings of others to prop up his intellectual poverty.

The representatives of the rich bourgeoisie characterize themselves as the parvenus of learning, exhibiting their newly acquired knowledge by spouting maxims and *exempla*. They are the fifteenth century's pedantic name-droppers, who tend to mix up their information and so become a caricature of learning (see *Ep.* 33).

The servants' speech is less innocent than that. Their discourse is that of flatterers and aims to ingratiate, regardless of the truth. Their words are characterized by fallacies and sophistries – a much more serious disease, according to Seneca, as it goes against both Nature and Reason (see *Ep.* 45).

Celestina's character is, of course, completely defined by her speech, but her affectation is not so much a sign of shaky knowledge or dubious flattery as it is the vice commonly ascribed to lawyers and rhetoricians. Her discourse is directed at destroying the opposition under an avalanche of words, always retaliatory, always intent to win. The result is as untruthful as in the speech of masters and of servants (cf. *Ep.* 40). Moreover, her job as go-between exemplifies the intimate relation between verbal and sexual excess and thus renders concrete Seneca's metaphor of depravity in language and morals (*Ep.* 114).

6

Readers ask for more:
the *Tragicomedia de Calisto y Melibea*

In the fifteenth century reading was neither a silent nor a private activity. On the contrary, judging by Rojas' reflections in the Prologue on what might happen 'cuando diez personas se juntaren a oir esta comedia', it took place during social gatherings. His remarks evoke a group of people intently listening to one reader who brings to life a world of conflicting passions solely through the impact of his voice. Indeed, reading was a form of acting, as Rojas' editor Proaza makes clear in the book's concluding verses. He recommends, for instance, that the reader should move his listeners with different nuances of his voice, acting out each part with varying emotions: 'a veces con gozo, esperanza y pasión / a veces airado con gran turbación' (S. 238; M. 271). In turn, his listeners would not sit around silently, but would express their own views in an equally vocal manner. Since a certain disagreement is inevitable in any group discussion, Rojas goes on to say, who will deny 'que haya contienda en cosa que de tantas maneras se entienda' (S. 43; M. 12). Later on, he lists all these 'dísonos y varios juicios' as the reason for his reluctant decision to side with the majority: 'que querían que se alargase en el proceso de su deleite de estos amantes' (S. 44; M. 13).

If his readers played such an important role in the transition from *Comedia* to *Tragicomedia*, we might assume that they also influenced Rojas in the nature of these changes. Just how much say they had in the revisions is difficult to assess. In fact, the composition of the *Tragicomedia de Calisto y Melibea* is riddled with unanswered and mostly unanswerable questions. We are involved not only with additions, but also with deletions and substitutions, some of which had already occurred in the 16-act *Comedia*. It is possible that the changes and additions were the work of a team headed by Rojas himself, or that Rojas carefully listed his readers' contrasting views and incorporated them as best he could in a new continuation. Another possibility is that

Rojas was only responsible for the prolongation of the love affair and that an entirely different author wrote the so-called 'Tratado de Centurio' (Acts 15, 17 and 18).

Another scenario could be that the editor, as spokesman for the majority of readers, sat down with Rojas to discuss how to make the *Comedia* more acceptable to a wider public of readers. Considering the intimate co-operation between authors and editors in the early days of printing, this could well be the most likely story. Then, as now, editors closely watched the market and kept a finger on the pulse of their prospective clientele. It is possible that Proaza foresaw that readers were losing interest in the intellectual content of the story and that they would prefer a more emotional emphasis, stressing the force of love, overpowering grief or raging revenge.

Thus Rojas was asked to go back to the drawing-board, although he considered this 'tan extraña labor y tan ajena de mi facultad' (S. 44; M. 13). It was indeed a strange task, not so much because it took him away from his legal studies as on account of his training, which disciplines the mind to judge people's actions and words dispassionately. However, Rojas agreed to insert five acts toward the end of the story, and to change the original text accordingly. He even complied with the printers' wishes to add rubrics to each act, although for Rojas this was 'una cosa bien excusada, según lo que los antiguos escritores usaron'. In the end, the interpolations, additions and subtle pointers in the rubrics proved to be so significant that he had to change the title from *Comedia* to *Tragicomedia*.[1]

The main reason for all the strife surrounding the reception of his book, Rojas says in the Prologue, is his readers' 'diferencia de condiciones' (S. 43; M. 12). Interestingly enough, recent psychological research into readers' response has called our attention to precisely these differences in its attempt to explain the variations in the interpretation of a work. Texts not only 'mean' something, they also 'do' something to the reader.[2] What Act 1 'meant' to Rojas was an entertaining and challenging intellectual exercise, and what it made him 'do' resulted in a continuation of the sketch according to his own Senecan 'condition'. However, Rojas' *Comedia* met with a much more complex response than did the first act, since on this occasion the text was received not by one but by a whole group of readers. Some accepted the Stoic message; others, of a more Epicurean bent, regretted the abrupt ending of the lovers' simple quest for pleasure; others (these of a more passionate disposition) sided with the servants and clamoured for revenge, while yet others wished to emphasize the basic sexuality of the lovers' desire.

Rojas was exceptionally sensitive to his readers' opinions and tried to accommodate each and every version. Nevertheless, he remained apprehensive about the final result, to judge by his concluding words in the Prologue: 'que no han de faltar nuevos detractores a la nueva adición'. Whether he incorporated the additional acts first and adjusted the existing text later, or the other way around, is difficult to ascertain. More within the scope of this study, however, is the question of what changes had to be made in order to please the widest possible readership.

The interpolations

Broadly speaking, additions to the original text fall into three categories: *sententiae*, explanations and emotions.

In the main, the interpolated *sententiae* are of Petrarchan origin and so could well have been inserted by Rojas himself, especially as they fulfil the same function as before. On the one hand they reflect a Senecan realism; on the other they illustrate the dubious poetics of the speakers.

As far as the Senecan content is concerned, the mutability of our feelings is supported in Act 3 with the Petrarchan quotation 'que la costumbre luenga amansa los dolores, aloja y deshace los deleites, desmengua las maravillas' (S. 80; M. 65; D. 146). In Act 7 Celestina predicts Parmeno's final surrender with the Petrarchan *sententia* 'múdanse las costumbres con la mudanza del cabello y variación' (S. 119; M. 122; D. 74). Parmeno, in turn annoyed with Sempronio's persistent hostility in Act 8, quotes Petrarch to warn him that his patience is wearing thin: 'Cata que es muy rara la paciencia que agudo baldón no penetre y traspase' (S. 136; M. 148; D. 44). Similarly, in Act 9 Celestina adds to her reflections on the instability of life 'Pero bien sé que subí para descender', etc. (S. 150; M. 170; D. 76), while she ends her long quotations from Petrarch's *De Remediis* in Act 12 with 'el duro adversario entibia las iras y sañas' (S. 183; M. 216; D. 77). One cannot help wondering whether here Rojas' particular choice of quotations reflected his readers', and possibly his own, changing views.

Act 4 has a long interpolation on the pernicious effects of riches; this is introduced by Celestina's Stoic remark that 'aquel es rico que está bien con Dios'. She then produces the Senecan misquotation 'más segura cosa es ser menospreciado que temido' (S. 91; M. 81). Instead of saying 'menospreciado', Celestina should have said 'amado' (cf. Anth. 48, fol. 50v), particularly when she goes on to mention how she herself is loved because of her character, but a rich man would be loved for his estate. The long interpolation then quotes Petrarch's *De Remediis* I on 'honesta pobreza', which itself goes back to Seneca's *Epistula* 2, 6. Similarly, the Petrarchan maxims 'no hacen señor, mas mayordomo' and 'más son los poseidos de las riquezas que no los que las poseen' (D. 69) reflect many of Seneca's thoughts as expressed in his letters (cf. *Ep.* 22, 119, etc.) and condensed in a trio of *Proverbios*, in turn supported by other *sententiae* such as 'Este no posee las riquezas, mas las riquezas poseen a él' and 'conviene mandar el dinero, no servirle' (numbers 284–6; R. 242–3).

Then there are those Petrarchan quotations which emphasize the speakers' pedantic name-dropping. In Act 13, Calisto compares himself to 'aquel gran capitán Ulises', who feigned madness to avoid serving in the Trojan War because he preferred to enjoy himself with 'Penélope su mujer' (S. 189; M. 226; D. 44). In this game of mixing and matching *sententiae*, Melibea needed to score more points than in the 16-act *Comedia*, and for this her last words to her father give her ample scope. In Act 20 she lists all those who have been cruel to their parents: 'Bursia, rey de Bitinia . . . Tolomeo, rey de Egipto . . . Orestes a su madre Clitenestra . . . Nero a su madre Agripina . . .' (S. 228; M. 256; D. 69). As if that were not enough, she then recites the names of those who have killed their beloved children without reason: 'Filipo, rey de Macedonia; Herodes, rey de Judea; Constantino, emperador de Roma; Laodice, reina de Capadocia, y Medea, la nigromantesa'. Finally, almost as an afterthought, she adds to the list a certain 'Frates, rey de los Partos', who killed not only his old father but his only child and thirty of his brothers! All these examples come from Petrarch's *De Remediis* and clearly add a comic touch to Melibea's imminent suicide.

Stemming from a more direct Senecan tradition is the *sententia* sandwiched between two *Proverbios* quoted in the original Act 4. To Melibea's remark 'Porque hacer beneficio es semejar a Dios', the interpolation adds: 'y más que el que hace beneficio lo recibe cuando es a persona que lo merece' (S. 94; M. 85). This inserted *sententia* is a mixture of the title of *Proverbio* 45, 'El que dio beneficio al digno, dándole recibióle', and of its gloss, which explains: 'mas si das la limosna al pobre que es digno de la recibir, en haciendo este beneficio, oviste mérito' (R. 53).

Other additions consist of *exempla* which amplify the topic under discussion. For instance, the hazard of 'el número uno' in Act 7 is dwelt upon with domestic examples of how one tires of eating the same dish every day, how a single witness is useless and how one set of clothes soon wears out. All this is tagged on to the proverb 'una golondrina no hace verano' (S. 130; M. 137). Then, on the same topic, the advantages of having a pair of everything are proved by the equally domestic evidence of our two feet, two hands, two sheets and two shirts – again with the support of appropriate proverbs.

When we look at the interpolations which list random examples, we are tempted to agree with María Rosa Lida de Malkiel that here we are dealing with team-work. It is as if readers individually and collectively proposed whatever came to mind, and that Rojas duly noted their suggestions. Of the same nature are the additions incorporating animal imagery in Act 4. To Celestina's mention of the benevolent unicorn one reader wanted to add the Aristotelian *exemplum* of the dog, 'si le echan en el suelo, no hace mal, esto de piedad' (S. 94; M. 85); and, where the altruism of the rooster towards its hens is concerned, somebody remembering the popular bestiaries proposed the generosity of the pelican and the stork (S. 95; M. 86).[3]

All in all, however, the new *sententiae* and *exempla* do not alter the orientation of the *Comedia*. Only with the explanations of the speakers' behaviour do we begin to feel that here the groundwork for the 21-act *Tragicomedia* is being laid.

The explanatory interpolations are of many types and serve various purposes. Some of the characters needed rounding out, in other cases a change of mind was deemed too brusque. Parmeno's character fascinated the reader; Celestina's 'oficios' were ambiguous; Melibea and Lucrecia needed more say in the matter, and so did Areusa and Elicia, in view of their active parts later on in the added acts. But then there were dissenting voices as well. For some, Melibea's surrender was the result of Celestina's witchcraft, while others explained her change of heart in terms of Stoic psychology.

Generally speaking, however, there seems to have been a consensus about the need to explain feelings and actions more fully. This is surprising, since Rojas comes through as the undisputed master in character portrayal. His interlocutors are anything but types; they are moody and beset by self-doubt, susceptible to one another's words and deeds, self-interested, changeable and far from self-sufficient. In short, they are living examples of Seneca's analysis of the foibles of mankind. But most readers failed to see this and as a result felt that some of the characters needed more clarification.

For instance, at the end of Act 2 Parmeno's sudden capitulation was felt to be too abrupt – hence the superfluous addition that the servant's despair was triggered by anger and frustration at his master's folly (S. 78; M. 61). Similarly, readers felt that his murder of Celestina needed to be made more plausible and his tragic end more acceptable. With this in mind, the interpolations in Act 6 (S. 109; M. 107), Act 11 (S. 166; M. 192) and Act 12 (S. 175; M. 204) portray the servant as a sanctimonious moralist on the surface and a suspicious coward underneath.

In a way, the interpolations come to fill the gaps, a task which had originally been left to the reader. In the 16-act *Comedia* readers were invited to supply their own mental comment, which more often than not was coloured by their knowledge of the Senecan subtext. The additions now leave less for the reader to do and in fact make it an 'easier' text. For some readers, however, this may have meant a loss of intellectual challenge.[4]

Sempronio's character only needed rounding out as far as his own background was concerned. In the fearful conversation with Parmeno outside Melibea's door in Act 12 the interpolation reveals him as yet another servant of many masters (S. 176; M. 206); while soon after, as he claims the golden chain, his threats to Celestina are expanded with the obscene insult 'Yo dígole que se vaya y abájase las bragas; no ando por lo que piensas . . .' (S. 182; M. 215). In the same dubious taste is the explanation of 'pájaras' as 'mochachas . . . de las que no saben volar' (S. 104; M. 99) and the Petrarchan quotation on 'tresquilar ovejas' which accompanies Melibea's half-hearted defence of her virginity (Act 14; S. 191; M. 229). Given the *Comedia*'s restraint in this sort of language, one cannot help thinking that Rojas bowed to his readers' dictates in this respect as well.

Of the minor characters in the *Comedia*, Elicia only needed to be developed into a half-hearted career girl to prepare the reader for her role as Celestina's reluctant successor in the added acts. At the end of Act 7 she welcomes Celestina home with a rambling disquisition on the relative merits of working for a living, the dubious advantages of getting rich and the certain benefits of a good night's rest.

By contrast, Areusa's murderous plotting in the added acts needed more preparation. This happens in the addition to Act 9, where she expresses her hatred for the ruling classes. Her long diatribe against modern mistresses is extended by a list of the small pleasures which are denied to servants. Interestingly, to the 'deleite' and 'los dulces premios de amor' the interpolation adds not love's sweet rewards, but rather the sad consequences of living without relatives on whom to drop in for a heart-to-heart chat. Her accusations then conclude with the Petrarchan quotation 'Oh tía, y qué duro nombre y qué grave y soberbio es "señora" continuo en la boca' (S. 149; M. 167; D. 146). Due to the new preponderance of domestic *exempla* on the plight of serving-maids, the Senecan analogy of masters and slaves gradually fades into the background. Indeed, the written interpolation here seems to be taking the place of the unspoken Senecan subtext.

Similarly, the cruelty of modern masters is exemplified with the addition in Act 13, where Sosia recounts the servants' last moments before their beheading. For the benefit of Tristan (and Rojas' readers), he recalls how, half-conscious, one of them with great difficulty lifted his eyes 'como preguntando [si me] sentía de su morir' (S. 186; M. 222). On this Tristan comments that the servant was probably wondering whether Calisto had come too. The interpolated dialogue, apart from explaining the servants' last feelings, adds a note of sympathy for the servant, with an implicit condemnation of the master's cruel indifference.

In view of Lucrecia's expanded role in the added acts, she too needed more say in previous developments. The first interpolation concerning her involvement happens in Act 4, where she thanks Celestina for promising her a remedy against bad breath. Celestina seizes this opportunity to reprimand her for her un-co-operative attitude and malicious whispering, which only increase her mistress' anger: 'No provoques a ira a tu señora más de lo que ella ha estado', Celestina adds (S. 101; M. 95). The mention of 'ira' here confirms Melibea's sudden change in Act 4 as a fit of rage – an interpretation which Rojas' readers were clearly still ready to accept.

During the second visit to Melibea's house in Act 10, Lucrecia's commitment to her mistress is again brought out, first when Celestina tries to send her away with the simile of the surgeon's concentration being hampered by the weak at heart (S. 157; M. 180), then in Lucrecia's apt description of Melibea's 'señales de pena' (S. 161; M. 185). The latter interpolation makes the maid speak out for the first time, revealing how, the more Melibea tried to hide the fire that was consuming her, the more its flames were obvious: 'en la color de tu cara, en el poco sosiego del corazón, en el meneo de tus miembros, en comer sin gana, en el no dormir'. Thus another series of circumstances is assembled in the customary medieval style of amplification, but when the series finishes with the observation 'fuera mejor el áspero consejo que la blanda lisonja' the Senecan stance on truthful versus flattering language is allowed a timid reappearance. However, with Lucrecia's revelations about the unspoken signs of love the interpolation focuses on the romance, not the moral tale. Clearly this was the message most readers were receiving as the drama reached its climax.

Calisto's character as a love-sick youth needed no further introduction. The only interpolation that concerns him occurs in Act 12, when the master agrees to go well armed to his first encounter with Melibea. Nevertheless, the addition brings out an interesting side of Calisto's character. Like Parmeno and Melibea, he is short-tempered, albeit forgiving in the end. After unjustly scolding his servants for being vague about the hour of night, and having been told by Parmeno that the time would be better employed in getting his armour together than in picking quarrels, Calisto concedes: 'Bien me dice este necio. No quiero en tal tiempo recibir enojo . . . Quiero dar espacio a la ira, que o se me quitará o se me ablandará . . .' (S. 169; M. 196). Thus we see how, at least for the first readers of the *Comedia*, *ira* was still an essential ingredient of the principal characters' psyche.

By contrast to this little adjustment of Calisto's character, it was felt that Melibea needed much more attention. In the same act she gives some gratuitous advice on how to reward Calisto's 'esforzados sirvientes', who, Calisto assures her, will protect them whatever happens. Her expressed hope that Calisto's rewards will guarantee secrecy is now expanded with ideas on how to reprimand servants without upsetting or angering them (S. 177; M. 207). Her advice seems to come straight out of a *Good Housekeeping* manual but with the implicit (Stoic) irony that in this very act both Calisto and Melibea had openly professed themselves not master or mistress, but 'siervos y cativos'.

Melibea's mention of a servant's irritability of course reflects her own irascible character, and indeed many interpolations dwell on Melibea's anger. In this connection, and for the benefit of those readers who needed convincing that Melibea's main weakness was uncontrolled rage, Rojas added a long adaptation of Seneca's *De Ira* 1, 1, 1–7.

Act 4, which describes Melibea's irate reaction to Calisto's name, seemed too long to accommodate additional information. By contrast, Act 6, in which Celestina recounts Melibea's fury, had room for expansion. Thus to Celestina's description of Melibea's shock at hearing Calisto's name the interpolation adds the many 'ignominiosos nombres' which Melibea hurls at the go-between, followed by a vivid description of her mad behaviour. Interestingly, Melibea's frantic movements closely resemble the many signs Seneca diagnoses as the symptoms of rage. In Celestina's words, her fury shows in every part of her body: 'turbado el sentido, bullendo fuertemente los miembros todos a una parte y a otra, . . . retorciendo el cuerpo, las manos enclavijadas, como quien se despereza, que parecía que las despedazaba, mirando con los ojos a todas partes, acoceando con los pies el suelo duro', etc., etc. (S. 111; M. 109–10). Similarly, Seneca's *De Ira* starts out by listing these very signs as pertaining to a fit of rage, only to prove that *ira* is a 'brevis insania', translated as 'locura, aunque dure poco tiempo' (Rubio 1961: 122). Again, in the words of the translator, the tell-tale signs of 'locos' and 'sañudos' are the same: 'el vulto ardid y amenazadero, la frente triste, y la faz turbada, y andar apresurado, y las manos non quedas, y la color mudada, y suspiros espesos, y fuertemente movidos'. The symptoms do not stop here: 'que los ojos se les encienden . . . las manos enclavijadas . . . y hieren y estriban los pies en tierra, y todo su cuerpo fuertemente levantado y orripilado, moviendo grandes amenazas de saña' (*ibid.*). Whoever suggested this interpolation clearly had Seneca's *De Ira* in mind, especially as Celestina finishes her description with the joyful comment that, 'entretanto que gastaba aquel espumajoso almacén su ira', she knew that Melibea's fit would soon be reaching breaking-point. However, then as now, not every reader agreed that Melibea was the victim of her own passion. There were others who preferred to see the power of magic at work.

Indeed, in Act 3, Celestina's long *conjuro* directed to Pluto was extended to include the classical Furies 'Tesifone, Megera, y Aleto', the infernal kingdom of Styx, Dis and Chaos, hydras and harpies (S. 85; M. 72–3). The addition may well have been patterned on Seneca's dramatic work *Medea*, where Medea's incantations also involve Furies, hydras, Styx, Dis and Chaos (cf. *Medea*, vv. 674–742).

With these two interpolations, one inspired by Seneca's *De Ira* and the other from the *Medea*, Rojas craftily satisfied two widely differing views of Melibea's surrender. Seneca's treatise on anger contented the moralists who attributed Melibea's capitulation to her own repressed passion, while the more literary-minded would have delighted in the allusion to Seneca's tragedy. Then there were readers of a more down-to-earth condition who wanted to have Celestina's hard-working qualities brought out. For them Rojas, in Act 4, added an explanation of Celestina's 'limpio trato', which stresses how she disappoints nobody and works 'como si tuviese veinte pies y otras tantas manos' (S. 98; M. 91). This is then followed by Melibea's Petrarchan quotation that one master in vice suffices to corrupt a whole city.

From these interpolations we can see how Celestina's intervention in the *Comedia* met with various interpretations. Her persuasive words were seen as magical by some and by others as the final kindling of Melibea's latent fire. Yet others attributed Celestina's success to her own skills in the trade. All these variables were present in the original text, and the explanatory amplifications, far from making things clearer, only added to the confusion by catering for each reader's differing experience and preferences.

Where readers' individual tastes are most prominent is in matters of wine, love and sex. On three different occasions the praises of wine are sung. In Act 3 Celestina's reminiscing about her erstwhile association with Parmeno's mother, 'Señora Claudina', revolves around the latter's talents in wine-tasting (S. 82; M. 66). In the next act, the reality of Celestina's present hardship is again brought out in connection with getting her daily drink (S. 94; M.85), while the banquet scene in Act 9 provides a great opportunity to extol the virtues of a good wine. Strange as this may seem, Seneca would here agree with Celestina. In his *De Tranquillitate Animi* he advises that hard work be alternated with distraction such as a slight drunkenness ('ebrietas'). This will dispel our worries, lift the heart and cure our sadness: 'eluit enim curas et ab imo animum movet et ut morbis quibusdam ita tristitiae medetur' (*De Tranq.* 17, 8).

In other respects, too, readers' 'diferencia de condiciones' directed their attention to a casual remark in the 16-act *Comedia*. Before leaving Parmeno alone with Areusa in Act 7, for instance, Celestina spurs him on so that she can see for herself what stuff he is made of. The interpolations expand the scene with Parmeno's compliance, to judge by Areusa's protestations: 'Ay, señor mío, no me trates de tal manera . . .', etc. This is followed by Celestina's assurances: 'que no sé yo, qué cosa es esto, que nunca vi estar un hombre con una mujer juntos . . .'. At this Areusa gives in: 'Madre si erré haya perdón y llégate más acá y él haga lo que quisiere' (S. 132; M. 140). Again, one is tempted to doubt whether Rojas would have condescended to this sexual explicitness were it not for readers' demand.

Other tastes, of course, centred around the force of love, as the readers followed Melibea's gradual surrender to passion. Celestina's remark in the third act that women in love curse the rooster's heralding of the dawn (S. 83; M. 68) is extended with appropriate metaphors, while Melibea's anxiety about Calisto's tardiness in Act 14 is expanded with examples of the many accidents that befall the unwary (S. 189; M. 227).

Melibea's last words to Calisto in the *Comedia*, then, sum up her deeply satisfied love, simultaneously preparing the reader for the prolongation of their nightly encounters. Melibea's wish to see Calisto again is now expanded with the words 'Y más, las noches que ordenares . . . porque siempre te espere apercibida del gozo con que queda esperando las venideras noches' (S. 192; M. 230). How different this Melibea sounds from the girl who in Act 1 had ordered Calisto out of her garden. Thus the woman who in Act 20 is made to add to her confession 'Del qual deleitoso yerro de amor gozamos casi un mes' (S. 230; M. 259) is clearly a composite character combining elements from the first author, Rojas and, finally, the readers of the *Comedia*.

The title

A shift in meaning brings with it a change in title.[5] Rojas had sided with the first author, who 'quiso darle denominación del principio que fue placer, y llamóla comedia' (Prologue). Clearly, for Rojas there seemed to be no reason for changing this heading, since he simply continued the first author's Senecan *contra-exempla*. By contrast, Rojas' own readers discarded the Senecan message and let their own *affectus* come into play. Emotions, by definition, are highly personal and therefore often conflicting. Realizing his readers' irreconcilable differences, Rojas decided to strike a compromise: 'viendo estas discordias, entre estos extremos partí agora por medio la porfía y llaméla tragicomedia' (S. 43; M. 13).

Plautus and Terence have been named as possible sources for Rojas' choice of the term 'Tragicomedia'. To these authorities one might add Seneca, who in Epistula 8, justifying his frequent quoting of Epicurus, draws the parallel with poets who similarly appropriate the famous sayings of philosophers and playwrights. For that reason, Seneca adds, they are halfway between comedy and tragedy, 'sunt inter comoedias ac tragoedias mediae' (*Ep.* 8, 8). It is just possible that Rojas applied Seneca's definition of the philosophizing poet to his own position half-way between writing a 'comoedia' and writing a 'tragoedia', thus satisfying all readers while still remaining faithful to his favourite Roman philosopher.

And then there was another reason why Rojas was willing to compromise with his readers. As an *aficionado* of Seneca, he must have been familiar with the philosopher's dramatic work as well, and for that reason Seneca should be included in Rojas' debt to classical playwrights.[6]

Perhaps the first drama to come to mind is *Medea*, which is well known for its witchcraft and magic. Before Medea starts her incantations, the nurse describes in every detail how, after having summoned all serpents and assembled all poisonous herbs, Medea mixes the serpents' venom and deadly herbs with unclean birds and the hearts and vitals extracted from live owls ('obscenas aves/ maestique cor bubonis et raucae strigis/ exsecta vivae viscera', vv. 732–4). Then, laying out some more objects of her craft, Medea starts her incantation with 'Comprecor vulgus silentum visque ferales deos/ et Chaos caecum atque opacam Ditis umbrosi domum' (vv. 740–1). Celestina's preparations for her *conjuro*, which involve 'la sangre de aquella nocturna ave' and the 'áspera ponzoña de las víboras de que este aceite fue hecho', are reminiscent of Medea's witchcraft. The later interpolations of the *Tragicomedia* reinforce this impression, as they complete the picture with the addition of the three Furies, 'las cosas negras del reino de Estigie y Dite', the 'sombras infernales y litigioso caos' and 'pavorosas hidras' (Act 6; S. 85; M. 71).

Other reminiscences of *Medea* can be detected in Melibea's final speech to her father from her tower; this parallels Medea's last words to Jason from the roof of her palace ('En ipsa tecti parte praecipiti imminet', v. 995). Although the circumstances are different, Medea's looking for Jason (v. 993) and Melibea's waiting for her father to appear at the foot of the tower have the same dramatic impact. In fact, Melibea's words as she throws herself off at the end of her speech – 'Toma, padre viejo, los dones de tu vejez . . . recibe allá tu amada hija' – are strongly reminiscent of Medea's last words to Jason: 'Recipe iam natos, parens' (v. 1024), with which she hurls down her slain sons.

Rage and murder are also the main issues of *Hercules Furens*. Here the hero, blinded by fury (*furor*) sent to him by Juno, murders his entire family as an illustration of how uncontrolled rage can destroy a complete household. Here, parallels with *Celestina* are not so much in the actual portrayal of *ira* but more as an illustration of the destructive repercussions of blind rage. Like Hercules, Melibea in Act 4 and the servants in Act 12 are the victims of fury and all three admit to being 'fuera de seso'. This loss of control is portrayed in *Hercules Furens* as a fainting fit, from which Hercules wakes after the atrocious deed has been committed. Melibea, too, faints after her fit of rage; the servants, however, have no chance to come to their senses as they jump to their death after murdering Celestina, thus exemplifying Hercules' words 'morte sanandum est scelus' (v. 1262).

The theme of *Hippolytus* is also passion and death, this time that of Phaedra for her young stepson Hippolytus. The scene which might have influenced Rojas is less probably Phaedra's fainting (v. 585) or calling herself a slave of the beloved (vv. 611–12) than the nurse's persuasion of Hippolytus. As the old woman sees the young lad approaching, she at first hesitates, but recognizes time and opportunity: 'Quid dubitas? dedit tempus locumque casus' (vv. 425–6). In her persuasion she urges the bashful youth to go out with friends, to love, to have fun – in short, to follow Nature and become a man of the world: 'proinde vitae sequere naturam ducem;/ urbem frequenta, civium coetum cole' (vv. 481–2). Many of the nurse's arguments remind us of Celestina's persuasion of Parmeno to go out and enjoy friendship and love, living according to Nature's law. But there are other parallels between scenes in *Hippolytus* and in *Celestina*. When, at the end of the former, Hippolytus' father beholds the shattered body of his son, he gathers together the broken limbs and complains at being left childless in his declining years, all the while fondling his child's mutilated body and bewailing his own sad lot: 'O triste fractis orbitas annis malum! . . . miserande, maesto pectore incumbens fove' (vv. 1253–5). This scene reminds us of Pleberio carrying his daughter, 'hecha pedazos', bemoaning the loss of his only child in his advanced years.

Pleberio's lament can also be traced back to another tragedy, and that is the *Troades*, where Hecuba bemoans her daughter's sacrifice (v. 1118) and her grandson's fatal leap from the high wall (v. 1151), to end with the desperate question of whither now: 'quo meas lacrimas feram? /ubi hanc anilis expuam leti moram?' (vv. 1167–8).

Clearly, Rojas had Seneca's tragedies in mind as he came to the close of his work. Pleberio's own mention of Paris, Helen,

Clytemnestra and Aegistus (S. 236; M. 267) reminds us of the *dramatis personae* in *Agamemnon*, a tragedy which also paints a violent picture of passion and death. Given the gradual appearance of this tragic mood toward the end of Rojas' fiction, it is not surprising that his readers preferred to call the story a tragedy rather than a comedy. In his attempt to please all his readers, Rojas may well have had another look at Seneca's dramatic works in search of inspiration as to ways of prolonging the love-story. However, rather than take his readers' wishes seriously, he parodied their preference for tragedy by changing Elicia and Areusa into two avenging Furies and portraying Calisto and Melibea's incipient love as reckless passion. The great difference between Seneca's tragedies and Rojas' *Tragicomedia* is that the moral concerns not kings and gods, but two *señoritos*, their servants and the lowest type of *vulgus* – thus bringing the tragedy down to the level of infatuation, domestic intrigue and petty crime.

The added acts

Who exactly was responsible for the great addition will remain a point of on-going debate. Marciales' claim that Rojas only wrote the continuation of Act 14, Acts 16 and 19 (i.e. the prolongation of the love affair) seems plausible. In that case, Acts 15, 17 and 18 (the 'Tratado de Centurio') may well be by that 'célèbre inconnu' Sanabria.[7]

However, on the basis of Seneca's and Petrarch's presence, it is more likely that Rojas was still the mastermind, if not the sole author, of all five acts. The thread of the Stoic message runs on unbroken, particularly in the 'Tratado de Centurio', where Areusa and Elicia's murderous plotting can be read both as an imitation of Seneca's tragedies and as an exemplification of his philosophy, accompanied by appropriate Senecan and Petrarchan *sententiae*.

The first challenge to be faced was how to adapt the existing Act 14 to the new mood. For the sake of prolonging the love affair, the first encounter in Melibea's garden with Calisto now closes with the latter's return home, where, for the first time, he realizes the full impact of recent events. Thus the act closes with an unusually long monologue which subtly analyses the lover's conflicting emotions of sorrow and pleasure. These two (Epicurean) extremes are seen by his servant Tristan as opposites which are too much for 'un flaco sujeto' (S. 197; 173). The contrasting emotions which take hold of Calisto are distress about his lost honour, resulting from the public execution of his servants, and the vivid memory of the delights in Melibea's garden. Sorrow at first takes the upper hand, when concern for his dishonour spills over into despair at his servants' death. This thought then triggers off many Senecan considerations on 'esta brevísima vida', supported by the Petrarchan quotation 'no hay hora cierta ni limitada ni aun un solo momento' (cf. *Ep.* 99, 9). This in turn leads to the Senecan condemnation of fleeting worldly pleasure.

However, the master's feelings soon concentrate on his personal dishonour, and turn into anger at the judge for having sentenced his servants to death. Calisto feels that, given the many favours this judge has received from Calisto's father, he should have protected the son – an opinion which is supported by the Petrarchan quotation 'que es menor yerro no condenar los malhechores que punir los inocentes' (S. 194; M. 234; D.76). But Calisto's mood changes again, this time to condone the judge's swift action, which he now perceives as a favour: 'por no me disfamar, por no esperar a que la gente se levantase y oyesen el pregón'. As in the case of his interpolated changing moods in Act 12, Calisto's anger subsides in feelings of gratitude. In typical legal jargon he then concludes: 'Y puesto caso que así no fuese, puesto caso que no echase lo pasado a la mejor parte' (S. 195; M. 235); he prefers to remember the good moments with Melibea, since no sorrow could possibly equal that gift of pleasure.

True to the Senecan analysis of carnal delights, Calisto's exultant exclamations are now followed by the lover's puzzled realization that he is not happy all the same. Unwilling to pursue this troubling thought any further, Calisto then produces another resolution which in itself is the perfect *exemplum* of an *affectus amantium*. Rejecting honour, glory, riches, parents and relatives, he decides to stay in his rooms all day and to spend the night 'en aquel paraíso dulce', Melibea's garden (S. 196; M. 236). This decision is in complete accordance with Seneca's diagnosis of the lovers' affliction. Obsessed with each other, they reject all other bonds and obligations: cf. 'Ipse per se amor omnium aliarum rerum negligens, animos in cupiditatem formae non sine spe mutuae caritatis accendit' (*Ep.* 9, 11). The very thought of Melibea thus makes Calisto rehearse all the glorious details of the night's encounter, which distract from the Senecan message but for that reason appeal all the more to readers' own fantasies.

To satisfy his readers' demands, Rojas also had to create a new Melibea, a woman obsessed by love. Her passionate disposition shows in her contempt for her parents' belated plans to find her a good husband: 'Déjalos parlar, déjalos devaneen', she exclaims in Act 16 (S. 205; M.241). Her scorn for her parents is then compounded by her thoroughgoing condemnation of the married state with the opinion 'más vale ser buena amiga que mala casada'. Her thoughts then turn to Calisto and how his servants died; his estate is at risk and he himself is locked up in his house, pretending to be absent, 'con esperanza de verme a la noche' (S. 206; M.243).

As in Calisto's case, her own *affectus amantium* makes her reject all other obligations and relations: 'que ni quiero marido ni quiero padre ni parientes', she exclaims angrily (S. 207; M. 243). Her obsession with love has been brought out earlier, with the Petrarchan quotation on how 'el amor no admite sino sólo amor por paga' (D. 96). Melibea's parents, too, express their concerns in Petrarchan quotations of Senecan content: for example, in their statements on approaching death, on being prepared at all times and on virtue's vulnerability to malicious gossip (S. 204; M. 240; D. 70, 75, 146–7).

The lovers' last encounter in Act 19 shows Melibea entirely 'apercibida al gozo'. While waiting for Calisto's visit, Lucrecia softly sings of love, soon to be joined by Melibea in a beautiful duet. When Calisto finally appears, Melibea continues the lyrically ecstatic expression of her love, but Calisto's usual impatience makes her change register with the words '¿cómo mandas a mi lengua hablar y no a tus manos que estén quedas?' (S. 222; M. 248).

With this the atmosphere changes. In tune with the rude interpolation on 'tresquilar ovejas' in Act 14, Rojas now makes Calisto say: 'Señora, el que quiere comer el ave, quita primero las plumas.' Similarly, he follows up the long voyeuristic interpolation in Act 7 with Lucrecia's running commentary on Calisto and Melibea's embraces in Act 19. In vain Melibea tries to send her maid away with the suggestion that she prepare them a collation. For Calisto, no snack can equal the possession of her beautiful body; after these words Lucrecia's more than explicit commentaries can leave the reader no room for doubt as to the turn events have taken. When Calisto mentions 'la noble conversación de tus delicados miembros', it is Melibea who openly professes her enjoyment: 'Señor, yo soy la que gozo, yo la que gano' (S. 223; M. 249).

Alternating with the acts in which Calisto and Melibea's love develops into reckless passion are Acts 15, 17 and 19, which focus on Elicia and Areusa as the merciless avengers of crime. It is here that we are reminded most of Seneca's tragedies, albeit in parodic fashion. Act 15 opens with Elicia's speeding to Areusa's house as the woeful messenger of death. Hearing Areusa's screams she fears that her friend may already have heard the news of Celestina's murder and the servants' death, thus spoiling her 'albricias de dolor que por tal mensaje se ganan' (S. 198; M. 274). Elicia's opening line thus reveals her as another victim of that *libido dolendi* which had characterized Pleberio's lament. As her lamentations, 'llore, llore, vierte lágrimas . . . Mese aquellos cabellos, . . .', make clear, Elicia's speech and appearance seem in many ways to be modelled on the typical messenger in Seneca's tragedies – an impression reinforced by Areusa's apprehensive reactions (cf. *Hippolytus*, vv. 991–6; *Troades*, vv. 1056–9; *Thyestes*, vv. 633–40). Scarcely recognizing her friend, Areusa waits in suspense as Elicia continues in her complaint, 'Gran dolor, gran pérdida', alternating with Areusa's impatient exhortations: 'dímelo, no te meses, no te rascuñes ni maltrates' (S. 199; M. 275–6). When, finally, Elicia announces the deaths of Parmeno, Sempronio and Celestina, Areusa is unstoppable in her lamentations: ¡Oh fuerte tribulación! ¡Oh dolorosas nuevas, dignas de mortal lloro! ¡Oh acelerados desastres! ¡Oh pérdida incurable!' (*ibid.*).

In striking contrast to this theatrical outpouring of woe one cannot help noticing Areusa's earlier crude insults and harsh recriminations against the ruffian Centurio. By placing two such opposite speech-patterns side by side, Rojas, in all likelihood, wanted to make the same points as in the original version. But while his target in the *Comedia* was scholastic and literary convention, in the *Tragicomedia* he mocks the dramatic pathos of the Senecan tragedy.

Recounting the whole sad story to Areusa, Elicia works herself up into such a frenzy that, like Melibea in Act 4 and the servants in Act 12, she loses control: 'Ay mezquina, que me salgo de seso' (S. 201; M. 278). And so her rage goes on, reaching its climax in her cursing of Calisto and Melibea, 'causadores de tantas muertes'.

Elicia's imprecations again remind us of Seneca's tragedies, and particularly of *Medea*, where the protagonist curses Jason and Creusa's wedding. But, while Medea in Seneca's tragedy defies the whole universe (vv. 397–425), Elicia's wrath is directed at the small details of Melibea's garden. May the soft grasses turn into serpents and songs into tears, she bursts out; let the trees become bare and the sweet-smelling flowers turn black. After these dramatic beginnings, Elicia lapses into crude language, lashing out against Calisto, 'aquel vil de poco sentimiento', who in spite of everything that has happened keeps visiting his 'estiércol de Melibea' (S. 202; M. 279).

Meanwhile, Elicia's recapitulation of events is interspersed with

Petrarchan quotations complemented by a Senecan moral on greed. Thus she explains how Calisto's desire for Melibea at one point seemed so unexpectedly close to fulfilment, that, in extreme gratitude, the lover gave Celestina the golden chain. This, in turn, made Celestina's greed for the precious metal so overpowering that she refused to share the booty with the servants, who, as a result, had become 'muy enojados'.

At this point Elicia, in tune with the interpolation in Act 13, clearly sides with the servants, explaining how they had been at a loss as to what to do until, on seeing Celestina's greed, they resorted to force. Elicia does not condemn the servants, but instead reports how, realizing their crime, they jumped out of a high window, were apprehended and then, without delay, beheaded.

Areusa's reaction to the disasters also goes through various stages. A first impulse upon hearing about Parmeno's death is regret concerning the short-lived pleasure she has enjoyed. But then, in truly Stoic fashion, she pulls herself together and tells Elicia to wipe away her tears. However, the very thought that crying is no remedy for sorrow in turn suggests a very non-Senecan remedy: 'Y muchas cosas se pueden vengar que es imposible remediar', she adds (S. 201; M.278).

With this suggestion Rojas again takes us back to the subject-matter of Seneca's tragedies. These, being a passionate *contra-exemplum* of Seneca's creed, deal with uncontrolled anger and love (cf. 'frenare nescit iras/Medea, non amores', *Medea*, vv. 866–7) and with crime avenged by greater crime (cf. 'scelera non ulcisceris,/nisi vincis', *Thyestes*, vv. 195–6). By contrast, in his moral philosophy Seneca insists on unconditional control of the *affectus*, and of anger especially, because this passion generates a desire for bloodthirsty revenge (*De Ira* 1, 5, 3). This particular passage of *De Ira* was also extracted in the 'Tratado de la ira' of the *Copilación*, to which the commentator added 'la cual venganza trae consigo muchos peligros' (*CL* 5). Interestingly, the sections on anger in the *Copilación* are followed by a 'Tratado de la venganza' extracted from Seneca's *De Clementia* 1. Here, the compiler highlighted the sweet satisfaction which results from avenging the perceived wrong. This the marginal gloss, basing itself on Aristotle, elucidates: 'aquello que de la saña bulló en el corazón del varón es más dulce que la miel, y esta dulzura y delectación y solaz han los que se vengan'. When summing up what Seneca says in a later passage, the commentator explains that successful revenge also gives the illusion of power. This is something on which Seneca does not dwell any further in *De Clementia*, but which is an important theme in his tragedies.

The illusion of power is eminently applicable to Areusa and Elicia, who in Act 9 expressed their contempt for and frustration with the idle rich. It is thus only logical that the girls' anger should now degenerate into revenge as they plot how to have Calisto killed by the same Centurio that Areusa had thrown out so unceremoniously moments before. With this excursion into the excessive effects of anger, the girls themselves join the cast of those slaves to their *affectus* whose life, for that reason, goes against nature. Indeed, both anger and revenge are considered contrary to nature (cf. *De Ira* 1, 5, 3 and 1, 6, 5), while mercy comes naturally to all: 'est ergo ut dicebam, clementia omnibus quidem hominibus secundum naturam' (*De Clem.* 1, 5, 2).

With the prospect of sweet revenge Elicia follows Areusa's advice and stops crying. Given the new emphasis on sorrow and tears, it is only natural that Rojas should have had another look at Seneca's *Consolationes*. The consolations written to Marcia and Helvia seemed not quite appropriate for the context of the *Tragicomedia*, as in one Seneca admonishes Marcia to stop grieving for the loss of a son, and in the other tells Helvia, his mother, not to feel too sorry about his own banishment. The *Consolatio ad Polybium*, however, seemed more in tune with the tragic ending of *Celestina*, as here the recipient of Seneca's consolatory words is a young man in mourning for his beloved brother. In fact, the definition of excessive grieving as 'libido dolendi' stems from this book (4, 1) and thus may well have provided the sub-text for the show of sorrow put up by Elicia and Areusa. There are, indeed, a few reminiscences of this particular *Consolatio* in the 'Tratado de Centurio'. For instance, the *sententia* which accompanies Areusa's admonishment to Elicia to wipe away her tears – 'como sea el primer oficio que en naciendo hacemos llorar' (S. 209; M. 283) – parallels Seneca's words to Polybius: '[natura] primum nascentium hominum fletum esse voluit' (*Poly.* 4, 3).

In this particular *Consolatio*, Seneca also talks about how easy it is to replace a deceased friend – 'in locum amissorum posset alios substituere' (*ibid.* 2, 4,) – of which we hear an echo in Areusa's quotation from Petrarch: 'con nuevo amor olvidarás los viejos' (S. 202; M. 280; D. 146).

In Act 17 Elicia takes up the argument again, painfully aware that mourning neither becomes her nor does much for her business. Realizing that Sempronio would not have mourned her death, she ceases to mourn him, thus making concrete the advice Seneca gives Polybius (cf. *Poly.* 5, 1). 'Quiero, pues, deponer el luto, dejar tristeza, despedir las lágrimas, que tan aparejadas han estado a salir', she decides (S. 208; M. 283) – a resolution which again parallels Seneca's words to Polybius: 'Proinde parcamus lacrimis nihil proficientibus . . . Qui si nos torquet, non adiuvat, primo quoque tempore deponendus est . . .' (*ibid.* 4, 1). The Senecan reminiscence is preceded by the Petrarchan quotation, taken from the Index, on 'vale más un día del hombre discreto que toda la vida del necio y simple' (D. 146) which echoes many similar sayings by Seneca. When Elicia then considers how all this crying damages her eyes, we are again reminded of Seneca's warning to Polybius: 'oculos tuos . . . sine ullo flendi fine et conturbat idem et exhaurit' (*ibid.* 5, 3).

The irony here is that Seneca urges Polybius to get on with his life since he is such a public figure. Elicia, too, realizes that all this mourning is bad for business and that she too is a 'public woman'. Confronted by these thoughts, she decides to put herself, her house and her garden in order, but not before visiting Areusa, for whom she now professes deep friendship. Meanwhile, for Areusa business has never been better; and here, too, we notice a change. In the *Comedia*, Areusa was not a real prostitute, but in the additional acts she is, in Tristan's words, a 'marcada ramera' (S. 219; M. 302) who is obviously relishing her freedom from Celestina's tutelage: 'Quizá por bien fue para entrambas la muerte de Celestina, que yo ya siento la mejoría más que antes', she confesses (S. 209; M. 284).

Clearly, Areusa has emulated her teacher in a spectacular way, including in her powers of verbal persuasion. Here, Celestina's rhetoric pales when compared to Areusa's skills in making Sosia reveal the secret of his master's next encounter with Melibea. Hinting at some false rumours that Sosia may inadvertently have spread, Areusa quotes the pseudo-Senecan *sententia* 'no confíes que tu amigo te ha de tener secreto de lo que le dijeres, pues tú no lo sabes a ti mismo tener' (S. 211; M. 286). As we have noted before, this was common knowledge and goes back to at least three sources: to the *De Moribus*, number 16, whence it passed to *Amonestamientos y doctrinas*, number 25, and Proverbio 310 (R. 263). Areusa thus manages to make Sosia divulge the real details of Calisto's next assignation, after which she dismisses him without further ado. Quite rightly, she feels she has outdone her teacher: 'que otra arte es ésta que la de Celestina' (S. 213; M. 288). Indeed, Celestina's art seems quite innocent when compared to Areusa's 'total war'.

The man Areusa has chosen to carry out her intent is Centurio. He accepts the job, offering a repertory of 770 types of murder. Areusa leaves it to him to decide what kind of death he wants to inflict, with the words 'de cualquier muerte holgaremos' (S. 217; M. 294). However, since Centurio is reluctant to carry out the commission, he decides to delegate the job to the lame Traso and his friends, whom he instructs only to scare Calisto and his servants off.[8] As a result, Areusa and Elicia are denied the sweet satisfaction of revenge, this being in accordance with the maxim expressed in *Medea* that hatred, if publicized, loses its chance for revenge ('professa perdunt odia vindictae locum', v. 154). Thus Act 19 skilfully blends in with the end of the original Act 14, where Calisto meets his unheroic death by falling off the ladder.

In many ways, the *Tratado de Centurio* is an adaptation and an emulation of foregoing events. Areusa becomes a superlative Celestina, and Centurio is baser than any representative of the *vulgus* we have met so far. The passions dealt with are despair and revenge, two extreme *affecti* analysed in Seneca's *Consolationes* and tragedies.

Meanwhile, Calisto and Melibea's prolonged love affair has reached extreme proportions as well. Their passion is consciously modelled on a Senecan *affectus amantium* knowing no other bond than the possession of each other (cf. *Ep.* 9).

Clearly the great addition heralds a taste for violence and passion which Seneca satisfied completely in his tragedies. This side of Seneca's writing was especially appreciated in the sixteenth century, when playwrights began to model their first attempts in the tragic genre on Seneca's dramatic work. The marked change in the tone of the added acts would therefore seem to point not to a different author, but to a shift from Seneca the philosopher to Seneca the tragedian, so making *Celestina* straddle two eras in literary fashion and two kinds of Senecan reception. On the one hand, the fifteenth-century *Comedia* transmits Seneca's moral philosophy through the fictionalization of an all-encompassing *affectus*, while the early sixteenth-century *Tragicomedia* conveys the extreme moods of blind *furor*.

In its final form, *Celestina* was intended to appeal to the widest possible readership. The neo-Stoics would delight in the persisting Senecan content, while the emerging taste for pathos was met by the various interpolations and additions.

The enduring achievement of Rojas, however, was the skill with which he accommodated all and every reader's preferences while remaining faithful to Seneca, the authority *par excellence* on man's varying afflictions. What made *Celestina* a book for all seasons and all readers was Rojas' own art in portraying what is described in the Prologue as the 'muchos afectos diversos y variedades que de esta nuestra flaca humanidad nos provienen'.

Conclusion

The fifteenth-century reader's knowledge of Seneca's philosophy was largely determined by a process which had through the ages expanded, distorted and reduced Seneca's words to a code of behaviour known as 'ciencia moral'. In addition, the extensive introductions, prologues and commentaries that accompanied contemporary translations had prepared the new readers for the 'right' reception of the classics, providing them with a handy short-cut to much Aristotelian, Epicurean and Christian thought as a bonus.

It was this potted wisdom that would find its literary expression as 'fontecicas de filosofía' in *Celestina* at the end of the century, making the book's dialogues one long collage of *sententiae* gathered together in a new and surprising setting. Underlying it all, however, is the *ars vivendi* of Seneca's *De Vita Beata*, which informed so much fifteenth-century thinking. *Bienaventurados* all of the characters aspire to be, whether they are in the pursuit of love, wealth or status. But each of them fails miserably in his quest, despite abundant quotations from moral philosophy.

The many *sententiae* in *Celestina* should not be seen as a regrettable or even, at best, a disposable ingredient of the characters' speech. On the contrary, they have a definite function, which is to illustrate the uses and abuses of language. The relation between speech and action is a topic closely related to Seneca's thinking on reason, simplicity and truth. Verbosity, jargon and the excessive use of maxims and metaphors all contravene Nature's harmony and beauty; the worst offence, however, takes place when a speaker's words are not in harmony with his deeds. 'Verbis opera concordent' (*Ep.* 20, 2) is an important point of philosophy, of which the speech-acts in *Celestina* are such an eloquent *contra-exemplum*. *Sentencia* and *ficción* are thus two inseparable elements in the *Tragicomedia*, although their relation and proportion vary at each consecutive stage in the composition of the book.

Although we know nothing of the author of the first act, one fact does emerge from the use he makes of the Senecan *sententia*. His references are less to the popular sentence-collections or the annotated translations, than to Seneca's work in the original Latin. The first author of *Celestina* is thus revealed as a sound Latin scholar who was nonetheless very familiar with those readers who only had a second-hand knowledge of Seneca's philosophy. It is their speech-patterns that he imitates in the dialogue, and it is their pseudo-knowledge of moral philosophy that he mocks through the art of quotation. The author's ingenious blending of the *sententia*'s original content into the new context reaches a climax in the final scene when Celestina and Parmeno are engaged in an unequal battle of quotemanship. Meanwhile, readers familiar with Seneca's work would have identified the ironic subtext of the debate as Seneca's *Epistulae Morales*.

From the very beginning of Act 1 the author directed his readers' attention to these letters through the name he chose for his protagonist. Epistula 47, which deals with the precarious relationship between master and slaves, using as illustration an anecdote about a certain Callistus, contains the moral message that very few can control their passions, which are portrayed as so many unruly servants. Once passion has taken hold of man, the natural order is disturbed and servants govern their masters, day turns into night, life becomes death.

Seneca's canon served as inspiration for many more themes. Sorrow (*dolor*) and pleasure (*deleite*), friendship (*amistad*) and gifts (*galardones*) and especially the danger of associating with the *vulgo* (Celestina's world) are all points of Seneca's philosophy which were waiting to be developed into a full-scale fiction.

We know only little more of the author of the 16-act *Comedia*. But two things are clear from the text: he was a student of law, and he added Petrarch to his frame of reference. Again it is the use of the *sententia* that tells us more about the author and his intent. On the one hand Rojas shared the first author's interest in Seneca's *Epistulae Morales* – indeed he owned a translation of it – and on the other he used Pero Díaz's *Proverbios de Séneca* as a handy checklist for his quotations.

That apart, Rojas' technique in mixing *sententiae* with the most down-to-earth language is very similar to that of the first author. By misquoting, twisting words or giving only half a *sententia*, both authors leave it to their readers to fill in the gaps. Thus the ironic juxtaposition of the borrowed text and its new setting subtly hint at both authors' hidden intention: a gentle mockery of the new readers' superficial knowledge of moral philosophy, as perceived through sentence collections and annotated translations.

The fact that Rojas adds Petrarch to his own frame of reference changes his target but not his intent. With his many quotations from Petrarch's prose work, Rojas may well have wanted to include the speech-patterns of the liberal arts student. In this way, Petrarch's Index joins the *Proverbios de Séneca* as a handy storehouse of proverbial wisdom and famous sayings. In addition, the Petrarchan quotations serve to underline the pedantry, poetic affectation and name-dropping of the speaker, thus not only imitating the speech-patterns of the parvenu in learning but also mocking the type of literary mind which venerated 'aquel orador y poeta Petrarca'. Seneca on the one hand and Petrarch on the other may well have become two cult figures whom Rojas felt the need to unmask. This does not mean that Rojas himself was unimpressed by the two authors; rather that he was amused by the new readers' show of erudition and 'poetics' while all the while hinting at the discrepancy between his characters' language and behaviour.

In other ways as well, Rojas made concrete the message contained in the first author's *sententiae*. The protagonists' passion is seen as the same disease (*morbus*) as underlies their artificial speech, while their 'affair' is developed along the same lines as the friendship between the servants. Both relationships are concrete forms of slavery (*servitus*), greed (*cupiditas*) and hard bargaining (*negotiatio*) and are presented in the light of an overriding madness (*insania*).

Rojas not only expanded the first author's Senecan thinking on the one and many faces of *affectus*; he also added anger as yet another form of insanity. In his *De Ira* Seneca qualifies rage, albeit a 'brevis insania', as the most destructive of all the passions. Judging by the fifteenth-century re-working of an earlier translation and the many extracts of that book in Cartagena and Pero Díaz, the average reader was familiar with the implications of this particular *affectus*. The 'Furia de Melibea' can thus be read as a manifestation of anger in the Senecan sense of the word – a reading which is supported by many quotations from Pero Díaz's *Proverbios* on the topic. The same anger, spilling into rage, is also at the root of the servants' murder of Celestina, and, last but not least, *ira* is what spurs Melibea's mad suicide. In all these instances Rojas stresses the fact that those in the grip of *ira* are 'sin seso': that is, they have lost their sense of reason and therefore control.

Anger, like all *affecti*, is a form of *cupiditas*, translated as 'codicia' in the Spanish versions of Seneca's writing. Anger, therefore, generates a 'codicia de venganza', in the same way as passionate love becomes a 'codicia de hermosura', false friendship a 'codicia de provecho' and wealth a 'codicia de honra y gloria'. Excessive *cupiditas* then turns into a *libido* which can be applied to the irrational decision to take one's life or excessive weeping for the loss of a beloved. Thus readers familiar with Seneca's philosophy would have recognized Melibea's demise as a *libido moriendi* and Pleberio's long lament as a *libido dolendi*.

To read Celestina as an *exemplum* of the one and many faces of *affectus* would seem to contradict the force of magic as an explanation for the tragic ending. But, although Stoic thinking ruled out any supernatural powers in the affairs of man, Seneca nevertheless structured his tragedy *Medea* around witchcraft and magic. Just as in this tragedy Medea's preparations and incantations add an extra touch of drama to the story of love, anger and revenge, so too Celestina's witchcraft adds a dramatic dimension of awe to the otherwise rational Stoic message.

Rojas' borrowing from the tragedies is, for the most part, limited to certain scenes and dialogue structures. The irony, however, is that along with these reminiscences Rojas conveyed, perhaps unwittingly, the tragic mood of Seneca's dramatic work to his readers.

It has been said that once words are uttered they cease to be the author's and become the property of the readers or listeners. Nowhere is this more true than in the reception of Rojas' *Comedia*. Judging by his remarks in the Prologue, most of his readers disagreed with his decision to continue the first author's sketch in the comic rather than the tragic vein and insisted on the prolongation of the love affair.

If anything, the transition from *Comedia* to *Tragicomedia* is even more puzzling than the step from first fragment to 16 acts. All we know here is that Rojas was annoyed at having to set pen to paper again.

As far as the interpolations are concerned, readers may well have had a say in how to change subtly the orientation of the *Comedia*. Ironically, the explanatory amplifications take the place of the unwritten subtext of the original version, thus diminishing the intellectual involvement of the reader. On the other hand, by catering to all his readers' 'dísonos juicios', Rojas only added to the confusion as far as the overall interpretation of his fiction was concerned.

The authorship of the five added acts will always be a point of debate. It has been argued that Rojas was not the author of 'the great addition'. However, judging by the continued ingenious use of the *sententia*, a technique requiring both skill and experience, we must deduce that Rojas was the mastermind behind, if not the sole author of, the added five acts. While it is true that the mood and tone change radically because of the changes necessary to turn the story into a tragi-comedy, a reason can also be found in Seneca's tragedies, which now begin to be a more explicit frame of reference.

In contrast to Seneca's prose, where his philosophy is illustrated with down-to-earth anecdotes, his tragedies are a full-scale poetization of his message through the extreme behaviour of kings and gods. Thus on the stage the diverse manifestations of *affectus* and *insania* are exaggerated into *libido* and *furor*, and rage turns into a desire for bloodthirsty revenge. Similarly, albeit always on the domestic level, in the *Tragicomedia* Areusa and Elicia are portrayed as two avenging furies, Calisto and Melibea's love turns into a reckless passion, and the *vulgus* becomes openly criminal.

In view of the great vogue which Seneca's dramatic work was to enjoy among the next generation of humanists, it is very likely that Rojas' contemporaries were beginning to appreciate Seneca's tragedies not because of their moral content, but precisely on account of their passionate form of expression. This being so, we might in turn share a conspiratorial chuckle with Rojas, because, by giving his readers that for which they were clamouring, he intensified his mockery of the literary student's tastes and sensibilities.

The suggestion that the love story of Calisto and Melibea was in fact a parody of the courtly love tradition has substantially altered our perception of the book. Taking the *sententia*, the backbone of the text, as a guide, I have attempted to show that we can extend the parody to include the medieval Senecan tradition as expressed in a pseudo-philosophy. In addition, Rojas broadened the range of targets by including the poetics of the Petrarchan quotation and the passionate mood of the Senecan tragedy.

And so we see that the *Tragicomedia de Calisto y Melibea* is perhaps not as serious or even as pessimistic as it might appear to be, because of the objective distance afforded by the mood of parody. The authors' target was clearly a literary fashion nurtured by, on the one hand, sentimental romances and Cancionero poetry and, on the other, by aphoristic literature and books of popular philosophy.

Whether or not the readers agreed, or even saw the point, the authors of *Celestina* did have a message, which we can only decipher through the speech-patterns of the dialogue. These, as has been shown, reflect both literary and scholastic conventions, mixed in with the realistic and often crudely explicit. When we then contrast the speakers' misuse of the *sententia* with the Stoic irony of the subtext, we must conclude that the authors of *Celestina* challenged tradition and questioned authority through the subtle means of parody.

In doing this, the authors were simply following Seneca's advice to the letter, because, ironically, the philosopher who had given his name to a tradition had advocated that his readers should not follow the example of the majority or act and speak 'al hilo de la gente'. Thus, with their fiction, the authors of *Celestina* show themselves to be of a truly Senecan independence of mind in an age of outmoded conventions and waning convictions.

Notes

1. Towards a Senecan tradition

1. See Paul Faider, *Etudes sur Sénèque* (Ghent, 1921); W. Trillitzch, *Seneca im literarischen Urteil der Antike* (Amsterdam, 1971); Miriam T. Griffin, 'Imago vitae suae', in C. D. N. Costa (ed.), *Seneca* (London, 1974), pp. 1–38; Karl Alfred Blüher, *Seneca en España* (Madrid 1983), translated from *Seneca in Spanien* (Munich, 1969).
2. Faider, pp. 83–107; J. N. Sevenster, *Paul and Seneca* (Leiden, 1961); L. D. Reynolds, *The Medieval Tradition of Seneca's Letters* (Oxford, 1965), pp. 82–9, 112–13; E. Liénard, 'Sur la correspondance apocryphe de Sénèque et de Saint Paul', *Revue belge de phil. et hist.*, 11 (1932), 5–23. For a modern edition of the correspondence, see C. W. Barlow (ed.), *Epistulae Senecae ad Paulum et Pauli ad Senecam (quae vocantur)* (Rome, 1938).
3. C. W. Barlow (ed.), *Martini Episcopi Bracarensis Opera Omnia* (New Haven, 1950).
4. See J. Loth, 'Un nouveau texte du traité de Sénèque *De Remediis Fortuitorum*', *Revue de Philologie*, n.s. 12 (1888), 120 n.; K. Munscher, *Senecas Werke. Untersuchungen zur Abfassungszeit und Echtheit*, *Philologus*, Suppl. 16 (Leipzig, 1923), pp. 62, 143; K. Heitmann, 'Le genesi del *De Remediis Utriusque Fortunae* del Petrarca', *Convivium*, 25 (1957), 9–30.
5. Nicholas G. Round, 'The medieval reputation of the *Proverbia Senecae*: a partial survey based on recorded MSS', *Proceedings of the Royal Irish Academy*, 72, sec. c, no. 5 (1972), 103–51.
6. M. B. Parkes, 'The influence of the concepts of *ordinatio* and *compilatio* on the development of the book, in J. J. G. Alexander and M. T. Gibson (eds.), *Medieval Learning and Literature: Essays presented to Richard William Hunt* (Oxford, 1976), pp. 115–41.
7. Round, 'The medieval reputation . . .', p. 134 n.; Blüher, pp. 131–6.
8. M. M. Phillips, 'Erasmus and the classics', in T. A. Dorey (ed.), *Erasmus* (London, 1970); M. W. Croll, 'Juste Lipse et le mouvement anticicéronien à la fin du XVIe siècle', *Revue du seizième siècle*, 2 (1914), 220–42; G. Williamson, *The Senecan Amble: A Study in Prose from Bacon to Collier* (London, 1951); Henry Ettinghausen, *Francisco de Quevedo and the Neo-Stoic Movement* (Oxford, 1972).
9. Jean Jacquot (ed.), *Les Tragédies de Sénèque et le théâtre de la Renaissance* (Paris, 1964); H. B. Charlton, *The Senecan Tradition in Renaissance Tragedy* (Manchester, 1974); Alfredo Hermenegildo, *La tragedia en el renacimiento español* (Barcelona, 1973).
10. A. R. D. Pagden, 'The diffusion of Aristotle's moral philosophy in Spain, ca. 1400–ca. 1600', *Traditio*, 31 (1975), 287–313; Nicholas G. Round, 'The shadow of a philosopher: medieval Castilian images of Plato', *Journal of Hispanic Philology*, 3

145

(1978), 1–36; Rosalba Mascagna (ed.), *La rhetórica de M. Tullio Cicerón* (Naples, 1969).

11. Letizia A. Panizza, 'Gasparino Barrizza's commentaries on Seneca's Letters', *Traditio*, 33 (1977), 297–358.

12. Alexander Birkenmajer, 'Der Streit des Alonso von Cartagena mit Leonardo Bruni Aretino', *Beiträge zur Geschichte der Philosophie des Mittelalters* (1922), 129–210; P. E. Russell and A. R. D. Pagden, 'Nueva luz sobre una versión española cuatrocentista de la *Etica a Nicomaco*: Bodleian Library, Ms. Span. D.1.', in *Homenaje a Guillermo Guastavino* (Madrid, 1974), pp. 125–46; Ottavio Di Camilo, *El humanismo castellano del siglo XV* (Valencia, 1976), pp. 203–26.

13. For the question of translating 'según el seso', see Margherita Morreale, 'Apuntes para la historia de la traducción en la Edad Media', *Revista de literatura*, 15 (1959), 3–10; Olga T. Impey, 'Alfonso de Cartagena, traductor de Séneca y precursor del humanismo español', *Prohemio*, 3 (1972), 473–94. On medieval translations in general, see M. Menéndez Pelayo, *Biblioteca de traductores españoles* (Santander, 1952); Jacques Monfrin, 'Humanisme et traductions au moyen âge', *Journal des Savants*, 3 (1963), 161–90; Peter E. Russell, *Traducciones y traductores en la península ibérica (1400–1550)* (Barcelona, 1985).

14. See J. N. H. Lawrance, 'Nuño de Guzmán and early Spanish humanism: some reconsiderations', *Medium Ævum*, 51 (1982), 55–85; *idem*, 'Nuño de Guzmán: life and works' (doct. diss., University of Oxford, 1983).

15. See Luciano Serrano, *Los conversos D. Pablo de Santa María y D. Alonso de Cartagena* (Madrid, 1942); Francisco Cantera Burgos, *Alvar García de Santa María y su familia de conversos* (Madrid, 1952).

16. Juan de Lucena, *Diálogo de vita beata*, in Giovanni M. Bertini (ed.), *Testi Spagnoli del secolo XV* (Turin, 1950), p. 102.

17. See Peter E. Russell, 'Las armas contra las letras; para una definición del humanismo español del siglo XV', in *Temas*, pp. 207–39; Ottavio Di Camillo, *El humanismo castellano del siglo XV* (Valencia, 1976), and N. G. Round's review, *Bulletin of Hispanic Studies*, 56:1 (1979), 59–61; Jeremy N. H. Lawrance, *Una epístola de Alfonso de Cartagena sobre la educación y los estudios literarios* (Barcelona, 1979); and especially *idem*, 'The spread of lay literacy in late medieval Castile', *Bulletin of Hispanic Studies*, 62 (1985), 79–94.

18. Mario Schiff, *La bibliothèque du Marquis de Santillane* (Paris, 1905), pp. 104–11; M. Eusebi, 'Le piú antiche traduzione francese delle *Lettere Morale* di Seneca e i suoi derrivati', *Romania*, 91 (1970), 1–47.

19. Angel Gómez Moreno, 'Una carta del marqués de Santillana', *Revista de filología española*, 63 (1983), 15–22; Ruth J. Dean and Samuel G. Armistead, 'A fifteenth-century Spanish book list', *The Library Chronicle*, 40: *Bibliographical Studies in Honour of Rudolf Hirsch* (1974), 73–87; F. del Valle Lersundi, 'Documentos referentes a Fernando de Rojas', *Revista de filología española*, 16 (1929), 385–96.

20. Nicholas G. Round, 'Las traducciones medievales catalanas y castellanas de las tragedias de Séneca', *Anuario de estudios medievales*, 9 (1974–9), 187–227.

21. Nicholas Round, 'Pero Díaz de Toledo: a study of a 15th-century "converso" translator in his background' (doct. dis., University of Oxford, 1967); Barbara Riss, 'Pero Díaz de Toledo's *Proverbios de Séneca*: an annotated edition of MS S-II-10 of the Escorial Library (Spanish text)' (doct. diss., University of California, 1979), pp. iv–lvii.

22. Diosdado García Rojo & Gonzalo Ortiz de Montalbán (eds.), *Catálogo de incunables de la Biblioteca Nacional* (Madrid, 1945), pp. 435–9; F. J. Norton, *Printing in Spain, 1501–1520* (Cambridge, 1966); T. S. Beardsley, *Hispano-Classical Translations printed between 1482 and 1699* (Pittsburgh, 1970).

23. Karl Kohut, 'La posición de la literatura en los sistemas científicos del siglo XV', *Iberoromania*, n.s. 7 (1978), 67–87.
24. See the edition by R. Foulché-Delbosc, in *Revue Hispanique*, 10 (1904), 5–154.

2. Senecan commentary as a frame of reference

1. Commentaries were not limited to works of philosophy alone. Villena's version of the *Aeneid* and López de Ayala's translation from the French of Livy's *Decades* I–III include their own glosses as well as those added by earlier transmitters. Nor do we find commentaries only in translated works. Pero Díaz de Toledo wrote glosses to Santillana's *Proverbios morales*; an anonymous commentator annotated Mena's *Laberinto*; and Pulgar provided commentary to the *Coplas de Mingo Revulgo*. For more ample references, see Julian Weiss, 'The poetic concept of his art: Castilian vernacular poetry circa 1400–1600' (doct. diss., University of Oxford, 1984). The following translations of Seneca's genuine and apocryphal works are without glosses: *El libro de Séneca de la ira y saña* (Escorial S-II-14); *Obra y tratado de las costumbres* (BN 6962); *Cartas que escribió Séneca a Paulo y Paulo a Séneca* (BN 10806) and *Las tragedias de Séneca* (BN 7088).
2. See R. R. Bolgar, *The Classical Heritage and its Beneficiaries* (Cambridge, 1954); idem (ed.), *Classical Influences on European Culture A.D. 500–1500* (Cambridge, 1971); Harold Hagendahl, *Latin Fathers and the Classics* (Goteborg, 1958); J. E. Sandys, *A History of Classical Scholarship* (New York, 1967).
3. For good introductory reading, see Edward Vernon Arnold, *Roman Stoicism* (London, 1911; re-issued 1958); Ludwig Edelstein, *The Meaning of Stoicism* (Cambridge, Mass., 1966); Arthur Bodson, *La morale sociale des derniers Stoiciens, Sénèque, Epictète et Marc Aurèle* (Paris, 1967); William Hamilton Baird, *The Tenets of Stoicism* (Toronto, 1973); A. L. Motto, *Seneca*, Twayne World Authors Series, 268 (Boston, 1973); C. D. N. Costa (ed.), *Seneca* (London, 1974); M. T. Griffin, *Seneca, a Philosopher in Politics* (Oxford, 1976); John M. Rist (ed.), *The Stoics* (Berkeley, 1978).
4. For an introduction to reception aesthetics, see Hans Robert Jauss, *Toward an Aesthetic of Reception* (Minneapolis, 1982), translated from the German; idem, 'Literary history as a challenge to literary theory', in Ralph Cohen (ed.), *New Directions in Literary Theory* (London, 1974), pp. 11–41; idem, 'The alterity and modernity of medieval literature', in *New Literary History*, 10:2 (1979), 181–227.
5. On the subject of Fortune and Providence, see Juan de Dios Mendoza Negrillo, S. J., *Fortuna y Providencia en la literature castellana del siglo XV*, BRAE, 27 (Madrid, 1973).
6. See María Rosa Lida de Malkiel, *La originalidad artística de La Celestina* (Buenos Aires, 1962), p. 169, n. 2; Stephen Gilman, *The Spain of Fernando de Rojas* (Princeton, 1972), p. 82.
7. See J. M. Rist, *Epicurus: an Introduction* (Cambridge, Mass., 1972). Controversy between Epicureanism and Christian dogma was not taken up publicly until the seventeenth century, following the publication of Pierre Gassendi's *De Vita et Moribus Epicuri Libri Octo* (Lyon, 1647). See on this issue J. S. Spink, *French Free Thought from Gassendi to Voltaire* (London, 1960), chapter 8, 'The rehabilitation of Epicurus' (pp. 133–68); Joseph A. Mazzeo, *Renaissance and Revolution* (London, 1967), chapter 6, 'The idea of progress' (pp. 275–336) and my 'The Jesuits as masters of rhetoric and drama', *Revista Canadiense de Estudios Hispánicos*, 10 (1985–6), 375–87.
8. See Angel Alcalá, 'El neoepicureismo y la intención de *La Celestina*: notas para una re-lección', *Romanische Forschungen*, 88 (1976), 224–45; idem, 'Rojas y el

neoepicureismo', in Manuel Criado de Val (ed.), *La Celestina y su contorno social,*
Actas del I congreso sobre *La Celestina* (Barcelona, 1977), pp. 35–50.

9. See Leslie P. Turano, 'Aristotle and the art of persuasion in *Celestina*' (doct. diss.,
University of London, 1985); also L. Ijsseling, *Rhetoric and Philosophy in Conflict: an
Historical Survey* (The Hague, 1976).

10. See N. G. Round, 'Conduct and values in *La Celestina*', in F. W. Hodcroft *et al.*
(eds.), *Mediæval and Renaissance Studies on Spain and Portugal in Honour of P. E. Russell*
(Oxford, 1981), pp. 38–52.

3. The 'antiguo autor' as a reader of Seneca

1. See Rudolf Hirsch, *Printing, Selling and Reading, 1450–1550* (Wiesbaden, 1967); F.
J. Norton, *Printing in Spain, 1501–1520* (Cambridge, 1966); Stephen Gilman, *The
Spain of Fernando de Rojas* (Princeton, 1972), p. 317.

2. See Herman Meyer, *The Poetics of Quotation in the European Novel* (Princeton, 1968),
translated from the German (Stuttgart, 1961 and 1967), p. 32. See also D. A.
Russell, 'De imitatione', in David West and Tony Woodman (eds.), *Creative
Imitation and Latin Literature* (Cambridge, 1979), pp. 1–16; and for parody, see
Linda Hutcheon, *A Theory of Parody* (London, 1985).

3. The following source studies have noted Senecan quotations. MS BN 17631,
commonly known as 'Celestina comentada', more or less correctly records the
provenance of various *sententiae*: see P. E. Russell, 'El primer comentario crítico de
La Celestina: cómo un legista del siglo XVI interpreta la *Tragicomedia*', in *Temas de
"La Celestina"* (Barcelona, 1978), pp. 293–332; F. Castro Guisasola, *Observaciones
sobre las fuentes literarias de "La Celestina"*, Revista de filología Española, Anejo 5
(1924); Blüher, pp. 161–5; and J. L. Heller and R. L. Grismer, 'Seneca in the
celestinesque novel', *Hispanic Review*, 12 (1944), 29–48.

4. See J. M. Aguirre, *Calisto y Melibea, amantes cortesanos* (Zaragoza, 1962); A. D.
Deyermond, 'The textbook mishandled: Andreas Capellanus and the opening
scene of *La Celestina*', *Neophilologus*, 45 (1961), 218–21. June Hall Martin takes up
the argument in *Love's Fools: Aucassin, Troilus, Calisto and the Parody of the Courtly
Lover* (London, 1972), pp. 73–8. Erna Ruth Berndt, *Amor, muerte y fortuna en la
Celestina* (Madrid, 1963), pp. 15–27, relates the scene to courtly love, Cancionero
poetry and Boccaccio. See also Theodore L. Kassier, 'Cancionero poetry and the
Celestina: from metaphor to reality', *Hispanófila*, 56 (1976), 1–28; John Devlin, *La
Celestina: a Parody of Courtly Love: Towards a Realistic Interpretation of the Tragicomedia
de Calisto y Melibea* (New York, 1971); David Wise, 'Reflections on Andreas
Capellanus' *De Reprobatione Amoris* in Juan Ruíz, Alfonso Martínez and Fernando
de Rojas', *Hispania* (Stanford, Calif.), 63 (1980), 506–13; Round, 'Conduct and
values . . .'

5. In Greek Stoicism, sight was considered the most 'divine' of the senses. Roman
Stoics admitted a certain doubt in the criterion of a so-called 'mind-picture',
however. For instance, Seneca himself concedes the weakness of sight: 'visus
noster solita imbecillitate deceptus' (*NQ* 12, 3). Cf. Vernon Arnold, *Roman
Stoicism*, chapter 4, 'Of reason and speech' (pp. 128–35).

6. For Melibea's name, Castro Guisasola has recorded a Vergilian source. However, the name could equally well have been suggested to the first author by a
reading of Seneca, who was himself a great 'taker' and more than once quotes
Vergil: cf. 'O Meliboee, deus nobis haec otia fecit/namque erit ille mihi semper
deus', *Eclogue* i, 6, quoted in *Ep.* 73, and 'insere nunc, Meliboee, piros, pone ordine
vites', *Eclogue* i, 74, quoted in *Ep.* 101. Equally, the name of Areusa might have a
Senecan ring. In the *Consolatio ad Marciam* reference is made to an unidentified
philosopher called Areus, who is reputedly an authority on consolation.

7. For a similar explanation of love in *Celestina*, see G. A. Shipley, 'Concerting through conceit: unconventional uses of conventional sickness images in *La Celestina*', *Modern Language Review*, 70 (1975), 324–32.

8. In Latin, *popularis* has two meanings: 1) belonging to the people; and 2) directed to the people, in which case it has the pejorative meaning of demagogic or populist rhetoric. Rhetoric in *Celestina* has been attracting an increasing number of studies. See A. Samonà, *Aspetti del retoricismo nella 'Celestina'* (Rome, 1953); Charles F. Fraker, 'Rhetoric in the *Celestina*: another look', in *Aurum Saeculum Hispanum: Festschrift für Hans Flasche* (Wiesbaden, 1983), pp. 81–90; *idem*, 'Argument in the *Celestina*, and in its predecessors', *Revista de estudios hispánicos* (Puerto Rico), 9 (1984 for 1982): *Homenaje a Stephen Gilman*, pp. 81–6; Malcolm K. Read, *The Birth and Death of Language: Spanish Literature and Linguistics: 1300–1700* (Madrid, 1983), chapter 4, 'The rhetoric of social encounter: *La Celestina* and the Renaissance philosophy of language' (pp. 70–96); Leslie Turano, 'Aristotle and the art . . .'.

9. 'Los diez libros de las Eticas de Aristóteles presentados al muy magnífico y al muy virtuoso Juan de Guzmán Señor de la Algava', Bodleian MS Spanish d 1, fol. 100r. There are two printings of the *compendium*: Saragossa, 1488–91, and Seville, 1493. See A. Pagden, 'The diffusion . . .'

10. Cf. *Las epístolas de Séneca*, nos. 3, 6, 10, 19, 35, 37; the 'Tratado del amigo' of the *Copilación*, the *Amonestamientos y doctrinas*, nos. 3 and 7, the *Obra y tratado de las costumbres*, the *Título de la amistanza o del amigo*, etc.

11. Marciales gratuitously 'corrects' Rojas' text here by inserting 'no' before 'dexar' (M. 50). It is clear from his tampering with the text that the irony of the misquotation escaped him.

12. Cartagena obviously took a liking to this *sententia*, as he uses it himself in the Prologue to his translation of *De Providentia Dei*: 'Ca pues el hombre es una criatura mediana entre las sustancias apartadas que llamamos los ángeles y los animales irracionales y brutos, deleitarse debe más en aquello que le es común con la natura angelical que en aquello que mejor o tan bien como él sienten las bestias.' Finally, Juan de Lucena takes up the line in his *Diálogo de vita beata*, where he puts these words in Cartagena's mouth (168).

4. Fernando de Rojas continues the story: the 'Comedia de Calisto y Melibea'

1. The inventory in Rojas' will lists *Las epístolas de Séneca* under the rubric 'Libros de Romance'. These Rojas had willed to his wife, as against the 'Libros de Leyes', which were to go to his son, the lawyer. For a detailed list of the 49 Spanish titles, see F. del Valle Lersundi, 'Documentos'. For a partial discussion of Rojas' library, see Gilman, *The Spain*, pp. 430–56.

2. Richard M. Gummere's translation of this particular passage in Loeb's bilingual edition (1917) is a striking example of a nineteenth-century misconception of the Stoic *affectus*. With reference to the *affectus amantium*, Seneca says: 'ipse per se amor omnium aliarum rerum neglegens animos in cupiditate formae non sine spe mutuae caritatis accedit' (*Ep.* 9, 11). Gummere translates 'ipse per se amor' as 'true love' which 'kindles the soul with desire for the beautiful object, not without the hope of a return of the affection'. The fifteenth-century translator, mindful of Seneca's equation of this *affectus amantium* with an *insana amicitia*, and unencumbered by romantic notions of love and affection, translates the same passage in terms of lust (*codicia*) and sex (*común amor*).

3. See my refutation of Marciales above, chapter 3, note 11.

4. Juan de Lucena's *Diálogo de vita beata* argues exactly the same point. Here, in his role of 'El obispo', Cartagena scorns Juan de Mena for the same mistake Parmeno

is making: 'llaman los vulgares bien lo que las más veces es malo y si no malo, no bueno . . . despláceme tan grave varón, como tú, Joan de Mena, que te vayas como niño al hilo de gentes' (p. 116).

5. Seneca's ideas on anger have recently attracted attention from the psychologists: see W. S. Anderson, *Anger in Juvenal and Seneca* (Berkeley, 1964); A. Ellis, *Reason and Emotion in Psychotherapy* (New York, 1962); Hans Toch, 'The management of hostile aggression: Seneca as applied social psychologist', *American Psychologist* (1983), 1022–6.

6. See Berndt, *Amor, Muerte y Fortuna.*

7. For Pleberio's lament, see Bruce W. Wardropper, 'Pleberio's lament for Melibea and the medieval elegiac tradition', *Modern Language Notes*, 79 (1964), 140–52; E. M. Gerli, 'Pleberio's lament and two literary topoi: *expositor* and *planctus*', *Romanische Forschungen*, 88 (1976), 67–74; Peter N. Dunn, 'Pleberio's world', *PMLA*, 91 (1976), 406–19; Henry Mendeloff, 'Pleberio in contemporary *Celestina* criticism', *Romance Notes*, 13 (1971–2), 369–73; Charles F. Fraker, 'The importance of Pleberio's soliloquy', *Romanische Forschungen*, 78 (1968), 515–29; David Hook, ' "Para quién edifiqué torres?" ': a footnote on Pleberio's lament', *Forum for Modern Language Studies*, 14 (1978), 25–31.

8. Keith Whinnom, ' "El plebérico coraçon" and the authorship of Act 1 of *La Celestina*', *Hispanic Review*, 65 (1977), 195–9.

9. Marciales gives Clytemnestra as the most likely name. Severin's text reads 'Hipermestra', from Hypermnestra, one of the Danaides: cf. S. 256, n. 339.

5. 'Res et verba' in Seneca, Petrarch and Rojas

1. Deyermond lists Enrique de Villena, Iñigo López de Mendoza, Marqués de Santillana and Alonso de Cartagena among those who had knowledge of Petrarch's Latin works (*The Petrarchan Sources*, p. 19).

2. See K. Heitman, *Fortuna und Virtus. Eine Studie zu Petrarcas Lebensweisheit* (Cologne–Graz, 1958); E. F. Rice, *The Renaissance Idea of Wisdom* (Cambridge, Mass., 1958); P. O. Kristeller, *Eight Philosophers of the Italian Renaissance* (Stanford, 1964); Charles Trinkhaus, *The Poet as Philosopher: Petrarch and the Formation of Renaissance Consciousness* (New Haven–London, 1979).

3. See K. O. Apel, *Die Idee der Sprache in der Tradition des Humanismus von Dante bis Vico* (Bonn, 1963); Turano, 'Aristotle . . .'

4. For the humorous treatment of language in *Celestina*, see Dorothy S. Severin, 'Humour in *La Celestina*', *Romance Philology*, 32 (1978–9), 274–91. For the ultimate uselessness of the *sententia* in *Celestina*, see George A. Shipley, 'Usos y abusos de la autoridad del refrán en *La Celestina*', in Manuel Criado de Val (ed.), *La Celestina y su contorno social*; Actas del I Congreso Internacional sobre *La Celestina* (Barcelona, 1977), pp. 231–44; and especially *idem*, 'Authority and experience in *La Celestina*', *Bulletin of Hispanic Studies*, 62 (1985), 95–111.

5. See D. J. Gifford, 'Magical patter: the place of verbal fascination in *La Celestina*', in *Mediæval and Renaissance Studies on Spain and Portugal in Honour of P. E. Russell*, ed. F. W. Hodcroft *et al.* (Oxford, 1981); Turano, 'Aristotle', p. 165. For the role of magic in *Celestina*, see P. E. Russell, 'La magia, tema integral de *La Celestina*', *Temas . . .* 241–76.

6. Cf. Barbara Riss Dubno & John K. Walsh, 'Pero Díaz de Toledo's *Proverbios de Séneca* and the composition of *Celestina*, Act IV, *Celestinesca*, 11:1 (1987), 3–12.

7. See Charles F. Fraker, 'Declamation and the *Celestina*', *Celestinesca*, 9:2 (1985), 47–64.

8. Cf. the wording in the 'Título de la amistanza o del amigo': 'los que quieren desechar el amor deben escusar de ver ni oir cosas algunas por las cuales pueden se ducir a su memoria la su enamorada' (BN 6962, fol. 263).

9. The first goes back to Hecaton and Seneca, and from there to the *Título de la amistanza* and proverbial wisdom; the second to *Ep.* 10, *De Moribus* ('amicus certus in re certa cernitur'), the *Proverbios de Séneca*, no. 49, the 'Tratado de los amigos' of the *Copilación*, the *Amonestamientos y doctrinas*, cap. 5, no. 17, the *Margarita poetica*, and so on.

10. Of course, the word *galardón* was also used in the courtly love convention to denote the final reward of love. See Keith Whinnom, *La poesía amatoria de la época de los Reyes Católicos*, Durham Modern Languages Series, HM2 (Durham, 1981), 34–6.

11. See Lloyd Halliburton, 'Symbolic implications of the *cadenilla* in *La Celestina*: unity, disunity and death', *Romance Notes*, 22 (1981–2), 94–7.

12. The *Margarita poetica*'s condensed *sententia*, 'ex animo dantis censetur munus magnum', serves as a testimony to the relevance of this statement for the fifteenth-century reader. For this and other borrowings from the *Margarita poetica*, see Ivy A. Corfis, 'Fernando de Rojas and Albrecht von Eyb's *Margarita poetica*', *Neophilologus*, 68 (1984), 206–13.

13. Cf. *Ep.* 15, 'Cuanto más habemos tanto más deseamos' (Anth. 15), and *Ep.* 73, 'porque ella [la codicia] tanto más crece cuanto más recibe' (Anth. 62); *De Ben.* 2 27, 3, 'maiora cupimus, quo maiora venerunt', and *ibid.* 3, 3, 2, '[uti] mortalibus mos est ex magnis maiora cupiendi'.

6. Readers ask for more: the 'Tragicomedia de Calisto y Melibea'

1. For the question of authorship of the *Tragicomedia*, see María Rosa Lida de Malkiel, *La originalidad*, pp. 11–26. For a view on the different authorship of the 'Tratado de Centurio', see Marciales, vol. 1; Dorothy Severin, 'Fernando de Rojas and *Celestina*: the author's intention from *Comedia* to *Tragicomedia de Calisto y Melibea*', *Celestinesca*, 5:1 (1981), 1–5. For Proaza's role in the composition of *Celestina*, see D. W. McPheeters, *Estudios humanísticos*, pp. 71–98.

2. Cf. Norman Holland, 'Unity identity text self', *PMLA*, 90 (1975), 813–22; *idem*, *The Dynamics of Literary Response* (Oxford, 1968); *idem*, *5 Readers Reading* (New Haven, 1975).

3. For animal imagery, see George Shipley, 'Bestiary imagery in *la Celestina*', in *Homenaje a Stephen Gilman*, pp. 211–18.

4. For reader's participation, see Wolfgang Iser, *The Implied Reader: Patterns of Communication in Prose Fiction from Bunyan to Beckett* (Baltimore, 1974); Umberto Eco, *The Role of the Reader* (Bloomington, 1979); Cathleen M. Bauschatz, 'Montaigne's conception of reading in the context of Renaissance poetics and modern criticism', in Jane P. Tomkins (ed.), *Reader-Response Criticism* (Baltimore, 1980).

5. See Erna Berndt-Kelley, 'Peripecias de un título: en torno al nombre de la obra de Fernando de Rojas', *Celestinesca*, 9:2 (1985), 3–46.

6. The only person to have drawn our attention to Seneca's tragedies in *Celestina* is Leo Spitzer in 'A new book on the art of *The Celestina*', *Hispanic Review*, 25 (1957), 1–25. In n. 5 he relates the dramatic and rhetorical dialogue of *Celestina* to Seneca's tragedies, e.g. *Medea*.

7. See Marciales, *Celestina*, vol. 1. Basing himself on those editions which also contain the *Auto de Traso* (1526, 1538, 1541) and have the specific mention 'el cual fue sacado de la comedia que ordenó Sanabria', Marciales concludes that Acts 15, 17 and 18, plus the hypothetical *Auto de Iza*, needs must constitute Sanabria's *comedia*. His contention, then, is that, in his search for additional material, Rojas adapted what must have been more like an *entremés*, while making adjustments at the end of Act 14 and the beginning of Act 20.

8. See David Hook, 'The genesis of the "Auto de Traso"', *Journal of Hispanic Philology*, 3 (1978–9), 107–20.

Bibliography

(a) Table of editions

To facilitate reference, readily available editions have been used wherever possible.

I. Seneca's Latin works: Loeb Classical Library (London: Heinemann Ltd)

Epistulae Morales, trans. Richard M. Gummere

    Vol. 1 (no. 75): *Ep.* 1–65 (1917; repr. 1967)

    Vol. 2 (no. 76): *Ep.* 66–92 (1920; repr. 1962)

    Vol. 3 (no. 77): *Ep.* 93–124 (1925; repr. 1971)

Moral Essays, trans. John W. Basore,

    Vol. 1 (no. 214): *De Providentia; De Constantia; De Ira; De Clementia* (1928; repr. 1985)

    Vol. 2 (no. 254): *De Consolatione ad Marciam; De Vita Beata; De Otio; De Tranquillitate Animi; De Brevitate Vitae; De Consolatione ad Polybium; De Consolatione ad Helviam* (1932; repr. 1979)

    Vol. 3 (no. 310): *De Beneficiis*, Books I–VII (1935; repr. 1975)

Tragedies, trans. Frank Justus Miller,

    Vol. 1 (no. 62): *Hercules Furens, Troades, Medea, Hippolytus, Oedipus* (1917; repr. 1968)

    Vol. 2: *Agamemnon, Thyestes, Hercules Oetaeus, Phoenissae, Octavia* (1917; repr. 1961)

Naturales Quaestiones, trans. Thomas H. Corcoran,

    Vol. 1 (no. 450): Books I–III (1971)

    Vol. 2 (no. 457): Books IV–VII (1972)

II. Fifteenth-century translations in print:

    Las epístolas de Séneca (75) (Zaragoza, 1496). (Reference to this edition is Anth. + number of letter and folio number.)

    Los cinco libros de Séneca (Seville, 1491). (Since this edition only has sporadic folio numbering, reference is *CL* + number of book and number of chapter or short title of 'Tratado'.)

    Los proverbios de Séneca: Barbara Riss, 'Pero Díaz de Toledo's *Proverbios de Séneca*: an annotated edition of MS S-II-10 of the Escorial Library (Spanish text)' (doct. diss., University of California, 1979); available through University Microfilms International, Ann Arbor, MI 48106, USA. (Reference to this edition is R. and page numbers.)

'El tratado de ira de Séneca, traducido al castellano en el siglo XIII', ed. Fernando Rubio. *La Ciudad de Dios*, 174 (1961), 113–39. (A transcription of Book I, according to the Escorial Manuscript N-II-8.) (Reference will be by page number of this article.)

III. Spanish translations in manuscript:
Reference will be by catalogue number of the Biblioteca Nacional, Madrid (BN) or Escorial (S. or N.).
N.B. All spelling has been modernized.

IV. *Celestina*
All references mention two editions: Dorothy Severin's (Madrid, 1979; repr. 1981) (S. + page number), and Miguel Marciales' critical edition, ed. Brian Dutton and Joseph T. Snow, 2 vols. (Urbana–Chicago, 1985) (M. and page number).

(b) Table of Seneca's works

   I.   SENECA'S EXTANT CANON
        1. *Epistulae Morales*
        2. *De Providentia Dei*
        3. *De Constantia Sapientis*
        4. *De Ira*
        5. *De Clementia*
        6. *De Vita Beata*
        7. *De Otio*
        8. *De Tranquillitate Animi*
        9. *De Brevitate Vitae*
       10. *De Consolatione ad Marciam*
       11. *De Consolatione ad Polybium*
       12. *De Consolatione ad Helviam*
       13. *De Beneficiis*
       14. *Naturales Quaestiones*
       15. *Tragediae*
       16. *Divi Claudii Apocolocyntosis*
  II.   PSEUDO- AND SEMI-SENECAN TEXTS
       17. *Epistulae Senecae ad Paulum et Pauli ad Senecam* (anon.)
       18. *Formula Vitae Honestae* (Martin of Braga) = *De quattuor virtutibus*
       19. *De Moribus* (anon.)
       20. *Proverbia Senecae* (two-thirds by Publilius Syrus)
       21. *De Institutis Legalibus* (anon.)
       22. *Copia Verborum* (= extracts from no. 18)
       23. *De Remediis Fortuitorum* (anon.)
       24. *Controversiae* (Seneca the Elder)
       25. *Epitome Rei Militaris* (Flavius Vegetius)
 III.   ANTHOLOGIES AND EXTRACTS
       26. *Tabulatio et Expositio Senecae* (Luca Mannelli)
       27. *De Septem Artibus Liberalibus* = *Ep.* 88
       28. *De Paupertate* (anon.)
       29. *De Sapientia* (anon.)

IV. FIFTEENTH-CENTURY TRANSLATIONS

Anonymous:

30. *El libro de Séneca contra la ira y saña*, − = no. 4, Book 1

Alonso de Cartagena:

31. *Copilación por alfabeto* = anthology of 26
32. *El primer libro de Séneca de la providencia de Dios* = 2
33. *El segundo libro de Séneca de la providencia de Dios* = 38
34. *El primer libro de Séneca de la clemencia* = 5
35. *El segundo libro de Séneca de la clemencia* = 5
36. *De las siete artes liberales* = 27
37. *De la vida bienaventurada* = 6 + 7
38. *De la constancia* = 3
39. *Amonestamientos y doctrinas* = 21
40. *Declamaciones* = anthology of 24
41. *El libro contra las adversidades* = 23
42. *El libro de las cuatro virtudes* = 18
43. *Dichos de Séneca en el hecho de la caballería* = 25

Pero Díaz de Toledo:

44. *Obra y tractado de las costumbres* = 19
45. *Los proverbios de Séneca* = 20

Anonymous:

46. *Las epístolas de Séneca* (124) = 1
47. *Las epístolas de Séneca* (1–88) = 1
48. *Las epístolas de Séneca* (75) = 1
49. *Cartas que escribió Séneca a Paulo y Paulo a Séneca* = 17
50. *Título de la amistanza* = one chapter of 26
51. *Las tragedias de Séneca* = anthology of 15
52. *Juego de Claudio Emperador* = 16

V. FIRST PRINTINGS

Pero Díaz de Toledo, *Los proverbios de Séneca* = 45 (1482, 1491, 1495, 1500 (twice), 1512, 1528, 1535, 1552 (twice), 1555)

Alonso de Cartagena, *Los cinco libros de Séneca* (1491, 1510, 1530, 1548, 1551)

Contents:

Book I: De la vida bienaventurada = 37
Book II: De las siete artes liberales = 36
Book III: Amonestamientos y doctrinas = 39
Book IV: Primer libro de la providencia de Dios = 32
Book V*: Copilación por alfabeto = 31
          Declamaciones = 40

* Under the erroneous title of Segundo libro de la providencia de Dios

Anonymous, *Las Epístolas de Séneca* = 48 (1496, 1502, 1510, 1529, 1551, 1555)

Nos. 1–30 = *Ep.* 1–30; no. 31 = *Ep.* 43; no. 32 = *Ep.* 44; no. 33 = *Ep.* 45; no. 34 = *Ep.* 104; no. 35 = *Ep.* 32; no. 36 = *Ep.* 34; no. 37 = *Ep.* 35; no. 38 = *Ep.* 37; no. 39 = *Ep.* 38; no. 40 = *Ep.* 39; no. 41 = *Ep.* 40; no.

42 = *Ep.* 41;   no. 43 = *Ep.* 90;   no. 44 = *Ep.* 91;   no. 45 = *Ep.* 81;
no. 46 = *Ep.* 97; no. 47 = *Ep.* 99; no. 48 = *Ep.* 47; no. 49 = *Ep.* 101; no.
50 = *Ep.* 107; no. 51 = *Ep.* 69; no. 52 = *Ep.* 33; no. 53 = *Ep.* 42; no.
54 = *Ep.* 86;   no. 55 = *Ep.* 64;   no. 56 = *Ep.* 61;   no. 57 = *Ep.* 62;
no. 58 = *Ep.* 63;   no. 59 = *Ep.* 96;   no. 60 = *Ep.* 53;   no. 61 = *Ep.* 72;
no. 62 = *Ep.* 73; no. 63 = *Ep.* 50; no. 64 = *Ep.* 67; no. 65 = *Ep.* 89, 18–23;
no. 66 = *Ep.* 103; no. 67 = *Ep.* 52; no. 68 = *Ep.* 60; no. 69 = *Ep.* 49; no.
70 = *Ep.* 122; no. 71 = *Ep.* 111; no. 72 = *Ep.* 112; no. 73 = *Ep.* 113; no.
74 = *Ep.* 46; no. 75 = *Ep.* 119.

(c) Select Bibliography

Abel, Günther. *Stoizismus und Frühe Neuzeit.* Berlin–New York, 1978
Aguirre, J. M. *Calisto y Melibea, amantes cortesanos.* Zaragoza, 1962
Ajo, C. M. Sainz de Zúñiga, *Historia de las Universidades hispánicas,* 2 vols.
   Madrid, 1957
Alcalá, Angel, 'El neoepicureismo y la intención de *La Celestina*: notas para
   una re-lección', *Romanische Forschungen,* 88 (1976), 224–45
   Rojas y el neoepicureismo, Actas del I Congreso Internacional sobre *La
   Celestina.* Barcelona, 1977
Anderson, W. S. *Anger in Juvenal and Seneca.* Berkeley, 1964
Apel, K. O. *Die Idee der Sprache in der Tradition des Humanismus von Dante bis Vico.*
   Bonn, 1963
Arnold, E. V. *Roman Stoicism.* London, 1911; repr. 1958
Auerbach, Erich. *Literary Language and its Public in Late Antiquity and in the
   Middle Ages.* London, 1965 (pp. 235–338)
Baird, William Hamilton. *The Tenets of Stoicism.* Toronto, 1973
Barlow, C. W., ed. *Epistolae Senecae ad Paulum et Pauli ad Senecam (quae
   vocantur).* Rome, 1938
   Martini Episcopi Bracarensis Opera Omnia. New Haven, 1950
Basore, John W., trans. *Seneca: Moral Essays,* 3 vols. London, 1928, 1975,
   1979
Bauschatz, Cathleen M. 'Montaigne's conception of reading in the context of
   Renaissance poetics and modern criticism', in *Reader-Response Criticism,* ed.
   Jane P. Tompkins. Baltimore, 1980
Beardsley, T. S. *Hispano-Classical Translations Printed between 1482–1699.*
   Pittsburgh, 1970
Beer, Rudolf. *Handschriften Schätze Spaniens.* 1894; repr. Amsterdam, 1970
Berndt-Kelley, Erna Ruth. *Amor, Muerte y Fortuna en la Celestina.* Madrid,
   1963
   'Peripecias de un título: en torno al nombre de la obra de Fernando de
   Rojas', *Celestinesca,* 9:2 (1985), 3–46
Birkenmajer, Alexander. 'Der Streit des Alonso von Cartagena mit
   Leonardo Bruni Aretino', in *Beiträge zur Geschichte der Philosophie des
   Mittelalters* (1922), 129–210
Blüher, Karl Alfred. *Séneca en España.* Madrid, 1983 (translation of *Seneca in
   Spanien.* Munich, 1969)

Bobbio, A. 'Seneca e la formazione spirituale e culturale del Petrarca', *La Bibliofilia*, 43 (1941), 224–91

Bodson, Arthur. *La Morale sociale des derniers Stoiciens*. Paris, 1967

Bolgar, R. R. *The Classical Heritage and its Beneficiaries*. Cambridge, 1954
   Classical Influences on European Culture, AD 500–1500. Cambridge, 1971

Brinckman, Wolfgang. *Der Begriff der Freundschaft in Senecas Briefen.* Dusseldorf, 1963

Cantera Burgos, Francisco. *Alvar García de Santa María y su familia de conversos.* Madrid, 1952

Cartagena, Alfonso de. *La rhetórica de M. Tullio Cicerón*, ed. Rosalba Mascagna. Naples, 1969

Casas, Elena, ed. *La retórica en España*. Madrid, 1980

Castro Guisasola, F. *Observaciones sobre las fuentes literarias de la Celestina* Revista de Filología Española, Anejo 5, (1924).

Charlton, H. B. *The Senecan Tradition in Renaissance Tragedy*. Manchester, 1974

Chevalier, Maxime. *Lectura y lectores en la España de los siglos XVI y XVII*. Madrid, n.d. (chapter 3, 'La Celestina según sus lectores', pp. 138–66)

Corbitt, Theodore G. 'The cult of Lipsius: a leading source of early modern Spanish statecraft in Spain', *Journal of the History of Ideas*, 36 (1975), 139–52

Corcoran, Thomas H., trans. *Seneca: Naturales Quaestiones*, 2 vols. London, 1971, 1972

Corfis, Ivy A. 'Fernando de Rojas and Albrecht von Eyb's *Margarita poética*', *Neophilologus*, 68 (1984), 206–13

Costa, C. D. N. 'The tragedies', in *Seneca*, ed. C. D. N. Costa. London, 1974

Croll, M. W. 'Juste Lipse et le mouvement anticicéronien à la fin du XVI siècle', *Revue du seizième siècle*, 2 (1914), 220–42

Dean, Ruth J. & Armistead, Samuel G. 'A fifteenth-century Spanish book list', *The Library Chronicle*, 40 (1974), 73–87

Devlin, John. *La Celestina, a Parody of Courtly Love: Towards a Realistic Interpretation of the Tragicomedia de Calisto y Melibea*. New York, 1971

Deyermond, Alan D. 'Hilado – cordón – cadena: symbolic equivalences in *La Celestina*', *Celestinesca*, 1:1 (1977), 6–12
   The Petrarchan Sources of La Celestina. Oxford, 1961; repr. Westport, Conn., 1975.
   'The text-book mishandled: Andreas Capellanus and the opening scene of *La Celestina*', *Neophilologus*, 45 (1961), 218–21

Di Camillo, Ottavio. *El humanismo castellano del siglo XV*. Valencia, 1976

Diosdado, García Rojo, & Ortiz de Montalván, Gonzalo, eds. *Catálogo de Incunables de la Biblioteca Nacional*. Madrid, 1945

Dubno, Barbara Riss, & Walsh, John K. 'Pero Díaz de Toledo's *Proverbios de Séneca* and the composition of *Celestina*, Act IV', *Celestinesca*, 11:1 (1987), 3–12

Dunn, Peter. *Fernando de Rojas*, Twayne World Authors Series, 368. Boston, 1975
   'Pleberio's world', *PMLA*, 91 (1976), 406–19

Eco, Umberto. *The Role of the Reader*. Bloomington, 1979

Edelstein, Ludwig. *The Meaning of Stoicism*. Cambridge, Mass., 1966

Ellis, A. *Reason and Emotion in Psychotherapy*. New York, 1962

Estudios sobre Séneca, Ponencias y comunicaciones. Octava Semana Española de Filosofía. Madrid, 1966

Ettinghausen, Henry. *Francisco de Quevedo and the Neostoic Movement*. Oxford, 1972

Eusebi, M. 'Le piú antiche traduzione francese delle *Lettere Morale* de Seneca e i suoi derrivati', *Romania*, 91 (1970), 1–47

Faider, Paul, *Etudes sur Sénèque*. Ghent, 1921

Fairweather, Janet. *Seneca the Elder*. Cambridge, 1981

Fontán, Antonio. 'Algunos códices de Séneca en bibliotecas españolas y su lugar en la tradición de los diálogos', *Emérita*, 17 (1949) 9–41; 22 (1954), 35–65

    'Sobre Séneca, "De tranquillitate animi," y "De brevitate vitae"', *Emérita*, 18 (1950), 186–92

Fothergill-Payne, Louise. 'La Celestina como esbozo de una lección maquiavélica', *Romanische Forschungen*, 81 (1969), 158–75

    'La Celestina, un libro hondamente senequista', in *Actas del VIII Congreso Internacional de Hispanistas*, ed. D. Kossoff. Madrid, 1986 (pp. 533–40)

    'The Jesuits as masters of rhetoric and drama', *Revista Canadiense de Estudios Hispánicos*, 10 (1986), 375–87

Foulché-Delbosc, R., ed. 'Floresta de philósophos', *Revue Hispanique* (1904), 5–154

Fraker, Charles F. 'Argument in the *Celestina* and in its predecessors', *Homenaje a Stephen Gilman, Revista Española de Filología*, 1984, 81–6

    'Declamation and the *Celestina*', *Celestinesca*, 9:2 (1985), 47–64

    'The importance of Pleberio's soliloquy', *Romanische Forschungen*, 78 (1968), 516–29

    'Rhetoric in the *Celestina*: another look', in *Aureum Saeculum Hispanum: Festschrift für Hans Flasche*. Wiesbaden, 1983 (pp. 81–9)

Gassendi, Pierre. *De Vita et Moribus Epicuri Libri Octo*. Lyon, 1647

Gerli, E. M. 'Pleberio's lament and two literary topoi: expositor and planctus', *Romanische Forschungen*, 88 (1976), 67–74

Gifford, Douglas J. 'Magical patter: the place of verbal fascination in *La Celestina*', in *Mediæval and Renaissance Studies on Spain and Portugal in honour of P. E. Russell*, ed. F. W. Hodcroft *et al*. Oxford, 1981

Gilman, Stephen. *The Spain of Fernando de Rojas*. Princeton, 1972

Goldsmidt, E. P. *From Manuscript to Printed Book*. London, 1943

Gómez Moreno, Angel. 'Una carta del marqués de Santillana', *Revista de Filología Española*, 63 (1983), 115–22

Griffin, Miriam T. '*Imago vitae suae*', in *Seneca*, ed. C. D. N. Costa. London, 1974 (pp. 1–38)

    Seneca, a Philosopher in Politics. Oxford, 1976

Guillermo, Antolín P. *Catálogo de los códices latinos de la Real Biblioteca del Escorial*. Madrid, 1910

Gummere, Richard M., trans. *Seneca: Epistulae Morales*, 3 vols. London, 1917, 1920, 1925

Hagendahl, Harold. *Latin Fathers and the Classics*. Göteborg, 1958

Halliburton, Lloyd. 'Symbolic implications of the *cadenilla* in *La Celestina*: unity, disunity and death', *Romance Notes*, 22 (1981–2), 94–7

Heitman, Klaus. *Fortuna und Virtus. Eine Studie zu Petrarcas Lebensweisheit.* Cologne–Graz, 1958

'La genesi del "De remediis utriusque fortune" del Petrarca', *Convivium* (revista di lettere), 25 (1957), 9–30

Heller, J. L., & Grismer, R. L. 'Seneca in the Celestinesque novel', *Hispanic Review*, 12 (1944), 29–48

Hermenegildo, Alfredo. *La tragedia en el renacimiento español.* Barcelona, 1973

Hirsch, Rudolf. *Printing, Selling and Reading, 1450–1550.* Wiesbaden, 1967

Holland, Norman. *The Dynamics of Literary Response.* Oxford, 1968

5 Readers Reading. New Haven, 1975

'Unity Identity Text Self', *PMLA*, 90 (1975), 813–22

Hook, David. 'The genesis of the "Auto de Traso"', *Journal of Hispanic Philology*, 3 (1978–9), 107–20

'"¿Para quién edifiqué torres?": a footnote to Pleberio's lament', *Forum for Modern Language Studies*, 14:1 (1978), 25–31

Hutcheon, Linda. *A Theory of Parody.* London, 1985

Ijsseling, L. *Rhetoric and Philosophy in Conflict: An Historical Survey.* The Hague, 1976

Impey, Olga T. 'Alfonso de Cartagena, traductor de Séneca y precursor del humanismo español', *Prohemio*, 3 (1972), 473–94

Iser, Wolfgang. *The Implied Reader: Patterns of Communication in Prose Fiction from Bunyan to Beckett.* Baltimore, 1974

Jacquot, Jean, ed. *Les Tragédies de Sénèque et le théâtre de la Renaissance.* Paris, 1964

Jauss, Hans Robert. 'The alterity and modernity of medieval literature', *New Literary History*, 10:2 (1979), 181–227

'Literary history as a challenge to literary theory', in *New Directions in Literary Theory*, ed. Ralph Cohen. London, 1974. (pp. 11–41)

Toward an Aesthetic of Reception. Mineapolis, 1982

Kohut, Karl. 'Der Beitrag der Theologie zum Literaturbegriff in der Zeit Juans II von Kastilien: Alonso de Cartagena (1384–1456) und Alonso de Madrigal, genannt El Tostado (1400?–1455)', *Romanische Forschungen*, 89 (1977), 183–226

'La posición de la literatura en los sistemas científicos del siglo XV', *Ibero–romania*, n.s. 7 (1978), 67–87

Kristeller, Paul Oscar. *Eight Philosophers of the Italian Renaissance.* Stanford, 1964

Renaissance Thought, the Classic, Scholastic and Humanist Strains. New York, 1961

Lawrance, Jeremy N. H. 'Nuño de Guzmán and early Spanish humanism: some reconsiderations', *Medium Ævum*, 51 (1982), 55–85

'Nuño de Guzmán: life and works', doct. diss. Oxford, 1983

'The spread of lay literacy in late medieval Castile', *Bulletin of Hispanic Studies*, 62 (1985), 79–94

Un tratado de Alonso de Cartagena sobre la educación. Barcelona, 1979

Lersundi, F. del Valle. 'Documentos referentes a Fernando de Rojas', *Revista de Filología Española*, 16 (1929), 385–96

Liénard, E. 'Sur la correspondance apocryphe de Sénèque et de Saint Paul', *Revue Belge de Philosophie et Histoire*, 11 (1932), 5–23

Lihani, John. 'The intrinsic and dramatic values of Celestina's gold chain', in *Studies in Honor of Gerald E. Wade*. Madrid, 1979 (pp. 151–65)

Loth, J. 'Un nouveau texte du traité de Sénèque *De Remediis Fortuitorum*', *Revue de Philologie*, n.s. 12 (1888), 120 n.

Lucena, Juan de. *De la vita beata*, ed. Bertini, G. M., in *Testi Spagnoli del secolo XV*. Turin, 1950

McPheeters, D. W. *Estudios humanísticos sobre 'La Celestina'*. Potomac, 1985

Malkiel, María Rosa Lida de. *La originalidad artística de la Celestina*. Buenos Aires, 1962

Maravall, José Antonio. *El mundo social de La Celestina*, 2nd edn. Madrid, 1968
  Estudios de historia del pensamiento español, vol. 1. Madrid, 1973

Marciales, Miguel, ed. *Celestina. Tragicomedia de Calisto y Melibea*, 2 vols. Urbana–Chicago, 1985

Marín, Luis Astrana Marín. *Vida general y trágica de Séneca*. Madrid, 1947

Martin, June Hall. *Love's Fools: Aucassin, Troilus, Calisto and the Parody of the Courtly Lover*. London, 1972

Martínez, Salvador. 'Cota y Rojas: contribución al estudio de las fuentes y la autoría de *La Celestina*', *Hispanic Review*, 48 (1980), 37–55

Mazzeo, Joseph A. *Renaissance and Revolution*. London, 1967

Mendeloff, Henry. 'Pleberio in contemporary *Celestina* criticism', *Romance Notes*, 13 (1971–2), 369–73

Mendoza Negrillo, Juan de Dios, SJ. *Fortuna y Providencia en la literatura castellana del siglo XV*. Madrid, 1973

Menéndez Pelayo, M. *Biblioteca de traductores españoles*, ed. Enrique Sánchez-Reyes, 4 vols. Santander, 1952–3

Meyer, Herman. *The Poetics of Quotation in the European Novel*. Princeton, 1968

Miller, Frank Justus, trans. *Seneca: Tragedies*, 2 vols. London, 1917

Monfrin, Jacques. 'Humanisme et traductions au moyen âge', *Journal des Savants*, 3 (1963), 161–90

Morgan, Erica. 'Rhetorical technique in the persuasion of Melibea', *Celestinesca*, 3:2 (1979), 7–18

Morón Arroyo, Ciriaco. *Sentido y forma de La Celestina*. Madrid, 1974

Morreale, Margherita. 'Apuntes para la historia de la traducción en la Edad Media', *Revista de Literatura*, 15 (1959), 3–10
  'El tratado de Juan de Lucena sobre la felicidad', *Nueva Revista de Filología Hispánica*, 2 (1955), 1–21

Motto, A. L. *Seneca*. Twayne World Authors Series, 268. Boston, 1973

Münscher, K. 'Seneca's Werke. Untersuchungen zur Abfassungszeit und Echtheit,' *Philologus*, Suppl. 16, Leipzig 1923, 62, 143

Norton, F. J. *Printing in Spain, 1501–1520*. Cambridge, 1966

Pagden, Anthony R. D. 'The diffusion of Aristotle's moral philosophy in Spain, ca. 1400–1600', *Traditio*, 31 (1975), 287–313

Panizza, Letizia A. 'Gasparino Barrizze's commentaries on Seneca's letters', *Traditio*, 33 (1977), 297–358

Parkes, M. B. 'The influence of the concepts of *ordinatio* and *compilatio* on the development of the book', in *Medieval Learning and Literature: Essays presented to Richard William Hunt*, ed. J. J. G. Alexander and M. T. Gibson. Oxford, 1976 (pp. 115–41)

Penney, Clara Louisa. *The Book called Celestina*. New York, 1954

Petrarcha, Francisco. *Opera Omnia* (Basle, 1554); facsimile edn Ridgewood, NJ, 1965

Phillips, M. M. 'Erasmus and the classics', in *Erasmus*, ed. T. A. Dorey. London, 1970

Rank, Jerry R. 'The uses of Dios . . .', *Revista Canadiense de Estudios Hispánicos*, 5 (1980), 75–91

Read, Malcolm K. *The Birth and Death of Language: Spanish Literature and Linguistics: 1300–1700*. Madrid, 1983
    'La Celestina and the Renaissance philosophy of language', *Philological Quarterly*, 55 (1976), 166–77
    'Fernando de Rojas' vision of the birth and death of language', *Modern Language Notes*, 93 (1978), 163–75

Reckert, Stephen. 'La textura verbal de *La Celestina*', in *Medieval Hispanic Studies Presented to Rita Hamilton*, ed. A. D. Deyermond. London, 1976 (pp. 161–74)

Reynolds, L. D. *The Medieval Tradition of Seneca's Letters*. Oxford, 1965

Reynolds, L. D., & Wilson, N. G. *Scribes & Scholars*, 2nd edn. Oxford, 1974

Rice, E. F. *The Renaissance Idea of Wisdom*. Cambridge, Mass., 1958

Riquer, Martín de. 'Fernando de Rojas, y el primer acto de *La Celestina*', *Revista de Filología Española* (1957), 374–95

Riss, Barbara. 'Pero Díaz de Toledo's *Proverbios de Séneca*: an annotated edition of MS S-II-10 of the Escorial Library (Spanish text)', doct. diss. University of California, 1979

Rist, John M. *Epicurus: An Introduction*. Cambridge, 1972
    ed. *The Stoics*. Berkeley, 1978

Rodríguez de Castro, D. Joseph. *Biblioteca Española. Tomo segundo, que contiene la noticia de los escritores gentiles españoles, y de los Cristianos hasta fines del siglo XIII de la Iglesia*. Madrid, 1786 (pp. 21–62)

Ross, G. M. 'Seneca's philosophical influence', in *Seneca*, ed. C. D. N. Costa. London, 1974

Round, Nicholas G. 'Conduct and values in *La Celestina*', in *Mediæval and Renaissance Studies on Spain and Portugal in honour of P. E. Russell*, ed. F. W. Hodcroft *et al*. Oxford, 1981 (pp. 38–52)
    'The medieval reputation of the *Proverbia Senecae*: a partial survey based on recorded MSS', *Proceedings of the Royal Irish Academy*, 72:C:5 (1972), 103–51
    'Pero Díaz de Toledo: a study of a 15th-century "converso" translator in his background', doct. diss. Oxford, 1967
    'The shadow of a philosopher: medieval Castilian images of Plato', *Journal of Hispanic Philology*, 3 (1978–9), 1–36
    'Las traducciones medievales, catalanas y castellanas de las tragedias de Séneca', *Anuario de estudios medievales*, 9 (1974–9), 187–227

Rubio, Fernando, ed. 'El tratado *De Ira* de Séneca traducido al castellano en el siglo XIII', *La ciudad de Dios*, 174 (1961), 113–39

Russell, D. A. 'De imitatione', in *Creative Imitation and Latin Literature*, ed. David West and Tony Woodman. Cambridge, 1979 (pp. 1–16)

Russell, Peter. *Temas de "La Celestina" y otros estudios*. Barcelona, 1978.

Traducciones y traductores en la península ibérica (1400–1500). Barcelona, 1985

Russell, Peter & Pagden, A. 'Nueva luz sobre una versión española cuatrocentista de la *Etica a Nicómaco*', in *Homenaje a Guillermo Guastavino*. Madrid, 1974 (pp. 125–46)

Salazar, Abdón M. 'El impacto humanístico de las misiones diplomáticas de Alonso De Cartagena en la Corte de Portugal entre medievo y renascimiento', in *Medieval Hispanic Studies Presented to Rita Hamilton*, ed. A. D. Deyermond. London, 1976

Samoná, A. *Aspetti del retoricismo nella 'Celestina'*. Rome, 1953

Sandys, John Edwin. *A History of Classical Scholarship*. New York, 1967

Schiff, Mario. *La Bibliothèque du Marquis de Santillana*. Paris, 1905

Serrano, Luciano. *Los conversos D. Pablo de Santa María y D. Alonso de Cartagena*. Madrid, 1942

Sevenster, J. N. *Paul and Seneca*. Leiden, 1961

Severin, Dorothy S. 'Aristotle's *Ethics* and *La Celestina*', *La Corónica* 10:1 (1981–2), 54–8

'Humour in *La Celestina*', *Romance Philology*, 32 (1978–9), 274–91

'Fernando de Rojas and *Celestina*: the author's intention from *Comedia* to *Tragicomedia de Calisto y Melibea*', *Celestinesca*, 5:1 (1981), 1–5

ed. *La Celestina*. Madrid, 1981

Shipley, George. 'Authority and experience in *La Celestina*', *Bulletin of Hispanic Studies* (1985), 95–111

'Bestiary imagery in *La Celestina*', *Homenaje a Stephen Gilman*, *Revista de Estudios Hispánicos* (Puerto Rico), 9 (1984), 211–18

'Concerting through conceit: unconventional uses of conventional sickness images in *La Celestina*', *Modern Language Review*, 70 (1975), 324–32

'*Non erat hic locus*: The Disconcerted Reader in Melibea's Garden', *Romance Philology*, 27 (1973–4), 286–303

'Usos y abusos de la autoridad del refrán en *La Celestina*', in *La Celestina y su contorno social*. Barcelona, 1977, 231–44

Snow, Joseph. *Celestina by Fernando de Rojas: An Annotated Bibliography of World Interest, 1930–1985*. Madison, 1986

Spink, J. S. *French Free Thought from Gassendi to Voltaire*. London, 1960

Spitzer, Leo. 'A new book on the art of *The Celestina*', *Hispanic Review*, 25:1 (1957), 1–25

Toch, Hans. 'The management of hostile aggression: Seneca as applied social psychologist', *American Psychologist* (1933), 1022–6

Trillitzsch, W. *Seneca im literarischen Urteil der Antike*, vols. 1 & 2. Amsterdam, 1971

Trinkhaus, Charles. *The Poet as Philosopher: Petrarch and the Formation of Renaissance Consciousness*. New Haven–London, 1979

Turano, Leslie T. 'Aristotle and the art of persuasion in *Celestina*', doct. diss. London, 1985

Weiss, Julian. 'The poetic concept of his art: Castilian vernacular poetry circa 1400–1600', doct. diss. Oxford, 1984

Whinnon, Keith. *La poesía amatoria de la época de los Reyes Católicos.* Durham, 1981

    La Celestina, The Celestina and L2 Interference in L1', *Celestinesca* 4:2 (1980), 19–21

    'Interpreting *La Celestina*: the motives and the personality of Fernando de Rojas', in *Mediæval and Renaissance Studies in Spain and Portugal in honour of P. E. Russell,* ed. F. W. Hodcroft *et al.* Oxford, 1981 (pp. 53–68)

Williamson, G. *The Senecan Amble: A Study in Prose from Bacon to Collier.* London, 1951

Wise, David, O. 'Reflections of Andreas Cappellanus' *De Reprobatione Amoris* in Juan Ruiz, Alfonso Martínez and Fernando de Rojas', *Hispania,* 63 (1980), 506–13

Zanta, L. *La Renaissance du Stoicisme au XVI siècle.* Paris, 1914

Zarco, Cuevas. *Catálogo de los MSS castellanos de la Real Biblioteca de El Escorial.* Madrid, 1924

Index of Senecan *sententiae*

a. Near-textual quotations

'. . . los peregrinos tienen muchas posadas y pocas amistades, porque en breve tiempo con ninguno [no] pueden fincar amistad. Y el que está en muchos cabos, [no] está en ninguno etc'. (Act 1; S. 68; M. 47) – 'Nusquam est qui ubique est, vitam in peregrinatione exigentibus hoc evenit, ut multa hospitia habeant, nullas amicitias etc.' (*Ep*. 2, 2). Translated as 'ca ciertamente el que ha su corazón en muchas partes no lo ha en ninguna, así como los que van en peregrinajes y romerías que mudan tantos albergues que con ninguno no toman amor etc.' (Anth. 2, fol. 3r). See pp. 60–2.

'Tengo por honesta cosa la pobreza alegre' (Act 1; S. 69; M. 49) – '"Honesta" inquit "res est laeta paupertas"' (*Ep*. 2, 6), translated as 'honesta cosa es, dijo Epicuro, alegre pobreza' (Anth. 2, fol. 3ʀ). See p. 62.

'No los que poco tienen son pobres; mas los que mucho desean' (Act 1; S. 69; M. 49) – 'Non qui parum habet sed qui plus cupit pauper est' (*Ep*. 2, 6), translated as 'ni es pobre el que ha poco, mas el que mucho desea' (Anth. 2, fol. 3r). See p. 62.

'Quien torpemente sube a lo alto, más aína cae que subió' (Act 1; S. 69; M. 49) – 'Quien por maneras torpes sube a lo alto más aína cae que subió' (*Amonestamientos y doctrinas*, CL 3, 1, 2). Also quoted in Act 5 (S. 104; M. 99). See pp. 63 and 105.

'Extremo es creer a todos y yerro no creer a ninguno' (Act 1; S. 70; M. 49) – Utrumque enim vitium est, et omnibus credere et nulli' (*Ep*. 3, 4), translated as 'porque lo uno y lo otro es vicio, fiarse de todos y dudar de todos' (Anth. 3, fol. 3v). See p. 64.

'Un ejemplo de lujuria o avaricia mucho mal hace' (Act 1; S. 70; M. 50) – 'Unum exemplum luxuriae aut avaritiae multum mali facit' (*Ep*. 7, 7), translated as 'un solo ejemplo de lujuria o de avaricia basta a hacer asaz dañõ' (Anth. 7, fol. 6r). See p. 64.

'La mujer o ama mucho a aquel de quien es requerida o le tiene grand odio' (Act 3; S. 83; M. 68) – 'Aut amat aut odit mulier: nihil est tertium' (*Proverbia Senecae*; R. 359), translated as 'La mujer ama o aborrece, no hay tercera cosa' (Proverbio 6; R. 39). See p. 101.

'Porque aquellas cosas que bien no son pensadas, aunque algunas veces hayan buen fin, comunmente crían desvariados efectos' (Act 4; S. 86; M. 75). – 'Ca las cosas que no son bien pensadas, aunque algunas veces hayan buen fin, más comunmente habrán desvariados efectos' (gloss to Proverbio 59; R. 65). See p. 102.

'Porque hacer beneficio es semejar a Dios' (Act 4; S. 94; M. 85) – 'Qui dat beneficia, deos imitatur' (*De Ben*. 3, 15, 4), paraphrased as 'Quid es dare beneficium? deum imitari' (*De Moribus*; R. 373), translated as '¿Qué cosa es dar beneficio? Semejar a Dios' (Proverbio 305; R. 258). See p. 104.

b. Altered quotations

'De enfermo corazón es no poder sufrir *el bien* (Act 1; S. 70; M. 50) – 'Infirmi animi est pati non posse *divitias*' (*Ep.* 5, 6), translated as 'El corazón enfermo y flaco no puede fuir [*sic*] las riquezas' (Anth. 5, fol. 4v). See p. 64.

'Con aquellos debe hombre conversar, que le hagan mejor, y aquellos *dejar* a quien él mejores piensa hacer (Act 1; S. 71; M. 50) – 'Cum his versare qui te meliorem facturi sunt. Illos *admitte* quos tu potes facere meliores' (*Ep.* 7, 8), translated as 'conversa y usa con aquellos que te puedan emendar, y recibe en tu compañía aquellos a quien tú puedas corregir y emendar' (Anth. 7, fol. 6r). See p. 65.

'De ninguna *cosa* es alegre posesión sin compañía' (Act 1; S. 71; M. 50) – 'Nullius *boni* sine socio iucunda possessio est' (*Ep.* 6, 4), translated as 'No es alegre ni dulce alguna posesión sin compañía' (Anth. 6, fol. 5r). Also quoted in Act 8: 'De ninguna *prosperidad* es buena la posesión sin compañía' (S. 135; M. 146) See p. 65.

'Yerro es no creer y culpa creerlo todo' (Act 1; S. 71; M. 50). Cf. 'Extremo es creer a todos' above and p. 66.

'Y sin duda la presta dádiva su efecto ha doblado...' (Act 1; S. 73; M. 53) – 'Inopi beneficium bis dat qui dat celeriter' (*Proverbia Senecae*; R. 365), translated as 'Dos veces da al pobre limosna quien se la da prestamente' (Proverbio 178; R. 173). See p. 67.

'Más presto se curan las tiernas *enfermedades* en sus principios que cuando han hecho curso en la perseveración de su oficio' (Act 10; S. 155; M. 177) – 'facile est enim teneros adhuc *animos* componere, difficulter reciduntur *vitia* quae nobiscum creverunt' (*De Ira* 2, 18, 2). See p. 110.

'Gran parte de la *salud* es desearla (Act 10; S. 155; M. 177) – 'pars magna *bonitatis* est velle fieri bonum' (*Ep.* 34, 3), translated as 'parte de la bondad es querer hombre ser bueno y desearlo' (Anth. 36, fol. 34r). See p. 110.

'Más segura cosa es *ser menospreciado* que temido' (Act 4 interpolation; S. 91; M. 81) – '*colant* potius te quam timeant' (*Ep.* 47, 18), translated as 'porque seas dellos más amado que temido' (Anth. 48, fol. 50v). See p. 120.

c. Hidden quotations

['Pues aquellos no deben menos hacer... sino] *vivir a su ley*' (Act 1; S. 69; M. 48) – '[... facere docet philosophia, non dicere, et hoc exigit], *ut ad legem suam quisque vivat*, [ne orationi vita dissentiat]' (*Ep.* 20, 2), translated as 'Philosophia no muestra bien hablar, mas bien obrar. Esto es lo que ella demanda y requiere, *que cada uno viva a su ley* y que su vida no sea desacordante de sus palabras' (Anth. 20, fol. 18r). See p. 62.

'Este es el deleite; que lo al, mejor lo hacen los asnos en el prado (Act 1; S. 71; M. 51) – 'Hominis bonum quaero, non ventris, qui pecudibus ac beluis laxior est; (*DVB* 9, 4), translated as 'E aun lo (i.e. deleite) sienten mejor los animales brutos y las bestias fieras' (*De la vida bienaventurada*, *CL* 1, 10). See pp. 65–6.

'¿Y cuándo me pagarás esto? Nunca, pues a los padres y a los maestros no puede ser hecho servicio igualmente (Act 1; S. 71–2; M. 51) – '"Sed patris' inquit, "beneficium est... Et praeceptoris mei... multum inter prima ac maxima interest..."' (*De Ben.* 3, 34). See p. 67.

'... porque la (dádiva) que tarda, el prometimiento muestra negar y arrepentirse del don prometido' (Act 1; S. 73; M. 53) – '[Ingratum est beneficium] quod diu inter dantis manus haesit, quod quis aegre dimittere visus est et sic dare, tamquam sibi eriperet' (*De Ben.* 2, 1, 2) paraphrased as 'ca no es gracioso aquel beneficio que tarda mucho entre las manos del que lo da, ni el que parece ser dado de malamente. E asi lo dan como lo tomasen por fuerza' (*Copilacion*; *CL* 5). See p. 67.

'Ninguno es tan viejo, que no pueda vivir un año' (Act 4; S. 92; M. 82) – 'Nemo tam senex qui non possit annum vivere' (Petrarch, Index; D. 43). Cf. Seneca: '[Primum ista (mors) tam seni ante oculos debet esse quam iuveni. Non enim citamur ex censu.] Deinde nemo tan senex est, ut improbe unum diem speret' (*Ep.* 12, 6), translated as 'Yo te digo que tan bien la ve ante sus ojos el mozo como el viejo porque no es más seguro de la muerte el mozo que el viejo. No hay hombre tan viejo que no espere de vivir un día (Anth. 12, fol. 10v). See p. 103.

'Es más penoso al delincuente esperar la cruda y capital sentencia que el acto de la ya sabida muerte' (Act 5; S. 105; M. 101) – 'quod antecedit tempus, maxima venturi supplicii pars est, [ita maior est muneris gratia, quo minus diu pependit'] (*De Ben.* 2, 5, 3). Cf. Seneca the Elder, *Controversia* 3: 'mortem timere crudelius est quam mori'. See p. 106.

'Es menester que ames si quieres ser amado' (Act 7; S. 102; M. 123) – 'Si vis amari, ama' (Petrarch, Index; D. 39) Cf. Seneca: 'Hecaton ait; "[Ego tibi monstrabo amatorium sine medicamento, sine herba, sine ullius veneficae carmine;] si vis amari, ama"' (*Ep.* 9, 6), translated as 'Catón dijo "Yo te mostraré una manera de hacer amigo sin arte de medicina y sin confación de hierbas y sin encantamiento. Si tú quieres ser amado, ama"' (Anth. 9, fol. 7v). See pp. 75 and 109.

'Denostadas, maltratadas las traen, contímuo sojuzgadas, que hablar delante (de) ellas no osan' (Act 9; S. 149; M. 164) – 'At infelicibus servis movere labra ne in hoc quidem, ut loquantur, licet, virga murmur omne conpescitur . . . Sic fit, ut isti de domino loquantur, quibus coram domino loqui non licet' (*Ep.* 47, 3–4), translated as 'Y los desaventurados siervos están ante ellos en pie y no osan hablar, y si alguna palabra dicen luego son heridos y denostados como canes . . . y de aquí viene que ellos dicen mal de sus señores detrás de ellos porque ante ellos no osan hablar' (Anth. 48, fol. 49v). See pp. 51 and 72.

'Como todo don o dádiva se juzgue grande o chica respecto del que lo da, no quiero traer a consecuencia mi poco merecer, ante quien sobra en cualidad y en cuantidad' (Act 11; S. 165; M. 190) – 'Respiciendae sunt cuique facultates suae viresque, ne aut plus praestemus, quam possumus, cui damus; quaedam enim minora sunt, quam ut exire a magnis viris debeant, quaedam accipiente maiora sunt' (*De Ben.* 2, 15, 3). See p. 112.

'Sobre dinero no hay amistad' (Act 12; S. 179; M. 210) – '"Quid ergo? Beneficia non parant amicitias?" [Parant, si accepturos licuit eligere, si conlocata, non sparsa sunt'] (*Ep.* 19, 12), translated as 'Pues dirás tu ¿qué es esto que el bien hacer no haga amigos? Por cierto sí hace cuando el don es bien asentado y en buen lugar y dado a buen hombre' (Anth. 19, fol. 18r). See p. 80.

'Quiero, pues, deponer el luto, dejar tristeza, despedir las lágrimas, que tan aparejadas han estado a salir' (Act 17; S. 208; M. 283) – Proinde parcamus lacrimis nihil proficientibus . . . Qui si nos torquet, non adiuvat, primo quoque tempore deponendus est et ab inanibus solaciis atque amara quadam libidine dolendi animus recipiendus est' (*Poly.* 4, 1). See p. 136.

General index

Spanish and Latin synonyms are entered under their English equivalent where appropriate.

adversity (adversidad, *adversitas*), 31, 37, 112, 114
advice (consejo), 59, 66, 79, 84, 88, 99, 101, 102, 124
affectus (afecto), 10, 31, 32, 35, 53, 54, 55, 58, 66, 83, 84, 85, 86, 89, 90, 92, 94, 95, 107, 108, 111, 115, 127, 134, 135, 137, 138, 141, 143
affectus amantium (loco amor) 43, 75, 95, 108, *131-2*, 137, 149 n.2
analogy (*proportio*), 48-9
anger (*ira*), 10, 16, 27, *32*, 33, 34, 40, 53, *83-7*, 88, 104, 109, 111, 123-5, 129, 131, 134, 135, 141, 142, 147 n., 150 n.5
Areus, 148 n.6
Aristotle (Aristóteles), 8, 15, 24, 29, 36, 37, 38, 39, 40, 41, 52, 56, 59, 60, 63, 64, 84, 85, 88, 121, 134, 145 n.10, 148 n.9, 149 nn.8 and 9; Aristotelian thinking, 36-8, 98, 138; *Ethics*, 8, 24, 37-41, 52, 60, 64, 98, 139, 146 n.12, 149 n.9; *Metaphysics*, 15; *Rhetoric*, 50
assent (*adsensio*), 48-9
avarice (avaricia), 65, 70, 71, 76
authority (autoridad, *auctoritas*), 3, 5, 7, 8, 13, 15, 31, 33, 36, 38, 39, 40, 41, 45, 46, 51, 52, 59, 63, 66, 67, 69, 89, 97, 138, 144, 150 n.4

Barrientos, Lope de, *Tratado de caso y fortuna*, 24
Basle, Council of: *see* Council of Basle
beauty (hermosura), 39, 43, 47, 48, 56, 75, 76, 91, 98, 139, 142
Beauvais, Vincent of: *see* Vincent of Beauvais
benefits (beneficio, *beneficium*), 34, *41-2*, 43, 44, 64, 66, 80, 81, 104, 106, 120. *See also gift*

Blüher, Karl Alfred, xiv, 6, 8, 11, 24-5, 145 n.1 and 7
Bocados de oro, 25
Boethius (Boecio), 29, 39, 56, 88.
Braga, Martin of, 4, 24, 145 n.3
Bruni, Leonardo, 8-9, 24, 146 n.12

Callistus, 50, 140
Cancionero, 143, 148 n.4
Cartagena, Alonso de, 3, 6, 8-11, 13-14, 17-18, 24-5, *26-38*, 39, 42, 48, 141, 146 nn.12-17, 149 n.12 and 4, 150 n.1
Cassiodorus (Casiodoro), 40
Castile, 8-9, 12
Castro Guisasola, F., xiv, 148 n.3 and 6
Cato (Catón), 29, 40, 59, 73
Centenera, Antón de, 16
chain (cadena, *catena*), 46, 58, 80, 86, 112, 122, 134
Christian: Seneca as, 2-3; times, 1-2; thinking, 2-3, 6, 14, *26-9*, 30, 49, 91, 139, 147 n.7
Cicero (Cicerón), 7, 8-9, 39-41, 146 n.8; *De Amicitia*, 9, *De Inventione*, 9, *De Senectute*, 9; Ciceronianism, 6; Anticiceronianism, 145 n.8
collatio rationis, 48-9, 98
compilation (*compilatio*), 5-6, 16
composition (*compositio*), 48-9
consolation (consolación, *consolatio*), 7, 31, 51, 52, 89, 135, 137
contra-exemplum, 32, 74-5, 79, 81, 83, 92, 97, 103, 127, 134, 139
control, 32, 57, 85-6, 93, 105, 129, 133-4, 140-1
Council of Basle, 11
courtly love, 47-8, 71, 87, 143, 148 n.4, 151 n.10
crowds (vulgo, *populus*), 13, 16, 33, 43, 55, 65, 70, *76-81*, 83, 92, 103, 109, 130, 137, 140, 143

167

For EU product safety concerns, contact us at Calle de José Abascal, 56–1°,
28003 Madrid, Spain or eugpsr@cambridge.org.

www.ingramcontent.com/pod-product-compliance
Ingram Content Group UK Ltd.
Pitfield, Milton Keynes, MK11 3LW, UK
UKHW010047140625
459647UK00012BB/1660